GOD
VERSUS
CAESAR

SUNY series, American Constitutionalism
Robert J. Spitzer, editor

GOD
VERSUS
CAESAR

Belief, Worship, and Proselytizing under the First Amendment

MARTIN S. SHEFFER

State University
of New York
Press

Published by
State University of New York Press, Albany

© 1999 State University of New York

All rights reserved

Production by Susan Geraghty
Marketing by Patrick Durocher

Printed in the United States of America

For information, address State University of New York
Press, State University Plaza, Albany, N.Y., 12246

Library of Congress Cataloging-in-Publication Data

Sheffer, Martin S.
    God versus Caesar : belief, worship, and proselytizing under the
First Amendment / Martin S. Sheffer.
        p.   cm. — (SUNY series in American constitutionalism)
    Includes bibliographical references and index.
    ISBN 0-7914-4175-X (alk. paper). — ISBN 0-7914-4176-8 (pbk. :
alk. paper)
    1. Freedom of religion—United States. I. Title. II. Series.
KF4783.S54 1999
342.73′0852—dc21   98-29185
                                                                      CIP

10 9 8 7 6 5 4 3 2 1

CONTENTS

ACKNOWLEDGMENTS

The author thanks the publishers of the following journals and books for permission to quote from these works:

The Harvard Law Review for Giannella, *Religious Liberty, Non-Establishment, and Doctrinal Development: Part I. The Religious Liberty Guaranty*, 80 HARV. L. REV. 1381, 1390 (1967).

The Yale Law Review for G. Braden, *The Search for Objectivity in Constitutional Law*, 57 YALE L.J. 571–94; and S. Shapiro, *Toward a Uniform Valuation of the Religion Guarnatees*, 80 YALE L.J. 77–106. Reprinted by permission of the Yale Law Journal Company and Fred B. Rothman & Company.

The New York University Law Review for N. Redlich & K. Feinberg, *Individual Conscience and the Selective Conscientious Objector: The Right Not to Kill*, 44 N.Y.U.L. REV. 875, 891 (1969).

The Michigan Law Review for Bernard, *Avoidance of Constitutional Issues in the United States Supreme Court: Liberties of the First Amendment*, 50 MICH. L. REV. 261 (1951).

The University of Chicago Law Review for Kurland, *Of Church, State, and the Supreme Court*, 29 U. CHI. L. REV. 1 (1961).

*The University of Michigan Law School, for Kauper, FRONTIERS OF LIBERTY (1956), 6–7, 100, 110–12.

The Columbia University Quarterly for Stone, *The Conscientious Objector*, 21 COLUM. U.Q. 253–72 (1919).

PREFACE

The first draft of this manuscript was originally written almost twenty years ago. After completion it simply sat and gathered dust. Upon rereading the work so many years after its completion I was struck by the fact that most of the initial analysis was absolutely correct and most of the solutions offered would have worked. In fact, with the exception of only one free exercise area—where, unfortunately, Supreme Court decision-making has raised more legal questions than supplied real legal answers—very little has changed regarding the meaning of the free exercise clause.

This volume therefore attempts two things: (1) to review the judicial development of the free exercise of religion clause—from one offering only protection for belief and certain forms of worship to a guarantee of religiously motivated behavior; and (2) to suggest possible guidelines for the future direction of the exercise of judicial review in free exercise cases. The attempt will be made as well to view law as it develops in response to changing social values *and* policy. For, as Eugene V. Rostow has said, the law must be reexamined and redefined by the Supreme Court to benefit "each generation seeking to solve the problems of its own experience."[1]

Henry J. Abraham has suggested that religion (like love), because of its very personal and irrational nature, should preclude any individual from claiming the ability to sit in judgment.[2] Any attempt by society to find and draw the line between the realm of God and the realm of Caesar is bound to be difficult at best. Yet in America the attempt has been made and the results have been (more often than not) satisfactory. Perhaps even more than any other First Amendment guarantee, the free exercise of religion clause has been protected from governmental intrusion. Nevertheless, problems concerning the free exercise of religion still do arise—currently the major problem deals with the religious use of controlled substances—and lines must still be found and drawn. One of my concerns within this volume is how and where and why lines are drawn between the guarantee of free exercise and the right of society to protect its citizens (the unorthodox religious minority is also included) from activity injurious to their health, welfare, safety, and morals.

What I propose in the pages that follow is to reinvoke a combination of several older First Amendment tests for exclusive use in the free exercise cases, along with modifications created in the free exercise cases themselves. The preferred freedom doctrine, coupled with the concepts of the reversal of the presumption of constitutionality and less drastic (or alternative) means, offers the most commonsense standard to use in protecting and promoting the free exercise of religion-conscience. However, the protection and promotion of religious liberty and conscience at the expense of the governing power and majority rule leaves the Supreme Court open to two accusations. One is that it is attempting to burden the law with tasks it cannot perform.[3] The other is that the Court and the law cannot perform these tasks without becoming a Leviathan.[4] It is the contention of this manuscript that the free exercise of religion is important enough for the Supreme Court to forsake such criticism because religious protection and promotion is far better for a democratic society than religious warfare.

Why, in 1998, would someone write a book on the legal development of the free exercise of religion clause? After all, free exercise is no longer the crucial and high-profile "religion" clause it once was. There are no wars and no draft and no conscientious objectors (given the all-volunteer army) to worry about. And certainly no one really concerns themselves with people who—even for purely religious reasons—violate the drug laws. These are the attitudes I had to take into account when I decided to update this manuscript for publication. I rejected (and I continue to reject) each of these arguments because I believe, as the framers did more than two centuries ago, that the continuing struggle for religious freedom and conscience will always be the crux of the basic struggle for freedom. In light with the above, I would also add that this volume claims to be neither complete nor comprehensive. It is not possible to discuss and analyze *all* the free exercise cases handed down by the Supreme Court from *Reynolds* to *Flores* in the amount of pages alloted to me here; and add to this number the very much larger one when you consider the volume of free exercise claims litigated by the lower federal (and state) courts. What I have done, therefore, is to have chosen select and (and in my opinion) crucial cases for discussion and analysis—cases representing the three areas of free exercise in order to provide sufficient background information on the long, sometimes tortuous development of free exercise.

The following scholars have read, commented on, and offered advice and corrections on this material at various stages: Professors (the late) Robert S. Hirschfield of Hunter College, CUNY, Henry J. Abraham of the University of Virginia, and Jacob Landynski and Marvin Schick of the New School for Social Research. This is a far better effort because of their gracious and generous help. All errors that remain are entirely my own. Special thanks is reserved for Clay Morgan, former Senior Editor of the State University of New York Press, for having faith in this work, and for my current editor, Zina Lawrence, for bringing it into print. And to my wife, Lois, an extraordinarily gifted historian and teacher, who offered historical direction, constant commonsense advise and encouragement, and my son Andrew, now a practicing attorney, who helped with some of the earlier research and gave crucial legal direction—both of whom believed in the project—this work is lovingly dedicated.

If only popular causes are entitled to enjoy the benefits of constitutional guarantees, they serve no purpose and could as well not have been written. [From Chief Justice Stone's draft of an undelivered opinion in *Martin v. City of Struthers,* 319 U.S. 141 (1943), quoted in A. Mason, *The Supreme Court from Taft to Warren* 156 (1968)].

We should therefore hesitate before approving the application of a statute that might be used as another instrument of oppression. Religious freedom is too sacred a right to be restricted or prohibited in any degree without convincing proof that a legitimate interest of the state is in grave danger. [From Justice Murphy's dissenting opinion in *Prince v. Massachusetts,* 321 U.S. 158, 176 (1944)].

INTRODUCTION

"The end of law is not to abolish or restrain, but to preserve and enlarge freedom," declared John Locke in his *Second Treatise of Civil Government*.[1] This volume considers freedom the indispensable ingredient of our legal system. But societies find that freedom is liable to abuse, so sometimes it must be subjected to restraints in the interest of the public welfare. Much of the constitutional history of the United States only can be understood as an attempt by the Supreme Court to create a balance between freedom and authority. My concern is with the Court's special role in interpreting law that develops in response to changing social policy. Although the Court does develop or "make" law passively as well as negatively,[2] my major interest lies in the way it develops law *positively* "by extending the provisions of the Constitution into areas of individual . . . activity where they did not formerly apply."[3] Consequently, if the law is to serve a free society, it must make an ethical response to changing fact situations in the social process;[4] it must establish an "ethical minimum."[5] Every society considers certain liberties essential and surrounds them with constitutional guarantees. The need for freedom does not change, but the immediate goals of a free society do change. An acceptable jurisprudence must determine the fairness and reasonableness of rules, principles, and standards comprising the normative social structure of the law.[6] Because freedom is a value and a desired condition, my concern is with what the law "ought to be," as well as with what it "is."

I will use the term "activist libertarian" to describe the legal philosophy of one group of justices on the Supreme Court, and also for a possible role to be played by the courts in our society. The activist libertarian believes a hierarchy of constitutional rights has been imposed on our society by history *and* the Constitution. In a society that allows individual initiative, conflict necessarily arises between the interests of the individual and the interests of organized society. A chief function of the law is to adjust and conciliate these conflicts.[7] The law must insure that political processes remain open to all. The activist libertarian believes that the protective role of the Court increases when the political or electoral process is threatened.[8] The activist libertarian believes that for every social wrong there should (whenever possible) be a judicial remedy.[9]

The activist libertarian believes in the primacy of the Bill of Rights, and particularly in the First Amendment, and acknowledges that all constitutional rights cannot be of equal importance. He (or she) believes that the special historical and sociological conditions of an age necessitate priority ranking. For him, judges and courts must never forget that judicial self-restraint and judicial abstention (as Stone would caution Frankfurter in his *Gobitis* dissent) are not the same thing. Even when invoking the former, the judiciary does not withdraw from the governing process. In addition, the activist libertarian cannot admit that the ultimate remedy lies solely in the ballot box. To sacrifice the rights of a minority (especially when an unorthodox religion is involved) for majority rule is to admit there is no remedy for abusive majority rule.[10] The activist libertarian jurist, in the words of Edmond Cahn, "brings deeper understanding, wider sympathy, and more intelligent analysis to the *moral aspects of legal problems.*"[11] He knows, as did Madison in *Federalist*, no. 51, that—although the best protection is the political system itself—there must be "auxilliary precautions." The activist libertarian believes that the Supreme Court is such a second line of protection.

EVOLUTION OF RELIGIOUS LIBERTY

"Congress shall make no law respecting an establishment of religion, or prohibiting the free exercise thereof . . ."

This opening section of the First Amendment speaks of two different prohibitions: one against laws restricting religious freedom, and the other against laws establishing a state religion. Though both refer to the same general principle they are by no means the same. On occasion they conflict with each other. For example, while governmental action prohibits restriction of the free exercise of religion, nothing is said about governmental action to aid or facilitate the free exercise. If there is such a limitation, it is in the establishment clause—usually interpreted to mean anything from a prohibition against aid to a command that any aid given must be on an impartial basis.[12] The establishment clause calls for separation, while the free exercise clause leaves Americans free to work for objectives dictated by their faiths. Together, they guarantee that the division mandated by the one will forever be tested because of the freedom assured by the other. My concern in this volume will be exclusively with the free exercise clause.

Initially I shall investigate the antecedent history of the free exercise of religion guarantee, and the reasons for its inclusion in the Bill of Rights. Beyond this, I shall explore reasons why a constitutional clause written by a religious people should now afford protection for nonreligious and nonbelieving people—atheists and agnostics.

Colonial Experience

The concept of religious freedom was a strong motivating force in the history of the American colonies. People of different religious faiths who settled here hoped for a measure of religious liberty for the first time. Most early settlements were founded by persons whose religious beliefs had exposed them to persecution in other countries. But these early settlers held the idea of a state-established and state-dominated religion and sought to form communities where all would be members of one congregation.[13] Many original charters required the establishment of a state religion by all, believers and nonbelievers alike. Thus the conditions of intolerance from which the settlers had fled were reestablished in the colonies. In early Virginia all ministers were required to conform to the tenets of the Church of England. Quakers were banished, Catholics were disqualified from public office, and their priests were not even permitted in the colony. In New York Peter Stuyvesant established the Dutch Reformed Church, which all settlers were required to support. Baptists who attempted to hold services in their homes were subject to fines, whipping, and banishment. Quakers were not even permitted in the colony. In the Massachusetts Bay Colony Anne Hutchinson was convicted in 1638 as a "blasphemer, and as a teacher of erroneous doctrines."[14]

During the initial years of Colonial America religious liberty evolved slowly. Religious toleration varied from colony to colony and time to time.[15] Nevertheless, religious liberty made headway in spite of the varying obstacles it faced. In 1649, largely due to Cecil Calvert (the second Lord Baltimore), Maryland granted toleration to all Trinitarian Catholics. In Rhode Island, through the efforts of John Clarke (a follower of Roger Williams), Charles II granted a charter in 1663 that provided almost complete religious freedom. In 1683 Pennsylvania received from William Penn its *Frame of Government*, which stated that all who believed in "one Almighty God" should be protected and all who believed in "Jesus Christ the Savior of the World" might hold civil office.

How has the concept of free religious exercise come to have such a deep-rooted and special position for the American people? The slow evolution from persecution to freedom was almost inevitable. Two factors were primary. First, the persecutions and exclusions during the sixteenth and seventeenth centuries in state religions reenforced religious discontent in sections of Colonial America. The colonial awakening involved secular as well as spiritual freedom. It strengthened and gave great meaning to the words of dissenters such as Roger Williams, Thomas Hooker, John Wise, and Jonathan Mayhew. The second primary factor favoring religious freedom was the intellectual atmosphere of freedom created by the Puritan ideas of local self-government (including literacy) and the principle of equality established through social contracts.[16]

The belief in religious liberty became rooted in the political and social mind of Colonial America for several reasons, according to Ralph Barton Perry:

> [T]he rejection of theocracy and the separation of Church and state in the seventeenth and eighteenth centuries marked the triumph of three ideas: the idea of the autonomy of religion as having both the right and need to live its own life in the faith and worship of its adherents; the idea of the neutral secular state—the protector of all religions, but the partisan of none; [and] the idea that liberality of outlook and temper is not a mere limitation forced upon all religions by the exigencies of civil order, but an excellence intrinsic to religion itself.[17]

This belief reinforced both values—freedom and religion. Reinhold Riebuhr says that historically both Christian and secular forces

> were involved in establishing the political institutions of democracy; and the cultural resources of modern societies are jointly furnished by both Christianity and modern secularism. . . . Free societies are the fortunate products of the confluence of Christian and secular forces. . . . As a matter of history, the later Calvinism and the Christian sects of the 17th and the rationalism of the 18th century equally contributed to the challenge of religiously sanctified political authority. In our own nation, the equal contributions which were made to our political thought by New England Calvinism and Jeffersonian deism are symbolic of this confluence of Christianity and secularism in our democracy.[18]

Virginia Experiment

When Richard Henry Lee of Virginia introduced his three resolutions of independence to the Second Continental Congress in June 1776, the need for greater religious freedom was gaining recognition. Each colony had experience with the church-state question. About half ended the colonial period with official churches. When the new state governments came into existence, their laws reflected that experience. Nevertheless, if American colonies could demand increased secular freedom, it was logical that they also would demand increased religious freedom.

Virginia continued the struggle for religious freedom and separation of church and state. The State Convention had severed political relations with England by the time, in June 1776, that it adopted a Declaration of Rights drafted by George Mason.[19] Shortly after formal adoption of this clause by the Virginia State Convention, Thomas Jefferson introduced his Bill for Establishing Religious Freedom, later known as the Virginia Statute of Religous Liberty. He did this while revising the Virginia Code to expand the first guarantee of religious freedom in the Declaration of Rights.

> [T]o suffer the civil magistrate to intrude his powers into the field of opinion, and to restrain the profession or propagation of principles, on [the] supposition of their ill tendency is a dangerous fallacy, which at once destroys all religious liberty, . . . ; that it is time enough for the rightful purposes of civil government for its officers to interfere when principles break out into overt acts against peace and good order; . . . that truth is great and will prevail if left to herself; that she is the proper . . . antagonist to error, and has nothing to fear from the conflict unless by human interposition disarmed of her natural weapons, free argument and debate; errors ceasing to be dangerous when it is permitted freely to contradict them.[20]

This additional religious protection was not enacted easily. The influence of Jefferson and Mason, as well as James Madison's *Memorial and Remonstrance*,[21] were necessary to persuade members of the Virginia House of Delegates to accept the measure in January 1786.

The evolution of religious liberty in Virginia—from persecution to exclusion to toleration to freedom—was almost complete at this point. The Virginia Statute of Religious Liberty, coupled with the religion clause of the Virginia Bill of Rights, indicated that the *struggle for religious freedom was the crux in the struggle for freedom in general.* When "libertarian" Virginia won religious liberty for herself she won it also for the newly created United States.[22]

Constitutional Guarantee

Religion was referred to in the Constitution only in Article VI, Clause 3: "[N]o religious test shall ever be required as a qualification to any office or public trust under the United States." This so-called "oath prohibition" meant only that no executive, legislative, or judicial officer of the United States would be required to pass a religious test as a qualification for public office. To the delegates at the Philadelphia Convention, religion was still a state matter.

In answer to the many promises given during the ratification debates in the states for certain additional protections against the new national government, Madison introduced two proposed constitutional amendments (during the Bill of Rights debate) that would have prevented both national and state governments from restricting individual religious liberty, as well as the rights of speech and press:

> The civil rights of none shall be abridged on account of religious belief or worship, nor shall any national religion be established, nor shall the full and equal rights of conscience be in any manner, or on any pretext, infringed. . . .
>
> No state shall violate the equal rights of conscience, or the freedom of the press, or the trial by jury in criminal cases.[23]

His proposals were modified during the debate. What was adopted by the House of Representatives read as follows:

> Congress shall make no law establishing religion, or to prevent the free exercise thereof, or to infringe the rights of conscience.
>
> The equal rights of conscience, the freedom of speech or of the press, and the rights of trial by jury in criminal cases, shall not be infringed by any state.[24]

The Senate failed to muster the votes necessary to approve the second part of this proposed amendment. The first portion was approved, but leaving out the final phrase "or to infringe the rights of conscience." Had this clause been included, religion would also have been recognized as the voice of individual conscience, and some of the more difficult questions concerning selective conscientious objection to military service might not have come before the courts. This problem will be raised in chapter 6.

As in a later period, the concept of "state rights" made its presence felt. Several states showed no immediate desire to disestablish their churches or accept ideas of religious equality. Nevertheless, the constitutional guarantee of religious freedom was ingrained by experience and tradition; and later it would become established by law. Its continued protection and expansion would require judicial decision-making that occasionally would be controversial in nature.

CONSTITUTIONAL PROBLEMS OF RELIGION'S EVOLUTION

The free exercise of religion guaranty speaks of freedom of religious belief and freedom of religious action. As such it is related to the other substantive rights of the First Amendment—namely, speech, press, assembly, and petition. At the same time, the phrase "prohibiting the free exercise thereof" is designed to mean what it says: Congress (and by the doctrine of incorporation the states as well) may not restrict or prohibit religious belief *and* exercise. Yet while the first is absolute, the second cannot be. As Justice Roberts once said:

> Conduct remains subject to regulation for the protection of society. The freedom to act must have appropriate definition to preserve the

enforcement of that protection. . . . The power to regulate must be so exercised as not, in attaining a permissible end, unduly to infringe the protected freedom.[25]

But drawing the line, here, raises as many questions as it seems to answer; and it involves, as well as emphasizes, the interrelationship between the free exercise and the guarantees of speech, press, and assembly.

More directly to the point, the free exercise clause (along with the establishment clause) attempts to mollify the uncertain relationship between the realm of God and the realm of Caesar. The words of the clause leave much unstated and seem to take much for granted. Is the clause primarily an expression of religious commitment? Or are the words intended to justify a democratic and secular experiment? The First Amendment simply does not explain itself. What is at least clear is the fact that the free exercise clause is not an isolated statement. It may be argued that—in the absence of a religion clause—the guarantees of speech, press, and assembly provide sufficient protection for religious belief, religious worship, and religious proselytizing. *It is my belief, however, that (since the free exercise clause is not redundant) it must be interpreted as having a more specific scope in protecting something not protected by the other First Amendment clauses.*[26]

The problem of defining the term free exercise of religion will be considered at various points within the body of this volume. Nevertheless, a brief comment here may be appropriate, at least to show that any definition will be difficult. Each individual is guaranteed the constitutional right to believe and worship and practice his or her religion, so long as that individual does not illegally conflict with the right of others.[27] Any legal definition of free exercise, if one is even possible, will come from the Supreme Court. Its acceptance or rejection by a majority of the people will depend ultimately on their willingness to have the Court substitute its current legal values (in defining free exercise) for their own psychologically oriented spiritual values. The have usually allowed the Court's definition to stand.

The free exercise of religion clause means more than no governmental infringement of that inner, spiritual belief already beyond governmental reach.[28] Nevertheless, *something* is protected against governmental intrusion. Let me suggest, as a beginning, what free exercise does not mean. Free exercise, for example, does not mean that the individual may resort to any action that he or she believes is sanctioned by his or her religion. At the same time, the individual cannot refuse to obey valid criminal law, even if it is contrary to his or her religion. In essence, there are limits to the freedom guaranteed by the free exercise clause. And the Court's line-drawing can set limits that are minimal as well as maximal.

I hope the reader will not find it confusing at this point if I briefly distinguish among the freedoms of belief, worship, and proselytizing—for each represents a different aspect of the free exercise of religion.

1. At a minimum, the freedom of religious belief means that the government cannot impose upon the individual an official (or even acceptable) belief, or one which he must say he believes in. But freedom of belief means much more than no allowable compulsion. It also means that the individual is guaranteed freedom from any intellectual conformity resulting from the embarrassment of his refusal to be initially compelled. And it means ultimately—in the words of Joseph Tussman—the right of individuals "to provide or maintain a general environment conducive to the development of desired moral and intellectual attitudes and beliefs."[29] All forms of coercion vis-a-vis religious belief *are* intolerable and *should be* constitutionally voided.

2. The individual is free to worship in his or her own way or reject all such ceremonies. In order to help secure this freedom we do not tax houses of worship or require attendance at religious services. But two difficulties arise nonetheless. First, there are ceremonial occasions not thought to be "religious"—flag saluting and oath taking—but that may seem to others to be idolatrous or in conflict with *their* religious beliefs. Second, there are limits imposed upon certain ceremonial rituals classified by some sects as forms of worship. Freedom of worship does not protect ritual actions (polygamy, snake-handling, human sacrifices) made criminal by law.

3. The freedom to proselytize includes the right to spread the faith by preaching to the unconverted, oftentimes in rather unorthodox ways. And although this freedom to communicate is already protected by the guarantees of speech, press, and assembly, certain decisions of the Supreme Court suggest that "religious" communication is subject to special consideration. These decisions concerning proselytizing by members of Jehovah's Witnesses (discussed in chapter 2) suggest religious communication can receive protection beyond limits imposed on the freedom of speech. By adding religious freedom to the freedoms of speech and press, the resulting religious communication seems to be given greater protection than other forms of communication.[30]

These problems, as well as numerous others, will be considered in greater detail within the body of this volume.

LAW AND THE PROBLEM OF FREE EXERCISE

The cornerstone of our constitutional liberties and form of government is the First Amendment guarantees of individual freedom. Any American definition of constitutional government gives these freedoms highest priority. This high position depends upon the emphasis placed on the free interplay of opinion within our free society, as well as the role of the individual judge (and the Supreme Court) in the judicial decision-making process. Burton C. Bernard has suggested that

> [t]he First Amendment is designed to guarantee freedom for the individual to express his beliefs. This freedom is essential to an accurate reflection of the sentiment of the people in the formation of public opinion and in the operation of government. . . . [T]he availability of the political process as a means of checking official abuse of . . . personal interests, is lessened when legislative . . . action curtails free expression. Accordingly, *an especial responsibility for safeguarding free expression should devolve upon the Court.* If this analysis is the sole basis for preference, then it is clear that for the most part only those personal interests protected by the First Amendment are to be preferred.[31]

When the free exercise of religion guarantee, as well as the other guarantees of the First Amendment, were made applicable to the states through the due process clause of the Fourteenth Amendment, judicial interpretation centered on the scope of the freedom—whether to interpret it broadly or narrowly. This continues to be the central question of constitutional law: "where to draw the line which marks the boundary between the appropriate field of individual liberty and right and that of government action for the larger good, so as to insure the least sacrifice of both types of social advantage."[32]

In adjudicating question of doubtful constitutionality, the Supreme Court faces issues that are ultimately political. Any solution to the problem of religious liberty versus governmental authority, according to Paul G. Kauper, reflects the scheme of the constitutional values of the nine men and women who compose the Supreme Court.[33] Of course, any attempt to separate the law from the political and social forces that bear upon its ultimate meaning can only be partially successful. No matter how "objective" a judge may claim to be, cases are never decided as pure classroom exercises.

> In the long run, logic is apt to yield to life, and technicality to justice and social need. . . . While a system of concepts and rules is necessary in order to guarantee the reign of law in society, it must always be kept in mind that such rules and concepts were created in order to meet the needs of life, and that care must be taken lest life be unnecessarily and

senselessly forced into the strait jacket of an overrigid legal order. Law cannot be reduced to a system of mathematics or scholastic logic. . . . Any attempt to keep the law completely insulated from the external social forces beating against the armor by which the law seeks to protect its internal structure will necessarily be doomed to failure.[34]

The words of the free exercise of religion clause (the right to believe and worship and proselytize) will remain the same, but the Supreme Court will continue to give them new meaning by its reappraisal and reconstruction of the judicial hierarchy of constitutional values. The development of the free exercise clause, and the problems it gives rise to, are significant because they deal with the limits of that reappraisal and reconstruction—and the lines that must be continually drawn.

CHAPTER 1

Criminal Conduct/Antisocial Behavior

James Madison placed the primary emphasis on freedom in framing the free exercise of religion guarantee of the First Amendment. In expanding this emphasis, the Supreme Court has ruled that religious freedom includes more than the right to believe and worship according to the dictates of one's own conscience. Religious freedom also means the right to proselytize—to engage in activities designed to win converts to the faith,[1] to distribute and sell religious literature free from license requirements and tax burdens,[2] to refuse to participate in secular practices against one's own religious beliefs,[3] to use public streets and parks for religious meetings,[4] and to make door-to-door solicitations free from local restrictions.[5] And the meaning of religious freedom has evolved in direct proportion to the Court's expansion of the outer limits and coverage of the First Amendment.

The starting point for a review of the constitutional meaning attached to the free exercise of religion guarantee by the Supreme Court is the case of *Reynolds v. United States*.[6] The most positive limitation on the exercise of individual religious freedom is its subjection to valid criminal law. While religious belief is protected, any practice made criminal by law is usually not protected regardless of the religious motivations involved. Practice in the form of criminal conduct must be balanced against the public welfare of the community as set forth by law.

Members of the Mormon Church since 1853 considered polygamous marriage a sacred duty. While Utah was still a territory, Congress enacted a statute making polygamy a criminal offense.[7] George Reynolds was duly convicted under this law. In his appeal on writ of error, Reynolds based his claim squarely on the free exercise of religion guarantee, as well as on the basic tenets of the Mormon Church. His counsel argued before the Court that (1) at the time of his second marriage he was a member of the Mormon Church and a follower of its doctrines; (2) the doctrine of his church prescribed the act of polygamy as a sacred duty; (3) polygamous marriage was a practice directly enjoined by God upon man in a "revelation" to the prophet Joseph Smith; and (4) the Mormon Church specifically taught that failure to practice the act of polygamy would lead to "eternal damnation." However, the Supreme

Court ruled that Congress did not violate Reynolds' right to the free exercise of religion, or violate (for that matter) any constitutional prohibition against the national government. The ruling stressed that this particular freedom prohibited the government from restricting religious belief, but not a religious practice (action) that violated valid criminal law.

Since the word "religion" was not defined in the Constitution, Chief Justice Waite (speaking for the Court) asked the crucial question: What is the religious freedom of the individual that is guaranteed against all infringements? His review of tradition and past experience of the United States led him to the documents of the Virginia experiment, to Madison's *Memorial and Remonstrance*, to Jefferson's concept of the balance between civil government and religious freedom as stated in his letter to the Danbury Baptists.[8] Such a constitutional guarantee, the Chief Justice believed, did not prohibit legislation regarding the distinction of what properly belongs to the church and to the state. Congress may have been deprived of all legislative power over mere opinions, but it still possessed the power to deal with actions considered criminal. Indeed, Congress could act to forestall behavior that it ordinarily had the power to prevent; and since it acted here in furtherance of a valid secular objective, the religious beliefs of Reynolds could not "decriminalize" his actions. What enters the picture, as a guide for future Supreme Court adjudication, is what Richard E. Morgan calls the "secular regulation rule":[9] "If the law is within the scope of governmental authority and of general application, it may . . . be applied without regard to the religious convictions of those whose acts constitute wilful violations of that law."[10]

The Chief Justice, obviously believing that polygamy violated some civil contract aspect of monogamous marriage, had no difficulty in finding a valid social interest that Congress had the power to legislate.[11] And in the process, the Court seemed to take the incredible step of equating "religion" (and all the concept entails) with Christianity. Of course, such an interpretation had not been the intention of Mason, Madison, and Jefferson. Furthermore, Waite suggested that the religious beliefs and practices of the individual, no matter how sincere the motivations, cannot be accepted as a justification for the commission of a crime.

> Laws are made for the government of actions, and while they cannot interfere with mere religious belief and opinions, they may with practices. Suppose one believed that human sacrifices were a necessary part of religious worship, would it be seriously contended that the civil government under which he lived could not interfere to prevent a sacrifice? . . . Can a man excuse his practices to the contrary because of his religious belief? To permit this would be to make the professed doc-

trines of religious belief superior to the law of the land, and in effect to permit every citizen to become a law unto himself. Government could exist in name only under such circumstances.[12]

Reynolds' offense consisted of a positive act that he knowingly committed. For the Court, therefore, "it would be dangerous to hold that the offender might escape punishment because he religiously believed the law which he had broken ought never to have been made."[13] The Court might accept ignorance of a fact as lack of criminal intent, but never ignorance of the law. The decision reiterated the congressional intent to outlaw polygamy and make its practice criminal.

Reynolds was the first of the Mormon cases. Other federal decisions were to follow. Each reiterated and strengthened the secular regulation rule, as well as the notion that the practice of one's religious beliefs cannot be used as a justification for the commission of a crime. Equally important, these decisions—following along the lines set out in Reynolds—continued to judicially define the term religion.

Polygamy, then as now, a criminal offense, constituted a disqualification for voting under territorial and other statutes. Samuel Davis was a Mormon who wanted to vote. He appeared before the appropriate registrar in the then Territory of Idaho and took the required oath.[14] He was subsequently indicted for, and convicted of, conspiring to obstruct the due administration of the territorial laws by falsifying his voter's oath. In essense, the lower federal court had upheld the disenfranchisement of members of the Mormon religion. Speaking for a unanimous Court in Davis v. Beason,[15] Justice Field rejected both the free exercise and establishment claims of Davis in language that reasserted the secular regulation rule:

> It was never intended or supposed that the Amendment could be invoked as a protection against legislation for the punishment of acts inimical to the peace, good order and morals of society. . . . However free the exercise of religion may be, it must be subordinate to the criminal law of the country, passed with reference to actions regarded by general consent as properly the subjects of punitive legislation.[16]

To outlaw polygamy was clearly proper, according to Field. By a delegation of power from the Congress, the territorial legislature of Idaho had the authority "to prescribe any qualifications for voters calculated to secure obedience to its laws."[17] If disenfranchisement of certain criminal segments of the community was deemed necessary to secure that compliance, then Idaho's action was not only reasonable but also a valid secular objective.

The logical conclusion was to define the concept of religion in narrow terms, including belief and some forms of worship, but excluding criminal action in the guise of religious practices.

The First Amendment to the Constitution, in declaring that Congress shall make no law respecting the establishment of religion, or forbidding the free exercise thereof, was in tended to allow everyone under the jurisdiction of the United States to entertain such notions respecting his relations to his Maker and the duties they impose as may be approved by his judgment and conscience, and to exhibit his sentiments in such form of worship as he may think proper, not injurious to the equal rights of others, and to prohibit legislation for the support of any religious tenets, or the modes of worship of any sect.[18]

Justice Field then continued:

With man's relations to his Maker and the obligations he may think they impose, and the manner in which an expression shall be made by him of his belief on those subjects, no interference can be permitted, provided always the laws of society, designed to secure its peace and prosperity, and the morals of its people, are not interfered with.[19]

And still continuing with the same theme, Field quoted (with obvious approval) Chief Justice Waite's similar view in his *Reynolds* opinion that laws may indeed interfere with religious action made criminal by law. Field defined religion in terms of individual commitment. Yet he could not accept any suggestion that a criminal act became "less odious because sanctioned by what any particular sect may designate as religion."[20] As George W. Spicer suggested, it was the intended purpose of the free exercise clause to allow everyone "to hold such beliefs respecting his relation to the Diety and his obligations thereunder as meet the approval of his judgment and conscience and to express his beliefs in such form as he may think proper, so long as there [was] no injury to the rights of others."[21]

The final Mormon case involved the successful attempt by Congress in 1887 to annul the charter of the Mormon Church in the Utah Territory, and to declare forfeited to the national government all church real estate except a small portion used exclusively for public worship. In 1862 Congress legislated against the practice of polygamy. But failing to stop the Mormon practice by legislation, Congress (in 1887) instructed the Attorney General to begin proceedings to forfeit and escheat to the United States the property of corporations obtained or held in violation of the 1862 statute. Both the Mormon Church and John Taylor (a trustee) sued. Justice Bradley, speaking for a majority of the Court in *The Late Corporation of the Church of Jesus Christ of Latter-Day Saints v. United States*,[22] believed that whenever the law of the land (in this case the law against polygamy) had been systematically violated by a charitable organization, it was within the power of Congress to disincorporate such an organization. Moreover, because of the national government's plenary power over the territories, "when a corporation is dissolved, its personal property, . . . ceases to be the subject of private ownership, and becomes subject to the disposal of the sovereign authority";[23] and the Congress may direct such property "to other charitable objects."[24]

Article I, Section 8, Clause 7 of the Constitution gives Congress the authority "to establish post offices and post roads." In exercising this provision, the Congress has enacted many postal rules under which the mails are processed and delivered. With the general welfatre of the community in mind, Congress enacted the postal law of 1889, which was concerned with the use of the mails for religious fraud. And in the case of *New v. United States,*[25] the national government prosecuted a professional faith healer for using the mails to defraud the public. The government charged that (1) the two defendants (John Fair New and Marie T. Leo) had pretended to believe that they attained a supernatural state of selfimmortality by righteous conduct, enabling them to conquer misery, poverty, disease, and death; (2) they could transmit this power to others for money; and (3) for the execution of their fraudulent scheme they used the mails of the United States.

The defendants questioned the validity of the indictment against them on the ground that it prohibited the practice of their religious beliefs. The Circuit Court of Appeals for the Ninth Circuit pointed out that the government did not attempt to force the defendants from holding the religious views

> the indictment alleges they pretended to entertain, or from honestly and sincerely endeavoring to persuade others, by any legitimate means, to embrace the same notions. But what the government did undertake to do, and what it had the statutory authority for doing, was to prevent by indictment the defendants . . . from pretending to entertain the views therein specifically alleged for the false and fraudulent purpose of procuring money or other things of value from third parties by use of its post office establishment, of which use the indictment alleges the defendants availed themselves for the said false, fraudulent, and illegal purpose.[26]

The court held that the government's action (i.e., prohibiting religious fraud through the use of the mails) was a valid secular objective; for the sole purpose of the law was to prevent the obtaining of money through the fraudulent use of the mails. Almost three decades later the precedent was to be reexamined by the Supreme Court, which based its new decision on criteria and reasons other than the furtherance of a valid secular objective.

In May 1940, the Supreme Court handed down its decision in *Cantwell v. Connecticut,*[27] and specifically ruled that the fundamental concept of liberty in the due process clause of the Fourteenth Amendment included the free exercise of religion guarantee. More important, the Court's decision raised three questions that would ultimately require judicial answers. First, *how far* in future decisions would it be willing to depart from the accepted distinction of the polygamy cases between protected belief and unprotected action?[28] Second, does the law have an *unlimited right* to protect people against the perpetration of *religious* frauds? Third, can an administrative official determine if a cause was in fact a bona fide religious one, so as to determine its right to survive? The Court now seemed willing to apply the logic of Cardozo in *Palko v. Connecticut*[29] and Stone in footnote four of his opinion in *United States v. Carolene Products Co.*,[30] to a First Amendment freedom in need of greater scrutiny and protection. For nearly a decade after *Cantwell* the Court would continue to narrow the older distinction between belief and action, although never to the point of being synonymous. There would be great victories for the cause of free exercise in all areas of adjudication save for "criminal" conduct. Here the victories would be slight and infrequent. And as hard as the Court would sometimes try, it could not seem to ever totally abandon the secular regulation rule.

The Ballard family had organized the so-called "I Am" movement in San Francisco during the late 1930s. They claimed (as messangers from God) the power to communicate with the "spirit world" and solicited money on the basis of the claim. They were indicted for religious fraud and for using the mails to accomplish their fraudulent scheme. With the consent of counsel for both sides, the trial judge instructed the jury that the government could not concern itself with either the truth or falsity of the Ballards' religious beliefs. This left the jury to consider only the question of whether the Ballard family honestly and sincerely believed in the claim they made. Thus, if the jury found that they did not honestly and sincerely believe their own representations, they must be found guilty.[31] The district court convicted the Ballard family for using, and conspiring to use, the mails to defraud. The Court of Appeals for the Ninth Circuit reversed the conviction on grounds that the trial court had restricted the jury to the issue of the good faith of the defendants, although the government should have proved the claims false. When the appeals court granted a new trial, the Solicitor General asked the Supreme Court to reinstate the jury verdict. A majority of the Court agreed that the contention of the court of appeals ought to be reversed—because of basic agreement with the position of the trial judge. And it was their intention (which they accomplished), according to Glendon Schubert, to quash the new trial and order the appeals court to consider the constitutional issues raised by the Ballard family in the original appeal.[32]

Justice Douglas, for a 5-4 (Jackson's dissent should more appropriately be listed as a concurrence of sorts making the decision 6-3) majority of the Court in *United States v. Ballard,*[33] side-stepped the issue of the defendants' good faith and concentrated on the reasons for excluding from governmental concern any inquiry into the truth or falsity of a religious belief. He accomplished this task by not applying the secular regulation rule and, at the same time, creating a so-called test of sincerity. Douglas maintained that the government must not concern itself with the question of truth or falsity of religious beliefs. The only issue for judges was whether the questioned belief was sincerely held. The free exercise of religion guarantee does not attempt to set up a preferred belief, but rather applies to all beliefs. "Freedom of thought, which includes freedom of religious belief," said Douglas, "is basic in a society of free men."[34] The constitutional guarantee of free exercise includes the right

> to maintain theories of life and of death and of the hereafter which are rank heresy to followers of the orthodox faiths. Heresy trials are foreign to our Constitution. Men may believe what they cannot prove. They may not be put to the proof of their religious doctrines or beliefs. Religious experiences which are as real as life to some may be incomprehensible to others. Yet the fact that they may be beyond the ken of mortals does not mean that they can be made suspect before the law. . . . [Our Founding Fathers] fashioned a charter of government which envisaged the widest possible toleration of conflicting views. Man's relation to his God was made no concern of the state. He was granted the right to worship as he pleased and to answer to no man for the verity of his religious views.[35]

Although the religious beliefs of the Ballard family might seem incredible, they cannot be subjected to verification of truth. "When the triers of fact undertake that task, they enter a forbidden domain."[36] And in applying the test of sincerity, Douglas seemed to conclude that the "I Am" movement was in fact a "religion" because the Ballards believed that it was. Consequently, it required the protection of the free exercise clause, no matter how unusual its doctrines.

Chief Justice Stone, along with Justices Roberts and Frankfurter, dissented from the opinion of the Court. Stone said in effect that the constitutional guarantee of religious freedom does not afford immunity from, or justification for, the commission of a crime. This was especially true where the interests in protecting society outweigh the interest in religion. "I cannot say that freedom of thought and worship includes freedom to procure money by making knowingly false statements about one's religious experiences."[37] Under such circumstances, Stone believed that the government should have been allowed to submit to the jury any proof available that the Ballards were religious fakers. In addition, Stone was concerned with the issue of the defendant's state of mind because such mental processes are as capable of

> fraudulent misrepresentation as is one's physical condition or the state of his bodily health. . . . Certainly none of respondents' constitutional rights are violated if they are prosecuted for the fraudulent procurement of money by false representations as to their beliefs, religious or otherwise.[38]

For him, as for the Solicitor General, the verdict of guilty should be reinstated. After all, the issue of belief had been submitted to the jury in good faith.

Justice Jackson also wrote a separate dissenting opinion, although he agreed in principle with the majority. For him, the justices composing the majority did not carry their opinion to a logical conclusion. The national government and the states cannot in any circumstances question the sincerity and honesty of the individual's religious beliefs. In a society where its constitutional guarantees protect the individual's free exercise of religion, religious sincerity cannot be tried apart from religious verity: "If we try religious sincerity severed from religious verity, we isolate the dispute from the very considerations which in common experience provide its most reliable answer."[39] Not content to stop there, Jackson then concluded his opinion by asking when

> does less than full belief in a professed credo become action able fraud if one is soliciting gifts or legacies? Such inquiries may discomfort orthodox as well as unconventional religious teachers, for even the most regular of them are sometimes accused of taking their orthodoxy with a grain of salt.[40]

In essence, he would not allow either the government or the courts to examine anyone's religious beliefs. Neither instrumentality was capable of doing so; and such prosecutions could lead only to religious persecutions. Milton R. Konvitz summarized Jackson's feeling about the Court's not carrying its decision far enough when he suggested that it was not possible to measure a person's

> honesty or sincerity when it comes to religious beliefs. . . . The human mind plays with subtleties, shadings of meanings, nuances, refinements of thoughts, ideas and shadows of ideas, myths, metaphors, parables, paradoxes, hyperboles, anthropomorphisms, circumlocutions, and a thousand and one other devices, which . . . the mind itself has made. . . . Who can weigh and measure the quantity and quality of honesty in professions of religious faith.[41]

And he also indicated that if inquisitions for heresy are alien to our Constituion, inquisitions for hypocrisy should also be alien.[42]

At first glance *Ballard* seems to abandon the secular regulation rule. It does not. Jackson's dissent (or more appropriately his concurrence regarding first principles) was not the opinion of the Court. And Douglas simply side-stepped the issue of good faith entirely. His sincerity test, although not what one would have hoped for in a result-oriented way, nevertheless allowed free exercise to emerge victorious. If the majority opinion "legitimized" the perpetration of religious fraud, it was a small enough price to pay for a free society. Elwyn A. Smith commented on the majority holding and its enlargment of free exercise in the following way;

> *Ballard* makes clear that so long as the courts are reluctant to define religion or even to specify, from a legal point of view, the sphere in which religion is conceived to lie, the area protected by the First Amendment tends to expand, encroachment on the state's sphere of operation tends to grow, and the rights of individuals and minorities over against those of the majority tends to increase.[43]

Inevitably, free exercise was more than the right to hold ideas. It also meant the right to express them.[44]

In contrast, *Prince v. Massachusetts*[45] illustrated succesful application of a state criminal statute against a form of "criminal" conduct. The decision continued the precedents of the polygamy cases—that a valid secular objective may taint certain forms of religious behavior with criminality. I might note one significant caveat: the Court did in fact distinguish between actions of an adult (which might fall under the protection of the free exercise clause) and actions of a child (which were not comparably protected).

The child labor statute of Massachusetts declared that no minor (boy under twelve or girl under eighteen) could sell any article of merchandise on the streets at night. The statute also made it unlawful to furnish a minor with items to be sold in violation of the law. A nine-year-old girl and her aunt (who was also her guardian) were convicted for selling publications of their religious sect on the streets at night. Both claimed to be ordained ministers of the Jehovah's Witnesses, and rested their case on the free exercise of religion clause. The aunt also entered a claim of parental right secured by the due process clause of the Fourteenth Amendment.

Speaking for a 5-4 majority, Justice Rutledge said that the family unit was not immune to regulation in the public interest even in the face of a free exercise claim. "[N]either rights of religion nor rights of parenthood are beyond limitation."[46] Indeed, when acting to protect the general welfare of the community on behalf of its children, the state as *parens patriae* may restrict the control of the parent and child in many ways. The state's authority over children's activities, according to Rutledge, was broader than like actions of adults.[47] And invoking a modified version of the secular regulation rule, Rutledge compared the relative importance of the competing interests involved and found that the statute was reasonable under all circumstances.

> We think that with reference to the public proclaiming of religion, upon the streets and in other similar public places, the power of the state to control the conduct of children reaches beyond the scope of its authority over adults, as is true in the case of other freedoms, and the rightful boundary of its power has not been crossed in this case.[48]

And once again, Rutledge was concerned with the adult-child distinction. Accordingly, "[p]arents may be free to become martyrs themselves. But it does not follow they are free, in identical circumstances, to make martyrs of their children before they have reached the age of full and legal discretion when they can make that choice for themselves."[49] Without that distinction—and the fact that parents are not free to make martyrs of their children—this decision might invariably have gone the other way.

The very same distinction that troubled Rutledge troubles me as well. In fact, I believe it to be a distinction without a difference. To suggest, as he did, that similar action by an adult would be protected by the free exercise clause, or that parents were free to make martyrs of themselves but not their children, was to disregard the meaning of religion for Jehovah's Witnesses. All—children and adults alike—believe themselves to be Witnesses of God, ordained ministers in His cause, with the primary task of proclaiming the impending Kingdom. To declare that the state may reinterpret the meaning of religion for the Witness sect—to distinguish between "witnesses" and "witnesses"—was to intrude upon basic belief, not actionable criminal conduct. Such an attitude on behalf of the state was to place a secular meaning upon the concept of religion. Such an attitude was to create a fictitious secular objective when no clear and present danger existed. It was one thing to draw a workable line between the realm of God and the realm of Caesar, but quite another thing for Caesar to be the only one to say what God was in fact entitled to.

Justice Jackson, along with Justice Frankfurter and Roberts, dissented, saying that the decision reached was inconsistent with the *Murdock* opinion.[50] He felt the case pointed out the basis of disagreement among Court members as expressed in earlier Jehovah Witness cases. And the basis of such disagreement involved the methods to be used in establishing limitations on the outer limits of the free exercise clause.

> My own view may be shortly put: I think the limits begin to operate whenever activities begin to affect or collide with liberties of others or

of the public. Religious activities which concern only members of the faith are and ought to be free—as nearly absolutely free as anything can be. . . . [But when churches engage in purely secular activities, these things are] Caesar's affairs and may be regulated by the state so long as it does not discriminate against one because he is doing them for a religious purpose, and the regulation is not arbitrary and capricious, in violation of other provisions of the Constitution.[51]

Also dissenting was Justice Murphy, who felt that no distinction should be made between the religious exercises of parent or child. Moreover, the actions of both parent and child must be allowed free exercise protection up to the point of a grave, immediate, and substantial danger.[52] In addition, reasoned Murphy, no sufficient proof was presented to justify the belief that lasting harm would come to Witness children distributing religious literature in public places. "[T]he bare possibility that such harms might emanate from distribution of religious literature is not, standing alone, sufficient justification for restricting freedom of conscience and religion."[53] Murphy then went on to argue that parents and/or guardians should not be subjected to criminal liability because of vague possibilities that their religious teachings might cause injury to the child. The evils that the state can protect children from must be grave, immediate, and substantial; a higher standard than "vague possibilities" was required by the free exercise clause.

Murphy's dissent also raised the issue of what logical conclusion might be reached in the application of the free exercise clause—and presumably the other First Amendment guarantees as well—and how far it might be extended in areas where a *vital secular claim* was not presented.

In dealing with the validity of statutes which directly or indirectly infringe religious freedom and the right of parents to encourage their children in the practice of a religious belief, we are not aided by any strong presumption of the constitutionality of such legislation. . . . On the contrary, the human freedoms enumerated in the First Amendment and carried over into the Fourteenth . . . are to be presumed to be invulnerable and any attempt to sweep away those freedoms is prima facie invalid. It follows that any restriction or prohibition must be justified by those who deny that the freedoms have been unlawfully invaded. The burden was therefore on the state of Massachusetts to prove the reasonableness and necessity of prohibiting children from engaging in religious activity of the type involved in this case.[54]

The significance of the issue raised by this forceful dissent, the actual reversal of the presumption of constitutionality concept, will be presented in the concluding chapters of this volume.

When the practice of a religious belief becomes criminal conduct, the Supreme Court will not accept the free exercise of religion guarantee as a justification. The precedent was established in the polygamy cases and has been reiterated many times.[55] What contrary holdings there have been—with the exception of *Ballard*—occurred in the lower federal and state courts;[56] and they have been the exception rather than the rule. In this one area of adjudication, the Court has been unwilling (one is tempted to say unable) to rid itself of the secular regulation rule. And so long as the distinction between belief and action remains (at least under the *Reynolds* and *Davis* definitions), the Court has two viable options open to it in criminal conduct cases: (1) it can continue to invoke the secular regulation rule in the obvious cases of polygamy and snake-handling; and (2) disregard the rule (and create a more favorable free exercise test) in the harmless cases exemplified by *Ballard* and *Prince*. I include here the problem of child-labor laws because I believe Rutledge and the majority were wrong in drawing both their distinctions and their lines. I would also add the harmless drug cases involving peyote, marijuana, and LSD, such as *People v. Woody*,[57] *United States v. Kuch*,[58] and *Oregon Department of Human Resources v. Smith*.[59] Since an acceptable (and useable) definition seems to be beyond the ability of man, the Court might consider the wisdom of such an approach—especially when our definitions of criminal conduct are subject to the same constant changes as society itself.

SUMMARY

What seems obviously apparent is that the judicial distinctions between belief and action still exist in the area of criminal conduct; and the use of such favorable free exercise tests (used in other areas of adjudication) as greater judicial scrutiny, clear and imminent danger, and preferred freedoms, have found little applicability here. The secular regulation rule, although not always acceptable in other free exercise areas, still finds here a large degree of support. But the problem is more complicated than this.

On the prime occasion when the test of sincerity replaced the secular regulation rule for a majority of the Court, it raised almost as many problems as it solved. As a test it was much more favorable to the free exercise claim—for it protected belief *and* many forms of action. Yet the test (as applied) did not set out any method of measuring sincerity. What might such criteria and standards be? Perhaps the length of time that the belief was held,[60] or the fervency with which the views were advanced.[61] How were either of these possibilities, or others that could be created, be measured? In other areas of free exercise adjudication the Court would attempt to grapple with the problem.

Another approach, begun in the polygamy cases, was to "test for religion." This required at least a coherent definition of the term. Unfortunately, the task proved not only more frustrating, but also more difficult. The creation and maintenance of such a definition required the Court to "examine the intrinsic quality of the beliefs asserted," as well as the "forms of worship or practice associated with the asserted beliefs."[62] Richard E. Morgan suggested this problem in the following way:

> To inquire into the quality of beliefs required that standards be set for determining what are assertions about the diety, about basic nature of man and about the human condition—standards which distinguish such assertions from trivial notions not worthy of the term religion. The mind boggles at the thought of judges hacking away, case by case, at this level of abstraction. Inchoate judicial subjectivism could be the only result.[63]

Morgan then continued:

> But to examine practices is even worse. Must there be regular meetings? Must there be exercises of a liturgical sort? It is hard to see how judges could avoid taking the familiar forms of religious worship as covert norms; the orthodox would be advantaged over the believer practicing in strange ways—just the sort of person whose behavior the free exercise [clause] is . . . being expanded to protect.[64]

Morgan also suggested that combining the two approaches did not guarantee coherence. Either everyone would qualify or judges (because of their personal predilections) would discriminate against the unorthodox and unfamiliar.[65] The dilemma has no answer. If the Court is to extend the free exercise clause to cover action, "it must define religion, and to define religion is to arbitrarily impose an orthodoxy."[66]

This, then, was—and is—the continuing dilemma. And the dilemma exists whether the free exercise clause is invoked by the "odd" few or a majority of religious fanatics. Remember, a right does not disappear because it is invoked or because of the increasing number of individuals choosing to invoke it.

There is one additional point to mention. I have saved the most difficult problem for last. The topic of this chapter is "criminal conduct/antisocial behavior." I used a double title because I am not convinced that all of the conduct discussed here is "criminal." Like H. L. A. Hart, I must wonder whether some of this so-called actionable behavior is not really a problem of morality—and its enforcement upon the "odd" few by a conformity-minded majority. Polygamy is the classic example here. According to Hart, if polygamy is being punished in order to protect the religious sensibilities of the majority, the polygamist is being punished as a nuisance for committing a public act.[67] But, on the other hand, if polygamy is labeled a crime—because the activity is practiced in private—by individuals who strongly condemn the act for sexual reasons, the polygamist is being punished for immorality.[68] I recognize that a very fine line of distinction may exist here, but it is a distinction nonetheless. And I believe that the *Reynolds* and *Davis* cases were incorrectly decided—and the resulting secular regulation rule erroneously constructed—because I am convinced that *it should not be the purpose of the law to punish immoral behavior* that does not endanger nonparticipants. The polygamy cases do just that; for the only religious sensibilities infringed were those of the Mormons themselves.

It must always be remembered that in virtually all jurisdiction where polygamy is punishable, the sexual cohabitation of the parties, although possibly a criminal offense, is seldom punished. If a married man cares to cohabitate with another woman—or even several other women—he may do so with impunity so far as the criminal law is concerned.[69] In fact, "[h]e may set up house and pretend that he is married . . . [b]ut if he goes through a [second] ceremony of marriage, the law steps in not merely to declare [the marriage] invalid but to punish the [polygamist]."[70] Should the law have the right to interfere at this point, after leaving the sexual cohabitation alone? Why is the extended period of sexual cohabitation not punished? Why does a simple marriage ceremony transform the act simultaneously into immorality and actionable criminal behavior?

It is not my purpose here to defend polygamy, or even condone it. Rather, I am concerned with the curious ritual that takes place in the minds and hearts of the community when certain forms of "antisocial behavior" become crimes simply because the community conveniently forgets about democratic principles and the guaranteed rights of the minority. John Stuart Mill's *On Liberty* rejected the idea that you could use punitive law to punish an act offensive to religious feelings;[71] and this would be especially true when the act itself was motivated by religious beliefs. Mill was not inconsistent on this point, even though he also suggested that coercion may be justifiably used to prevent harm to others. From Mill's perspective, you simply cannot—and should not—constitute as harm the possible distress occasioned by the thought that others are offending in private against public morality.[72] Even if the majority of the community is both neurotic and hypersensitive, and literally "made ill" by the thought, it cannot constitute harm under democratic principles.[73]

Hart suggested the nexus of the problem in the following language:

[A] right to be protected from the distress which is inseparable from the bare knowledge that others are acting in ways you think wrong, cannot be acknowledged by anyone who recognizes individual liberty as a value. . . . If distress incident to the belief that others are doing wrong is harm, so also is the distress incident to the belief that others are doing what you do not want them to do. To punish people for causing this form of distress would be tantamount to punishing them simply because others object to what they do; and the only liberty that could coexist with this extension of the utilitarian principle is liberty to do those things to which no one seriously objects. Such liberty plainly is quite nugatory. Recognition of individual liberty as a value involves, as a minimum, acceptance of the principle that the individual may do what he wants, even if others are distressed when they learn what it is that he does—unless, of course, there are other good grounds for forbidding it.[74]

If there is no harm to be prevented, and no potential victim to be protected, as is oftentimes the case when conventional "antisocial behavior" is involved (since there is usually consent, and the so-called victim is usually willing)—then the assertion that conformity is a value worth pursuing, and an appropriate end for the law to secure by the use of criminal sanctions, is completely unacceptable in a free society given the misery and sacrifice of freedom that it involves.[75] The price of human suffering forced upon people motivated by purely religious beliefs, the ability of society to inflict punishment as a symbol of moral condemnation, is simply too high a price to pay. Once again, Hart suggested what should be the last word:

[W]here there is no victim but only a transgression of a moral rule, the view that punishment is . . . called for as a proper return for the immorality lacks . . . support. Retribution here seems to rest on nothing but the implausible claim that in morality two blacks make a white: that the evil of suffering added to the evil of immorality as its punishment makes a moral good.[76]

Three decades ago, Alexander Meiklejohn suggested that "[t]o be afraid of ideas, any idea, is to be unfit for selfgovernment."[77] Punishing antisocial behavior as actionable criminal conduct is only one example in American law of the fact that most Americans are afraid to be free. The odd few, the dissenters and malcontents, the engagers in antisocial behavior, alert us to democracy's most fundamental truth: the imposition of conformity in the name of law and morality means no democracy and no freedom.

Nevertheless, by the 1940s the older distinction between belief and action would no longer suffice. Not only would the secular regulation rule be eroded, but it would not be carried over into other free exercise areas. Indeed, the Court (in these other areas) created a more favorable series of tests and tools and devices; and the new judicial techniques allowed judges to write their values concerning the free exercise clause into the First Amendment. And in the process it allowed action to be protected along with belief—while on several occasions making the two indistinguishable.

It is to some of these problems that I now turn.

CHAPTER 2

Previous Restraint

The free exercise of religion guarantee has come to mean that religious proselytizing must be exempt from previous restraint legislation. Municipal ordinances requiring the previous consent of local officials for the dissemination of religious literature and ideas have been challenged in the courts as infringements of religious freedom. But until the free exercise clause became nationalized in the *Cantwell* case, several judicial decisions against minority religious sects were handed down.

Many of the free exercise cases adjudicated by the Supreme Court (especially since *Cantwell*) have been brought by the Watchtower Bible and Tract Society (more commonly known as the Jehovah's Witnesses). Their efforts to preach religion to disinterested listeners, along with their attacks on other religious sects, have brought them into direct conflict with the majority view in communities.[1] In the case of *Coleman v. City of Griffin*,[2] a local ordinance of Griffin, Georgia, required a permit by the city manager for the distribution of literature of any type, whether offered free or for sale. A Jehovah's Witness was convicted of violating the ordinance. His contention that the ordinance interfered with his religious freedom was held without justification by the state courts. His appeal to the United States Supreme Court was refused on the ground that no substantial federal question had been raised.

In a series of decisions that followed the Court broadened its protective outlook with respect to this very basic liberty, although on grounds other than free exercise. In the first case, *Lovell v. City of Griffin*,[3] another Jehovah's Witness was convicted of violating the same city ordinance. Since members of this sect believe they are sent by the "Lord God Jehovah" to to His work, they regard acquiring a permit as an act of disobedience. Again state courts said denial of the "privilege" of distributing religious literature did not infringe on free exercise. But the Supreme Court now conceded that a substantial federal question was presented and assumed jurisdiction. Chief Justice Hughes, speaking for the Court, and basing his decision on the freedom of press guarantee, said that the ordinance of Griffin, Georgia, was applicable to more than literature conducive to criminal conduct. Indeed, it prohibited the distribution of all literature, religious and otherwise, without a permit from the city manager. No standards were set within the statute to guide administrative officials in the exercise of their permit power. If carried to its ultimate conclusion all objectionable beliefs could be censored. Thus, "the ordinance [was] invalid on its face" by striking "at the very foundation of the freedom of the press by subjecting it to license and censorship."[4]

In the second case, *Schneider v. Town of Irvington,*[5] the local ordinance required a written permit from the chief of police for door-to-door distribution of literature and for solicitation of funds. In addition, the chief of police had the discretionary power to withhold the permit if he was convinced the canvasser was not of "good character," or if he represented a fraudulent charity. The Jehovah's Witness involved was convicted of violating the police regulation for canvassing without a permit. The state courts dismissed the contention that such a regulation was a violation of religious freedom—saying the ordinance protected citizens from annoyance. The Supreme Court declared this ordinance an unconstitutional infringement of the freedom of press guarantee. The distribution of literature that was the evangelist's ability "to communicate with the residents of the town at their homes depend[ed] upon the exercise of the officer's discretion."[6] The spreading of ideas, religious or otherwise, could not be subjected to prior governmental consent, even under authority of the police power of the state. The Court pointed out that the police ordinance was not of a general type designed to regulate trespassing by hawkers. Rather, it banned "unlicenced communication by any views or the advocacy of any cause from door to door, and permitted canvassing only subject to the power of a police officer to determine, as a censor, what literature may be distributed from house to house and who may distribute it."[7] The opinion of Justice Roberts gave some indication of the direction activist libertarian jurists might travel given the proper circumstances. In a small way, it foreshadowed some of the reasoning of his *Cantwell* opinion.

In the landmark case of *Cantwell v. Connecticut,*[8] the Supreme Court again faced the conflict between the individual's religious freedom and legislation based on the state police power. A Connecticut law prohibited soliciting for religious and other causes except with a certificate issued by the secretary of the Public Welfare Council. The unorthodox methods of evangelism practiced by the Witnesses were demonstrated by the Cantwell family, a father and two sons. After refusing to secure the required permit, they chose a New Haven neighborhood that was 90 percent Roman Catholic and went door-to-door distributing literature, soliciting contributions, and playing a phonograph record that attacked the tenets of the Roman Catholic Church. They were convicted for canvassing without a permit. This time the Court accepted some of the wisdom of Stone's reasoning in footnote four—particularly with regard for the need to protect discrete and insular minorities. *See* Appendix A, *infra.*

Justice Roberts, in his opinion for the Court, said that not only were the Cantwells' unorthodox methods of evangelism legitimate, but that the Connecticut statute deprived them of due process of law. The Court accepted the need of municipalities to legislate with general and nondiscriminatory regulations under the state police power for the peace and safety of the community. Nevertheless, using the precedent established in the *Schneider* case, it refused to sanction a situation giving an administrative official censorial powers over the dissemination of religious ideas. For Roberts and a unanimous Court, the requirement for prior consent with respect to *religious proselytizing* constituted "a censorship of religion as a means of determining its right to survive."[9] A second charge against the Cantwell family was the common-law offense of inciting to breach of the peace. This conviction was disposed of by the Court on the ground that testimony disclosed angry words were spoken by and to the Cantwells—but no actual breach of the peace took place. Furthermore, this conviction rested only on a "common law concept of the most general and undefined nature."[10] The facts did not show a "clear and present danger of riot, disorder, . . . or other immediate threat to public safety, peace, or order."[11] In the end, the legislation was held a violation of the free exercise of religion guarantee of the First Amendment.

Roberts' opinion attempted to establish workable judicial guidelines giving definite meaning to what religious freedom actually constituted in a free society. In so doing, he carefully distinguished (and ultimately narrowed) the gulf between protected belief and unprotected action.

> On the one hand, [the constitutional prohibition on state legislation applicable to religion] forestalls compulsion by law of the acceptance of any creed or the practice of any form of worship. Freedom of conscience and freedom to adhere to such religious organization or form of worship as the individual may choose cannot be restricted by law. On the other hand, it safeguards the free exercise of the chosen form of religion. Thus, the amendment embraces two concepts,—freedom to believe and freedom to act. The first is absolute but, in the nature of things, the second cannot be. Conduct remains subject to regulation for the protection of society. The freedom to act must have appropriate definition to preserve the enforcement of that protection. In every case the power to regulate must be so exercised as not, in attaining a permissible end, unduly to infringe the protected freedom.[12]

Unlike the earlier nineteenth-century view, action now would receive a larger degree of protection.[13] According to the Court, the state must now be mindful that individual behavior involving the free exercise of religion (including the right to proselytize) must not be unduly infringed.

Earlier I raised the question of whether religious communication was subject to special considerations. Is religious communication—the result of adding religious freedom to the freedoms of speech and press—to be given greater freedom from regulation than other forms of communication? Roberts' opinion for the Court attempted (if not an answer) to at least deal with the question in more than a negative way. Prior to *Cantwell* the Court had constantly invoked the secular regulation rule, and, by implication, said no to the idea of special consideration. Now, by specifically incorporating free exercise into the due process clause (and making it applicable to the states), the Court did several things of major importance.

In drawing the line between freedom of religious belief and freedom of religious action, the Supreme Court invoked the clear and present danger plus "imminence" test[14] for the first time in free exercise cases. In so doing, the Court also suggested the use to which the reasoning of footnote four (in its nonpreferred freedom form) might later be put. Simply because an individual, in practicing his or her religion, resorted to exaggeration and abuse in arousing the public, it did not per se make him or her automatically liable to punishment if there was no clear and present danger to public order.[15] And it was (and still is) the role of the Court to determine—by subjecting legislation to a more seaching judicial scrutiny—whether such clear and present danger existed. A unanimous Court found that it did not exist in the present case. "[T]o condition the solicitation of aid for the perpetuation of religious views or systems upon a license, the grant of which rests in the exercise of a determination by state authority as to what is a religious cause, is to lay a forbidden burden upon the exercise of liberty protected by the Constitution."[16]

Moreover, the Court acknowledged that the words "free exercise thereof" are not redundant—that they have a meaning not covered by the other First Amendment guarantees. Although the Court was not yet prepared to say what that meaning was, the acknowledgment in and of itself began the erosion of the secular regulation rule.[17] Equally important, the Court's initial definition of free exercise afforded the opportunity for the activist libertarian justices to attempt establishing a meaning as complete for the freedom to act as for the freedom to believe. The attempt would never be totally successful. From this point on, the somewhat inconsistent approach of the Court in the free exercise decisions, as George W. Spicer suggested, was "evidence of the difficulty encountered by the Court in fashioning reliable criteria for the proper balancing of the right to free exercise of religion against the social interest of the community as expressed through the police power."[18]

Almost immediately after the *Cantwell* decision, however, the Court seemed to pull back from its attempt to accord the religious behavior of the Witnesses a greater degree of protection. Instead, the Court relied on several judicial restraint doctrines developed in the commerce cases, namely, legislative supremacy and judicial limitation, and no further application of footnote four seemed possible. And it was not until the *Murdock* decision in 1943, when the Court gained several new activist libertarian members, that the previously applicable restraint doctrines were changed to legislative limitation and judicial supremacy.[19] The Court, in effect, had developed a double standard of judicial review. The older doctrines remained the same in most areas of adjudication, while the new doctrines applied primarily to the First Amendment. The extent to which the Court would expand and/or contract the meaning of free exercise would ultimately depend upon the position occupied by religion (and its need for judicial protection) in the individual justice's hierarchy of constitutional values.[20]

Several decisions involving the religious proselytizing of the Witnesses followed shortly after the *Cantwell* case. Each decision was based on the older judicial selfrestraint doctrines that (1) governmental power to act is not narrowly limited by constitutional barriers, and (2) legislative judgments, even at the municipal or local school board level, were to be respected. In the cases of *Cox v. New Hampshire*[21] and *Chaplinsky v. New Hampshire*,[22] the Court ruled that the municipal ordinances challenged were reasonable police regulations to promote safety and order. In holding that the individual's civil liberties are not absolute, the Court implied that the existence of organized society and its ability to maintain public order was a superior value to that of religious freedom. The facts of the *Cox* case well illustrated the tactics of the Witnesses. They decided to hold a sidewalk parade in Manchester, New Hampshire, and not only failed to secure a permit, but marched single file in several groups of fifteen to twenty through the crowded business district on Saturday night. The Court in a unanimous decision, and speaking through Chief Justice Stone, rejected the Witness contention that the procession was a form of worship and local interference violated the due process clause of the Fourteenth Amendment. The authority of a municipality to regulate public highways in order to assure the safety and convenience of the people cannot be regarded as inconsistent with civil liberties.

The *Chaplinsky* case was also unanimously decided. This time speaking through Justice Murphy, the Court held valid a state statute that forbade anyone to address any "offensive, derisive or annoying" word or name to any other person lawfully in a public street or place.

Chaplinsky, a Jehovah's Witness, had been warned by a city marshal against inciting a public disturbance; and his response was to call the official a "God-damned racketeer," and "damned Fascist." Rejecting this language as an exercise of religious freedom, Murphy said that he could not "conceive that cursing a public officer is the exercise of religion in any sense of the term."[23] The action of Chaplinsky, by his use of insulting and "fighting" words, was outside the sphere of constitutional protection. Such words "are no essential part of any exposition of ideas, and are of such slight social value as a step to truth that any benefit that may be derived from them is clearly outweighed by the social interest in order and morality."[24]

There is little to suggest that the cause of free exercise was unreasonably curtailed by these two decisions against the Witnesses. Neither belief nor worship nor proselytizing was involved to any degree in these episodes. And there was no disruption (because of the actions taken by the municipalities) of the channels of the democratic process—consequently, there was also no need to consider these forms of behavior in a preferred status. The same cannot be said for the third anti-Witness decision. In *Jones v. City of Opelika*,[25] the Court split 5-4 in favor of the municipal ordiance. This was the first such vote in a Witness case. More important, the decision was the first evidence that a solid activist libertarian group existed. With the appointment of Justice Rutledge the following year, the group was to form the nucleus of a Court majority giving new meaning to the free exercise of religion guarantee.

In the *Jones* case, the Jehovah's Witnesses again challenged the constitutionality of a municipal ordinance that both required a permit for the distribution of literature, and imposed a license tax on total sales. The Supreme Court assumed that since the fees were nondiscriminatory they were simple taxes on the privilege of canvassing, and should also be treated as incidental to the question of religious freedom. The Court upheld the legislation on the ground that when a religious sect disseminated beliefs through the ordinary channels of communication, "[t]he First Amendment does not require a subsidy in the form of fiscal exemption."[26] For Justice Reed and the Court majority, even the provision allowing an administrative official to revoke a license without prior notice was not an infringement.[27] He then said:

> To subject any religious . . . group to a reasonable fee for their money-making activities does not require a finding that the licensed arts are purely commercial. It is enough that money is earned by the sale of articles. A book agent cannot escape a license requirement by a plea that it is a tax on knowledge. . . . When proponents of religious or social theories use the ordinary commercial methods of sales of articles

to raise propaganda funds, it is a natural and proper exercise of the power of the state to charge reasonable fees for the privilege of canvassing.[28]

The Court distinguished between censorship and regulation where such a distinction did not exist.

More important, the majority was guilty of making a false distinction as well. In one hand Reed waved the *Lovell* precedent, which held invalid a statute placing the grant of a license within the discretion of the licensing authority. "By this discretion," he said, "the right to obtain a license was made an empty right. Therefore the formality of going through an application was naturally not deemed a prerequisite to insistence on a constitutional right."[29] With the other hand he thrusts at the Witnesses the implication of *Cox* and *Chaplinsky*—that certain claimed religious actions were not at all religious, when in fact they were. Here (mysteriously) we have a very different situation, Reed suggested, where a license was required that may properly be required. "The fact that such a license, if it were granted, may subsequently be revoked does not necessarily destroy the licensing ordinance. The hazard of such revocation is much too contingent for us now to declare the licensing provisions to be invalid."[30] Yet *Lovell,* along with *Schneider* and *Cantwell,* had held unconstitutional that very same degree of discretionary control in the area of free exercise. To say now that the hazard of a properly granted license would be—or could be—improperly revoked was too slight for the Court to subject the ordinance to more searching judicial scrutiny was, at best, erroneous.

Chief Justice Stone, along with Justices Black, Douglas, and Murphy, dissented from the majority opinion. Referring to the *Lovell, Schneider,* and *Cantwell* cases, the Chief Justice indicated that the ordinance of Opelika, Alabama, gave local authority censorial power over the distribution of religious ideas. The purpose of the freedom

> cannot rightly be defeated by so transparent a subterfuge as the pronouncement that, while a license may not be required if its award is contingent upon the whim of an administrative officer, it may be if its retention and the enjoyment of the privilege which it purports to give are wholly contingent upon his whim. In either case enjoyment of the freedom is depend ent upon the contingency and the censorship is as effective in one as in the other.[31]

Stone then continued the point with even greater emphasis by saying that "[t]he constitutional protection of the Bill of Rights is not to be evaded by classifying with business callings an activity whose sole purpose is the dissemination of ideas, and taxing it as business callings are taxed."[32] To him, the license tax was a measure of previous restraint on religious publication. Sale of this literature was in fact a religious operation rather than a commercial one.

For Stone the activities in which the Witnesses were involved must be classified as the dissemination of religious and educational ideas. Any collection of funds for the propagation of those ideas, always incidental in such a religious cause, must also be accorded constitutional protection. The First Amendment guarantee of free exercise was not—and is not—confined solely to discriminatory attempts to destroy it. Rather, the Constitution (by virtue of the First and Fourteenth Amendments) has put this freedom in a "preferred position."[33] Its protection was "not restricted to cases where the protected privilege is sought out for attack."[34] Its protection extended "at least to every form of taxation which, because it is a condition of the exercise of the privilege, is capable of being used to control or suppress it."[35] Consequently, the Court must subject enactments abridging explicitly guaranteed First Amendment rights to a more searching judicial scrutiny and to look upon them with a jealous eye. Eleven months later Stone's views were accepted by a majority of the Court. Ultimately they were to be expanded beyond their original understanding.

By accepting the special responsibility set out by the dissenters in the *Jones* case, the Supreme Court virtually became a legislative drafting bureau for local policy regulations.[36] The new role was demonstrated in two related cases handed down the same day, *Jamison v. Texas*[37] and *Largent v. Texas*.[38] Each was decided upon the *Lovell-Schneider-Cantwell* precedent. In addition, the decisions ushered in a period of reexamination by the Court of the standing to act with respect to the practice of a religious belief; and ultimately one of redefinition of the concept of free exercise. In both cases members of the Jehovah's Witnesses were convicted of violating municipal ordinances—one prohibiting distribution of handbills, the other requiring a permit (revocable without notice by local officials) for selling books and other merchandise. In each case the defendant's contention that the ordinance was an infringement of religious freedom was set aside by the state courts. In these instances, however, the Supreme Court upheld the practice of religious beliefs on grounds set forth by the dissenting opinions in the *Jones* case.

The Court's willingness to accept this new judicial role was shown during the remainder of the 1942 term. Each case which followed *Jamison* and *Largent* involved violations of local anti-handbill ordinances by Jehovah's Witnesses. Individuals were required to procure permits as well as pay specified license fees for the privilege of canvassing on the streets of the community. Turning to the precedents of the *Lovell, Schneider, Cantwell, Jamison,* and *Largent* decisions, the

Court held each police regulation a violation of the free exercise of religion guarantee of the First Amendment. At the same time, the Court took the initial steps towards giving new meaning to this freedom.

The first ruling was a *per curiam* decision in the case of *Jones v. City of Opelika*,[39] were the earlier judgment was reversed for the reasons set forth in the second ruling, *Murdock v. Pennsylvania*.[40] Justice Douglas emphasized Stone's point in the first *Jones* case, which said soliciting funds for religious literature was not commercial. A license fee required by the Jeannette, Pennsylvania, ordinance was an outright tax on the exercise of a religious belief. In a three-pronged attack on the license fee Douglas said that "[t]he power to tax the exercise of a privilege is the power to control or suppress its enjoyment."[41] Moreover, a "state may not impose or charge for the enjoyment of a right guaranteed by the Constitution."[42] And finally, "[t]he way of the religious dissenter has long been hard. But if the formula of this type of [religious] ordinance is approved, a new device for the suppression of religious minorities will have been found."[43] Once this freedom to proselytize was liberated from the controlling precedent of the first *Jones* case, the majority seemed ready to extend judicial protection to "the liberties of itinerant evangelists who disseminate their religious beliefs and the tenets of their faith through distribution of literature."[44]

> The hand distribution of religious tracts is an age-old form of missionary evangelism. . . . It is more than preaching; it is more than distribution of religious literature. It is a combination of both. . . . This form of religious activity *occupies the same high estate* under the First Amendment as do worship in the churches and preaching from the pulpits. It has the *same claim to protection* as the more orthodox and conventional exercises of religion.[45]

At the same time Douglas *did not say* that all forms of religious behavior were immune from statutory regulation. Although there was little if anything in his opinion to indicate how or where such restraints might be imposed,[46] *he was not* suggesting a Meiklejohn interpretation of the absolute immunity of the First Amendment. On the contrary, Douglas (like Frankfurter before him) believed he was following the true meaning of Stone's concept of greater judicial scrutiny; and both would be erroneous in their interpretations. Yet it was the exceptional emphasis on freedom in general, and religious freedom in particular, contained in the *Murdock* opinion that became important to the further development of the free exercise clause.

In the case of *Martin v. City of Struthers*,[47] the Court faced the question of the validity of a Struthers, Ohio, ordinance that forbade knocking on doors or ringing of doorbells of a residence in order to deliver a handbill to the occupant without an invitation.

In holding the ordinance unconstitutional, the Court ruled that it was not aimed exclusively at commercial solicitation but was rather a blanket prohibition of all uninvited distributions, no matter what their substantive content. Speaking for the Court, Justice Black said that the free exercise of religion guarantee included the right to distribute, as well as receive, literature. He conceded that some abuse might arise when itinerant evangelists are free to practice actions considered antisocial by local law. But, in stressing the expansion of free exercise begun by Douglas in the *Murdock* case, he recognized that the "[d]oor to door distribution of circulars is essential to the poorly financed causes of little people."[48] This unorthodox evangelism always has been accepted as proper communication and dissemination of ideas, making the

> freedom to distribute information to every citizen wherever he desires to receive it . . . so clearly vital to the preservation of a free society that, putting aside reasonable police and health regulations of time and manner of distribution, it must be fully preserved.[49]

Once again describing the hand distribution of literature as an age-old form of missionary evangelism Black said it was—and is—entitled to the same judicial scrutiny and protection as the more usual religious practices, such as worshipping in churches and preaching from pulpits. And in subjecting the ordinance to more searching judicial scrutiny a majority of the Court presumed unconstitutionality in this case because the enactment was void on its face.[50] Two years later Chief Justice Stone would be among the dissenters when his tenative inquiry was expanded (in the *Marsh* and *Tucker* cases) to presume invalidity against virtually all legislation restricting First Amendment guarantees.

The fourth ruling during the 1942 term was the case of *Douglas v. City of Jeannette*.[51] Involved here was the same ordinance invalidated in the *Murdock* case. But in this situation members of the Witnesses attempted to have a district court issue an injunction to prohibit the local authority from enforcing the police regulation. In a unanimous decision by Chief Justice Stone the Court held that, in view of the previously-reached *Murdock* opinion, the injunction was unnecessary.

Justice Jackson wrote a separate concurring opinion. He set forth his reasons for agreeing with the results handed down by the Court in the *Douglas* case, while dissenting from the results in *Murdock* and *Martin*. The constitutional protection of the First Amendment assured the greatest possible latitude for exercising religious freedom and the freedoms of speech, press, assembly, and petition for redress of grievance. But when the limits of such communication were reached, he asked, can an individual go further by proclaiming an unorthodox religious belief? Jackson suggested that "[t]he real question is where their rights end and the rights of others begin."[52] Indeed, "[c]ivil government cannot let any group ride roughshod over others simply because their 'consciences' tell them to do so."[53] And going directly to the point, he asked: "How then can the Court today hold it a 'high constitutional privilege' to go to homes, including those of devout Catholics on Palm Sunday morning, and thrust upon them literature calling their church a 'whore' and their faith a 'racket?'"[54]

Taking a much narrower view of what constituted infringement than the activist libertarians, Jackson (invoking the secular regulation rule and the establishment clause) attacked the expanded—and it seemed to him expanding—definition of free exercise. The First Amendment guarantees of speech, press, and assembly—the guarantee of free expression, he called them—adequately protected the freedom of religious belief, worship, and proselytizing. The Constitution, he emphasized, did not provide any special exemption for religious behavior in conflict with an otherwise valid secular objective. Religious as well as nonreligious behavior could be regulated under the police power of the state. And he said: "I had not supposed that the rights of secular and nonreligious communications were more narrow or in any way inferior to those of avowed religious groups."[55] To Jackson, the free exercise guarantee gave individuals only "freedom from" legislative restraint in the orderly, peaceful practice of belief. It was one thing to preserve the essentials of freedom, but it was quite another to circumscribe the power to govern.

The *Jones, Murdock,* and *Martin* cases were all decided on a 5:4 basis, with Justices Reed, Frankfurter, Roberts, and Jackson (whose opinions have already been discussed) dissenting from the holding of the Court. Reed's dissent was little more than a reiteration of his majority opinion in the first *Jones* case. Frankfurter, taking up where Reed left off, isolated on the nondiscrimination issue: "The real issue here is not whether a city may charge for the dissemination of ideas but whether the states have power to require those who need additional facilities to help bear the cost of furnishing such facilities."[56] For Frankfurter it was simply not possible to reject the license fee requirements (as the majority did) because of the religious nature of the Witnesses' activities.[57] Perhaps the common ground of the dissenters was best emphasized by Jackson's point that *there is a difference* between the Court's obligation to protect the free exercise of individuals and its attempt to guarantee special treatment because of religious grounds.[58]

The last case relevant to this matter decided during the 1942 term was *Taylor v. Mississippi.*[59] Members of the Witnesses were convicted of disseminating information designed to encourage disloyalty to the United States and the state of Mississippi. This included the charge of creating an attitude of refusal to salute, honor, and respect the flag by means of the distribution of literature. The penalty for conviction was imprisonment until the conclusion of a treaty of peace, but not for a period exceeding ten years. Evidence showed that the appellant, Taylor, had told some women (whose sons had been killed overseas) that (1) sending troops abroad was wrong, (2) deaths in war are in vain, and (3) people should not salute the flag. The appellant maintained, however, that conviction denied him the rights guaranteed by the First and Fourteenth Amendments. He also maintained that the Mississippi law restricted his free exercise of religion because it was vague, indefinite, and uncertain so as to furnish no ascertainable standard of guilt.

The Court, speaking through Justice Roberts, held that the law violated the individual's free exercise of religion, and that the appellant was not shown to have (1) advocated subversive action, (2) done anything with evil or sinister purpose, or (3) threatened any clear and present danger to American institutions.[60] Equally important, the Court set aside the part of the law forbidding interference with saluting the flag, giving direct evidence of the result to be expected in the forthcoming *Barnette*[61] case.

> The statute here in question seeks to punish as a criminal one who teaches resistence to governmental compulsion to salute [the flag]. If the Fourteenth Amendment bans enforcement of the school regulation, a fortiori it prohibits the imposition of punishment for urging and advising that, on religious grounds, citizens refrain from saluting . . . the national emblem, then certainly it cannot punish him for imparting his views on the subject to his fellows and exhorting them to accept those views.[62]

Several other previous restraint cases decided by the "Roosevelt Court" remain to be considered in this chapter. Each built upon the new redefinition of free exercise. Each accorded the freedom to proselytize greatly enlarged protection. Each drew the line separating the realm of God and the realm of Caesar in favor of God. Each, following the precedents of *Murdock* and *Martin*, combined free exercise and clear and present danger into the notion of preferred freedom. And, ultimately, the warning of the dissenters became a selffulfilling prophesy.

In *Follette v. Town of McCormick*,[63] the Supreme Court ruled that requiring a municipal license and the paying of a fee for permission to sell religious literature was unconstitutional. Justice Douglas, emphasizing the new expansion of free exercise, stated that no distinction existed between the individual who preached from the pulpit and the individual who, because of circumstances, did not. The religious sect and its manner of seeking converts was not important when "[t]he exaction of a tax as a condition to the exercise of the great liberties guaranteed by the First Amendment is as obnoxious . . . as the imposition of a censorship or a previous restraint."[64]

> Freedom of religion is not merely reserved for those with a long purse. Preachers of the more orthodox faiths are not engaged in commercial undertakings because they are dependent on their calling for a living. Whether needy or affluent, they avail themselves of the constitutional privilege of a "free exercise" of their religion when they enter the pulpit to proclaim their faith. *The priest or preacher is as fully protected in his function as the parishioners are in their worship.* A flat license tax on that constitutional privilege would be as odious as the early "taxes on knowledge" which the framers of the First Amendment sought to outlaw.[65]

Douglas then concluded by proclaiming that both permanent and itinerant preachers have equal claim to Supreme Court protection. For him, the protection of the First Amendment was not limited to orthodox religious practices. Evangelists occupy the same preferred position as do traditional ministers. And as a logical conclusion to the new and expanded definition of free exercise, religious communication might be allowed to occasionally proceed beyond the limits imposed on the more secular forms of communication—simply because religion (as exercised by a religious people) is involved. And the Court will remain mindful of any intrusion into God's domain.

In two cases, *Marsh v. Alabama*[66] and *Tucker v. Texas,*[67] the Supreme Court ruled that the itinerant and community-based preacher must be allowed to distribute literature of their sects on the streets of a company-owned town and a federally-owned village as a valid exercise of religion. In these cases members of the Witnesses had been convicted of violating statutes prohibiting "any peddler or hawker of merchandise" from entering the property of another individual after having been warned not to by its owner. In both cases a majority of the Court upheld the Witnesses' contention that the legislation infringed on their free exercise of religion. Just as importantly, the dissenters in both cases raised the problem of the transgression of constitutional limits by individuals under the banner of religious freedom as set forth by Jackson in his concurring opinion in the *Douglas* case.[68]

The last of the "Roosevelt Court" decisions in the area of previous restraint was the case of *Saia v. New York.*[69] Involved here was a police regulation of Lockport, New York, prohibiting the use of sound amplification equipment in public places without a permit. Saia, an ordained minister of the Jehovah's Witnesses, had a permit, but when it expired the police department refused to issue another on grounds that there had been too many complaints about noise at previous meetings. The minister continued to hold his public meetings, however, and disseminated his religious beliefs through the use of a public address system. He was convicted of violating the local ordinance. The New York State Court of Appeals overrode his free exercise contention on the ground of public safety and order.

The Supreme Court held the ordinance unconstitutional on its face as a previous restraint on the individual's right to a free exercise of religion. Since local officials could revoke a permit without notice, the individual had no relief save for appeal to the state courts. Again, no standards were set for the exercise of this discretion. The statute contained no detail regarding time, place, volume, and so on. Justice Douglas and the majority viewed the result of such legislation as outright censorship rather than conducive to the general welfare.

> The right to be heard is placed in the uncontrolled discretion of the Chief of Police. He stands athwart the channels of communication as an obstruction which can be removed only after criminal trial and conviction and lengthly appeal. A more effective previous restraint is difficult to imagine. Unless we are to retreat from the firm positions we have taken in the past, we must give [religious communication] in this case the same preferred treatment that we gave freedom of religion in the *Cantwell* case.[70]

The Court ruled that such a "discriminatory" piece of legislation contained all the vices already struck down in numerous previous decisions.

More important, like many of the Witness cases previously decided, neither side in the 5-4 decision attempted to reach a fair accommodation over the competing interests involved—religious communication and the avowed need for privacy.[71] Rather than voiding the statute on its face the majority might have suggested various ways in which the necessary accommodation could in fact have been reached: limitation of time and place of the audio equipment, or the decibel volume allowable, or some allocation of space within the park, or the creation of a separate "Hyde Park" area specifically reserved for this type of communication.[72] For their part, also, the dissenters could have been less absolute in the values they attempted to balance. It was not at all necessary to set at odds the right of privacy versus "unwanted communication," especially when communicated by a legitimate religious minority. By isolating the values in such extreme form accommodation was impossible even to suggest.

Thomas I. Emerson suggests at least one way out of the dilemma:

> Any society sincerely interested in protecting the right of privacy is hardly likely to be at the same time hostile to the right of free expres-

sion. Both interests tend to have the same friends and the same enemies. The chief danger is that the right of privacy will be used as a
screen, by those not really interested in either interest, to infringe upon
legitimate expression. This danger can be met if the courts actively
insist upon a careful definition of a genuine right to privacy and upon
a fair accommodation of the two interests.[73]

The crucial point is once again the judicial insistence on *fair* rather than
plausible accommodation.[74] I cannot help but wonder, however, if the
losing litigant will ever be satisfied.

The cases the Supreme Court has considered since 1948 in the area
of previous restraint have presented no new opportunities to continue
the redefinition of the meaning of free exercise. The Witnesses had won
their day in court and had come away victorious. With the exception of
the *Cox* and *Chaplinsky* precedents (applicable not only to religion but
all First Amendment guarantees), the rights of belief, worship, and proselytizing were equalized and expanded about as far as the Court could
take them. Consequently, the decisions in the cases of *Niemotko v.
Maryland*,[75] *Kunz v. New York*,[76] and *Fowler v. Rhode Island*,[77] were a
reiteration of previous decisions by a more activist libertarian Court.
The death of Chief Justice Stone in 1946, followed by the deaths of Justices Murphy and Rutledge in 1949, left only Black and Douglas from
the old majority. In their attempt to continue the expansion of the judicial scrutiny concept they failed to create the necessary atmosphere of
urgency and activism among many of the new members of the Court. It
would be a decade before they would find themselves once again as part
of a majority.

SUMMARY

Taken in their entirety, the Court's decisions in the area of previous
restraint give us an unusually expanded and open-ended concept of free
exercise adequate to protect freedom of belief and worship, freedom to
proselytize the faith orally and by printed word, and the right to use
public places—streets, sidewalks, and parks—to achieve these purposes.
Throughout these decisions the relationship between free exercise and
other guarantees of the First Amendment has oftentimes been noted.
These other freedoms (namely, speech, press, and assembly), encom-
passing as they do various phases of freedom of expression, are in themselves adequate to protect various manifestations of free exercise—*but
not all*. Significantly, therefore, the bulk of cases decided from *Cantwell*
onwards have rested squarely on the almost limitless expansion of the
free exercise of religion clause.

In expanding the meaning of free exercise to include behavior not protected by the other First Amendment guarantees, the Court fairly well completed the erosion of the secular regulation rule—at least in the area of previous restraint. In so doing, the Court also devised various tests and intellectual devices in order to see the light at the end of the judicial tunnel. Primary among these tests were an expanded version of Stone's concept of greater judicial scrutiny, a revised clear and present danger plus imminence test, and the intriguing notion of "void on its face." In combination form, although not necessarily of equal parts, the activist libertarians created a preferred freedom doctrine. And applying that new standard to free exercise (one result was the partial erosion of the secular regulation rule) brought the Court face-to-face with the question of the reversal of the presumption of constitutionality. Yet time was denied the activist libertarians;[78] and while the effect of preferred freedom on the free exercise clause was significant, its effect on the ultimate meaning of the First Amendment was—and still is—less than significant. The doctrine died without ever losing a battle, much less the war—but by that time most of the Jehovah's Witness cases had been favorably decided. Ironically the doctrine died as the Court entered the McCarthy period; and the Court faced the uncertainties of a new age with a great void in its arsenal of protective devices.

The holdings of the Court in *Cantwell, Murdock, Douglas, Martin, Follette, Marsh, Tucker,* and *Saia* suggest two things of significance: (1) the free exercise clause can be interpreted to protect various actions not ordinarily protected by the other First Amendment guarantees;[79] and (2) religious communication oftentimes has been granted special consideration not extended to the freedoms of speech and press. Justices Reed and Frankfurter, in their dissents in *Murdock,* suggest that the majority holding can mean nothing else. Justice Jackson's dissent in *Martin* comes to the very same conclusion.

The Court's decisions in *Breard v. City of Alexandria*[80] and *Kovacs v. Cooper*[81] lend additional credence to the idea that the cases from *Cantwell* onward created a special religious exemption.[82] Breard, a salesman for a line of national magazines, was convicted of violating a municipal ordinance banning all door-to-door solicitations. In upholding the conviction, the Court specifically rejected Breard's free speech and press arguments on the ground that commercial canvassing was subject to local regulations. Justice Reed, speaking for the Court in a 6-3 decision, said that this ordinance (identical to many previously struck down in the Witness cases) did not impose upon Breard any unreasonable restraint on his right to engage in a legitimate occupation. Moreover, the state may regulate even a legitimate occupation (in the public interest) whenever reasonable bases for legislative action exist. Granting that the sale of the publication did not place it beyond the protection of the First Amendment, Reed—similar to his opinion in the first *Jones* case—nevertheless seemed to imply just the opposite by his overconcern with the purely commercial feature of the transaction. "Freedom of speech or press does not mean that one can talk or distribute where, when and how one chooses."[83] The right to do so must be adjusted to the rights of others. Indeed, the constitutionality of the ordinance—as applied to solicitors of magazine subscriptions—turns "upon a balancing of the convenience between some householders' desire for privacy and the publisher's right to distribute publications in the precise way that those soliciting for him think brings the best results."[84] This use of the balancing test inevitably supported the legislation.

The question must be raised—in line with the "piggyback" theory of religious communication—whether the outcome would have been different (and controlled by the free exercise precedents) if the magazine had been *Watch Tower* and the salesman a Jehovah's Witness?[85] The only way of distinguishing *Breard* from the religious cases in the area of previous restraint, as Morgan suggests, "is to assume that the latter established a free exercise right for religiously motivated persons to ring doorbells which those pursuing ordinary free speech errands must leave alone."[86] In other words, is it possible to conclude that the free exercise clause protects the very proselytizing activities that the freedoms of speech and press do not?

The *Kovacs* decision seems even more pertinent, because it was handed down before the deaths of Justices Murphy and Rutledge; and unlike *Breard* the holding cannot be dismissed simply on the ground that the composition of the Court changed. In *Kovacs* the Court seemed to overturn the *Saia* verdict of the previous year. I qualify my assessment because all that can be ascertained from the oftentimes conflicting opinions of the justices is that the law on the problem of loudspeakers is in a state of confusion. Kovacs was convicted of violating a Trenton, New Jersey, ordinance prohibiting the playing, use, or operation for advertising or any other purpose on the public streets of sound trucks or any instrument that emitted "loud and raucous noises." And in upholding the conviction, the state supreme court acknowledged that the ordinance was a complete prohibition of electronic equipment.[87]

In a 5-4 decision, Justice Reed (speaking for himself, Justice Burton, and Chief Justice Vinson) rejected the claim that "loud and raucous" were excessively vague terms as to deny due process of law. Rather, the ordinance (or so he believed) applied only to vehicles and sound amplifiers emitting disturbing noises—and it was within the power of the municipality to control such disturbances. Indeed, at least for Reed, the right of free speech is guaranteed to every citizen; but it does not include the license to inconvenience [how's that standard for a compelling state interest] other citizens.

> The *preferred position* of freedom of speech in a society that cherishes liberty for all does not require legislators to be insensible to claims by citizens to comfort and convenience. . . . That more people may be more easily and cheaply reached by sound trucks, . . . is not enough to call forth constitutional protection for what those charged with public welfare reasonably think is a nuisance when easy means of publicity are open. . . . There is no restriction upon the communication of ideas or discussion of issues by the human voice, by newspapers, by pamphlets, by dodgers. We think that the need for reasonable protection in the homes or business houses from the distracting noises of vehicles equipped with such sound amplifying devices justifies the ordinance.[88]

Reed also attempted to distinguish the present case from *Saia* on grounds inconsistent with the facts of the case. Acknowledging that the Lockport, New York, ordinance had placed uncontrolled discretion in the hands of the chief of police, Reed then suggested that the Trenton, New Jersey, regulation possessed none of its vices. If by vices he meant the fact that Lockport at least allowed sound-amplified speech once the permission of the authorities was granted,[89] Reed was quite right—for Trenton banned all such speech regardless of its content. It was a distinction difficult to accept, or even understand, as shown by its rejection in the opinions of six of the justices.[90] And he further confused the issue of the regulation of loudspeakers (and the preferred position of First Amendment guarantees) by resting his decision on the "loud and raucous" test—which was also rejected by the six other justices. Noel T. Dowling aptly observed that the test could be applied only if a justice were unwilling to handle the more difficult questions: "the justification that may support total prohibition of some manifestations of speech; the significance of the city's methods of control as well as the speaker's method of communication; [and] the [j]ustices' varying sensitivity toward a claim that a particular forum is necessary to enable the speaker to reach [his or her] audience."[91]

None of the justices paid any attention to the fact that Saia was a Jehovah's Witness and his speech—no matter how disturbing—was religious in content. On the other hand, *Kovacs* did not involve the issue of religious proselytizing.[92] I submit that here the real distinction exists. For in the hands of the activist libertarian majority of the "Roosevelt Court" the free exercise clause became a vehicle affording a greater degree of protection than they saw possible at that time under the other First Amendment guarantees. And the free exercise clause found itself—in the short period allowed this temporary majority—consistently accorded a very preferred position.

One additional note: The role of the Supreme Court increased in direct proportion to the expansion of the free exercise clause, as it assumed more and more responsibility for the health of the democratic process and the channels of communication. At the same time the secular regulation rule did not become a major methodological force for the justices in the area of previous restraint.

CHAPTER 3

Public Education

An important element of the free exercise clause is that the state cannot create an education monopoly (directly affecting religious training) or coerce an individual to participate in practices opposed to his or her religious beliefs. Legislation that demands such unreasonable requirements of teachers, parents, and students infringes individual rights of religious freedom. Actions such as the (1) compelling of students to attend public schools only, (2) restriction and regulation of foreign language studies in schools, and (3) making public expressions of loyalty, violate the free exercise clause. And in an earlier period, before incorporation in *Cantwell,* religious freedom was protected tangentially as a byproduct of the "liberty" guaranteed by the due process clause.

Our examination begins with the case of *Meyers v. Nebraska.*[1] Responding to the anti-German feelings during World War I, the state of Nebraska legislatively prohibited the teaching of foreign languages, especially the German language, in public and private schools. The law was aimed at Lutheran parochial schools that used German in their teaching programs. As a result, a German-language instructor from such a school was convicted of violating the statute.

The Supreme Court ruled that the Nebraska law was a direct violation of the "liberty" guaranteed to each individual by the due process clause of the Fourteenth Amendment. But the conception of liberty set forth by the majority opinion presented no guidelines to indicate which phase the state of Nebraska had violated.[2] The meaning attached to it, at least for Justice McReynolds (in speaking for the Court), included the following:

> Without doubt, it denotes not merely freedom from bodily restraint, but also the right of the individual to contract, to engage in any of the common occupations of life, to acquire useful knowledge, to marry, establish a home and bring up children, to worship God according to the dictates of his own conscience, and generally to enjoy those privileges long recognized at common law as essential to the orderly pursuit of happiness by free men.[3]

According to Samuel J. Konefsky, McReynolds believed this guaranteed liberty to include the right of an individual "to pursue the occupation of teacher, . . . as a phase of property."[4] Saliently, this liberty guaranteed the right of teachers, parents, and students to be constitutionally protected against an attempt by the state to establish an educational monopoly.[5]

Justices Holmes and Sutherland dissented. They said the attack on the Nebraska law was another instance of the resort to judicial review to check legitimate legislative discretion. Konefsky suggests that for Holmes the only debatable point was the lawfulness of the means toward the state's ends, not the social wisdom of the public policy.[6] In applying the "reasonable man" test to such legislation,[7] Holmes seemed to forget his majority and dissenting opinions in the freedom of speech cases[8] only a few years earlier that suggested a double standard for the review of economic and civil liberties cases. But here he refused to accept the wisdom of his previous opinions, which were to determine later majority decisions.

It was another seventeen years before free exercise was incorporated into the due process clause. Thus, McReynolds relied on earlier cases where the Court struck down regulatory measures restricting the new "freedom of contract." Religious liberty was given protection by the courts, but it was not subjected to an explicitly more exacting judicial scrutiny until the creation of a activist libertarian majority in the 1940s.

A similar decision was reached in *Pierce v. Society of Sisters of the Holy Names.*[9] It was decided by a unanimous Supreme Court that gave protection to religious freedom, though it necessarily based its opinion on other constitutional grounds. The case arose when the state of Oregon passed a compulsory public school education law. It required children between the ages of eight and sixteen to attend public schools, threatening the existence of parochial and private schools. The Court (once again speaking through Justice McReynolds) upheld the religious freedom claims of the defendants, but on nonreligious grounds. The Oregon law conflicted with the right of (1) parents to choose where their children would receive educational and religious training, (2) children to influence their parents' choice of a school, and (3) schools and teachers to engage in a business or profession.[10] Again the Court indicated (as in the *Meyers* case) that the business and property of parochial and private schools were constitutionally protected by the due process clause. The decision was handed down before the Court's ruling in *Gitlow*[11] and *Fiske*[12] began the nationalization of the First Amendment; and no standard with respect to the outright protection of religious freedom could in fact be made.

In 1898 New York enacted the first compulsory flag-salute act requiring an expression of loyalty by every public school pupil during certain classroom exercises. By 1939, the year when a U.S. district court handed down its decision in the *Gobitis* case and brought the entire issue into national prominence, more than thirty states had enacted similar "patriotic" laws.[13] Most of these flag salute programs were carried out in the following manner: first, pupils who refused to salute and pledge allegiance to the flag for religious and other reasons were suspended from school; and second, the parents of these suspended pupils were subjected to court action for violating the compulsory school attendance laws. Members of Jehovah's Witnesses were directly affected by this legislation since they believed the flag salute ritual was forbidden by the Holy Bible, Exodus 20:3–5.[14]

By the end of the 1930s the overwhelming majority of state and national court decisions sustained the constitutionality of these laws.[15] The courts viewed the compulsory salute and pledge as symbolic expressions of loyalty having no reference to religious beliefs practiced by those involved. When the issue first reached the Supreme Court in *Loeles v. Landers*[16] and *Hering v. State Board of Education*,[17] it was dismissed in two *per curiam* decisions on the curious ground that no substantial federal question had been presented. These opinions affirmed the decisions previously reached below, but the basic issue was not closed by the courts. In effect, all of the precedents were simply unfavorable to the anti–flag salute forces. The presumption of constitutionality rule was an established fact. Even the *Pierce* decision was not helpful, because the claim of parental control over the upbringing of a child was superseded (or at least neutralized) by the flag salute ceremony's indirect relation to "citizenship training." In addition, the secular regulation rule itself prohibited the very favored treatment Jehovah's Witnesses required; and one would suppose that the establishment clause would be applicable as well. Moreover, the free speech precedents—and the newly refined clear and present danger test—had not even been explored for possible use in the area of free exercise. Lastly, Stone's double standard in footnote four (and the notion that legislation touching the freedom of expression must bear a larger burden of proof) had not yet been articulated when the Court ruled in *Loeles* and *Hering*.[18]

According to David R. Manwaring, only two possible options were open to the anti–flag salute forces: (1) create a "right to silence" concept by turning the effect of the free speech decisions upside-down; or (2) combine the clear-and-present-danger test with footnote four and create a preferred freedom of religion to directly attack the secular regulation rule.[19] Although the latter would be the tack chosen in the area of previous restraint, the former proved more successful against coerced expression.

In *Gobitis v. Minersville School District*,[20] a U.S. district court handed down a contrary ruling to established flag salute precedent. The court's decision held that the enactment of the Minersville, Pennsylvania, school board was an infringement of the religious freedom guaranteed to the citizens of the state by the Pennsylvania Constitution. According to Judge Maris, this freedom included the right to practice, or not to practice, any religious belief that did not constitute a criminal act. If an individual sincerely bases his or her acts or refusals to act on religious grounds

> they must be accepted as such and may only be interfered with if it becomes necessary to do so in connection with the exercise of the police power, that is, if it appears that the public safety, health or morals or . . . personal rights will be prejudiced by them. To permit public officers to determine whether the views of individuals sincerely held and their acts sincerely undertaken on religious grounds are . . . based on convictions religious in character would be to sound the death knell of religious liberty. To such a pernicious and alien doctrine this court cannot subscribe.[21]

The court defined the individual, not an instrumentality of the state, as judge of the validity of his or her own religious beliefs.

The decision was affirmed unanimously in the U.S. Court of Appeals for the Third Circuit in *Minersville School District v. Gobitis.*[22] Going to the heart of the matter, Judge Clark suggested that

> compulsory flag saluting is designed to better secure the state by inculcating in its youthful citizens a love of country that will incline their hearts and minds to its more willing defense. That particular compulsion happens to be abhorrent to the particular love of God of the little girl and boy now seeking our protection. One conception or the other must yield. . . . Compulsion rather than protection should be sparingly exercised. Harm usually comes from doing rather than leaving undone, and refraining is generally not sacrilege. A fortiori departure from a ritualistic norm of patriotism is not clear and present assurance of future cowardice or treachery. And that is especially so, where compulsory adherence to that norm is neither logically consistent with, nor pedagogically indispensable to, the dissemination of courage or loyalty.[23]

The two most important aspects of the decision (after the holding itself), according to Manwaring, were (1) limiting the secular regulation rule precedents "to their actual fact situations and holdings—without the accompanying dicta,"[24] thus allowing the lower court to distinguish them; and (2) invoking the clear and present danger test of the free speech cases in the free exercise area, forcing the authorities to bear the burden of proof.[25] This ruling left the Supreme Court little choice but to grant *certiorari* and finally deal with this aspect of substantive religious belief and practice. When the *Cantwell* case followed shortly thereafter, it was hoped the Court would now reexamine and redefine the new meaning of free exercise as set forth by Justice Roberts. However, the time and circumstances surrounding the decision contributed toward making the Supreme Court, in *Minersville School District v. Gobitis*,[26] overrule the judgment of the lower courts. And in attempting to balance the competing interests of religious freedom against public welfare, the Court found the flag salute ceremony related to the ideal of national unity—the basis of national security and "an interest inferior to none in the hierarchy of legal values."[27]

Speaking for an eight-man majority, Justice Frankfurter implicitly confirmed Alexis de Tocqueville's reminder that men have always seemed ready "to fling away their freedom at the first disturbance . . . before they discover how freedom itself serves to promote it."[28] Europe was at war, and Frankfurter (in a letter to Stone—after he learned that Stone would dissent) explained his position by saying that "times and circumstances are surely not irrelevant considerations in resolving the conflicts that we do have to resolve in this particular case. . . . It is relevant to make the adjustment that we have to make within the framework of present circumstances and those that are clearly ahead of us."[29] For Frankfurter, the issue involved was one of reconciliation between two competing interests—freedom of the individual versus the power to govern. Yet his opinion showed little attempt at the reconciliation he believed necessary. The interpretation he placed on free exercise and the Court's role under the judicial scrutiny concept was absolute in the non-libertarian sense. He was as guilty of "absolutism" as the future activist libertarian majority that he was to criticize.

> Except where the transgression of constitutional liberty is too plain for argument, personal freedom is best maintained—so long as the remedial channels of the democratic process remain open and unobstructed—when it is ingrained in a people's habits and not enforced against popular policy by the coercion of adjudicated law.[30]

Frankfurter believed, as did Jackson a decade later, that courts should not be solely relied upon to safeguard the fundamentals of a free society. He felt that the people themselves must provide for the safety and continuation of their government.

The paramount lesson learned by the Court from the executive-judicial crisis of 1937, at least according to Frankfurter, was that justices must not substitute their own value judgments for those of the legislature. To do otherwise, he argued, "would in effect make us the school board of the country. That authority has not been given to this Court, nor should we assume it."[31] Frankfurter seemed to suggest, according to George W. Spicer, that "the flag salute statute raise[d] a political question which must be determined by public opinion and not by the judiciary."[32]

The Court was concerned with the power to govern rather than with the essentials of freedom. National unity was the central theme of the majority opinion, not the inability of a minority group to keep the remedial channnels of the democratic processs open.[33] Frankfurter, in giving tribute to flag salute symbolism, consciously failed to heed the warning of Circuit Judge Clark—that another form that false patriotism frequently takes is so-called flag-worship. For him, at least, requiring such a secular exercise was in no way to foist a religious belief on the Gobitis children. He therefore limited the meaning of the free exercise clause to the one it possessed in 1791,[34] and once again proclaimed the secular regulation rule:

> Conscientious scruples have not, in the course of the long struggle for religious toleration, relieved the individual from obedience to a general law not aimed at the promotion or restriction of religious beliefs. The mere possession of religious convictions which contradict the relevant concerns of . . . society does not relieve the citizen from the discharge of political responsibilities. The necessity for this adjustment has again and again been recognized.[35]

Once again the secular regulation rule emerged triumphant. The fact that the Minersville ordinance not only infringed upon held beliefs, but sought to impose additional ones, was quite immaterial.

Justice Stone was the sole dissenter. In reiterating the major philosophical underpinnings (as he understood them) of his *Carolene Products Co.* footnote, he gave the widest possible scope to religious belief and practice in a free society. The older distinction between belief and action was no longer applicable—except when the most paramount of social values were involved.[36] There must be a certain degree of reconciliation between government and the demands of free exercise; yet the majority opinion made no attempt at such a reconciliation. Rather, the majority considered only peripherally the important substantive issues of free exercise, although these issues had been dealt with by lower courts upholding the contention of the Gobitis family. A retreat by the justices, by invoking Frankfurter's version of the doctrine of selfre-straint, would mean that helpless minority groups would be victimized by a religious bigoted majority. All minority rights in the United States, as in Rousseau's *Social Contract*, would cease to exist.[37]

More importantly, Stone took exception to Frankfurter's doctrine of judicial abstention and countered with the view that the Court could never again avoid expressing an independent judgment on the wisdom of legislation conflicting with the First Amendment.

I am not persuaded that we should refrain from passing upon the legislative judgment "as long as the remedial channels of the democratic
process remain open and unobstructed." This seems to me no more
than the surrender of the constitutional protection of the liberty of
small minorities to the popular will. . . . Here we have such a small
minority entertaining in good faith a religious belief, which is such a
departure from the usual course of human conduct, that most persons
are disposed to regard it with little toleration or concern. In such circumstances careful scrutiny of legislative efforts to secure conformity
of belief and opinion by a compulsory affirmation of the desired belief,
is especially needful if civil rights are to receive any protection.[38]

For Stone, the Witnesses were an appropriate example of the "discrete
and insular" minority he had in mind when formulating paragraph three
of his *Carolene* footnote; and the ultimate importance to him of the free
exercise claim they advanced is a matter of conjecture.[39] Not content to
scrutinize only that legislation deliberately and directly aimed at minorities (as was Frankfurter), Stone believed the scrutiny must extend to all
legislation that simply operated to repress them.[40]

One final point: The problems which Stone found so difficult to
answer—that is (1) how far must the presumption of constitutionality
extend, (2) must the application be identical in all cases, and (3) what
burden of proof would be necessary to overturn it—Frankfurter had no
difficulty in answering. By refusing to distinguish between ordinary due
process and civil liberties cases (the double standard), he was able to
leave the secular regulation rule triumphant. By confining free exercise
to its earliest and narrowest meaning, and then limiting the role of the
Court to cases where the political process itself was in danger, Frankfurter at no time had to confront one of the central points of Stone's
footnote four: that the type of review to be engaged in by the Court
would depend upon whether alternative modes of correction actually
existed.[41] By both incorrectly stating and applying Stone's original meaning, no questions regarding means and effects had to be raised. And
under such circumstances it was quite easy for Frankfurter to conclude
that the flag-salute ceremony was not an infringement of religion, and
that Stone never really meant what he said in footnote four. Ultimately,
as Spicer suggests, "[t]he flag, intended as a symbol of freedom, had
become for many persons an instrument of oppression of a religious
minority."[42] It was "bitterly ironical that a free government should
inflict a penalty for refusal to salute a symbol of freedom."[43] Happily,
Stone would not have to wait long to see his reasoning become the
majority opinion of the Supreme Court.

Immediately following the Court's decision in the *Gobitis* case, the
state of West Virginia began requiring all of its schools to conduct

courses in history, civics, and both the federal and West Virginia constitutions—for the purpose of teaching, fostering and perpetuating the ideals, principles, and spirit of "Americanism," and increasing the knowledge of the organization and machinery of government. In 1942, the state Board of Education adopted a flag salute resolution that ordered the exercise to become a required part of the program of activities in the public schools. Members of the Jehovah's Witnesses once again refused to comply. When the case reached the Supreme Court on appeal, the *Gobitis* precedent was specifically overturned. And the basic meaning of substantive free exercise (as well as the broader concept of freedom of expression) was redefined and expanded by a new, more libertarian Court majority in *West Virginia State Board of Education v. Barnette.*[44] In his opinion for the Court, Justice Jackson refused to draw a fictitious legal distinction where none existed. When members of the Witnesses refused to salute or pledge allegiance they did not infringe upon the freedom of other public school children to do so. The conflict, Jackson believed, was not between two individual rights brought into confrontation, but rather between the authority of the state and the religious freedom guaranteed to each individual.

The American Civil Liberties Union (ACLU) had entered the case on behalf of the Witnesses as *amicus curiae.* Unlike its earlier position taken at the time of *Gobitis*, the new brief went far beyond even the ad hoc balancing approach suggested by the Committee on the Bill of Rights of the American Bar Association. The ACLU suggested that unless religious action constituted a clear and present danger to the community, it simply could not be regulated no matter how valid the secular objective. Indeed, the free exercise clause must be interpreted beyond the limits of freedom of speech (verbal behavior), so as to protect all religiously motivated nonverbal action up to the clear and present danger limitation. Seeking the total obliteration of the secular regulation rule, the ACLU also sought the establishment of a legitimate preferred freedom commitment by the Supreme Court.[45] Jackson, however, did not accept the entire thrust of the argument; and, consequently, the concurring opinions of Justices Black, Douglas, and Murphy based their argument exclusively on the free exercise clause and the clear-and-present danger test.[46]

By not relying upon the free exercise clause or limiting himself solely to the position of Stone in his *Gobitis* dissent, Jackson was able to raise the question (the entire crux of his opinion) of whether the flag salute requirement could even be imposed against those whose objections were not religious?[47] And to this question he answered in the negative.

The very purpose of a Bill of Rights was to withdraw certain subjects from the vicissitudes of political controversy, to place them beyond the reach of majorities and officials and to establish them as legal principles to be applied by the courts. One's right to life, liberty, and property, to free speech, a free press, freedom of worship and assembly, and other fundamental rights may not be submitted to vote; they depend on the outcome of no elections.[48]

Jackson then went on to reemphasize both the dissenting opinion in *Gobitis* and the original understanding of the judicial scrutiny concept, and stressed the point that the school board compelled a minority religious group to declare a belief alien to its faith. Constitutional limitations in a free society (at least until his Nuremberg experience) were to be applied

> with no fear that freedom to be intellectually and spiritually diverse or even contrary will disintegrate the social organization. . . . We can have intellectual individualism and the rich cultural diversities that we owe to exceptional minds only at the price of occasional eccentricity and abnormal attitudes. When they are so harmless to others or to the State as those we deal with here, the price is not too great. But freedom to differ is not limited to things that do not matter much. That would be mere shadow of freedom. The test of its substance is the right to differ as to things that touch the heart of the existing order.[49]

In directly answering Frankfurter's *Gobitis* opinion on the importance of national unity in a free society, Jackson suggested that such sentiment must never be imposed by outright compulsion. Using language equally appropriate to more recent constitutional history, he said that *"Those who begin coercive elimination of dissent soon find themselves exterminating dissenters. Compulsory unification of opinion achieves only the unanimity of the graveyard."*[50] Jackson believed (according to Glendon Schubert) that the Barnette children "sought to defend a passive right to internalize and accept certain (typically, nonmajoritarian) values, without having to divulge them, or to suffer punishment or deprivations for their nondisclosure."[51] Government simply could not enter this area of belief. And by specifically excluding the free exercise issue itself, Jackson was able to dispose of the West Virginia statute without really destroying the secular regulation rule.[52] Obliterating the distinction made by Stone in his *Gobitis* dissent—between a compulsory expression of belief (a form of punishment) and compulsion of belief itself[53]—Jackson suggested both are identical and could not stand. He emphasized the point again and again; and then concluded with the following enduring libertarian language: *"If there is any fixed star in our constitutional constellation, it is that no official, high or petty, can prescribe what shall be orthodox in politics, nationalism, religion, or other matters of opinion or force citizens to confess by word or act their faith therein."*[54]

Justice Frankfurter, joined by Justices Reed and Roberts, bitterly dissented. And by his passionate dedication to the creed of judicial self-restraint (the crux of a large part of his opinion), he implicitly attacked his brethren for acting beyond their warrants as judges.

> One who belongs to the most vilified and persecuted minority in history is not likely to be insensible to the freedoms guaranteed by the Constitution. Were my purely personal attitude relevant I should wholeheartedly associate myself with the general libertarian views in the Court's opinion, representing as they do the thought and action of a lifetime. But as judges we are neither Jew nor Gentile, neither Catholic nor agnostic. We owe equal attachment to the Constitution and are equally bound by our judicial obligations whether we derive our citizenship from the earliest or the latest immigrants to these shores. As a member of this Court I am not justified in writing my private notions of policy into the Constitution, no matter how deeply I may cherish them or how mischievous I may deem their disregard.[55]

Frankfurter here believed, as in *Gobitis,* that the rights guaranteed by the First Amendment were entitled to no greater degree of protection than the ordinary rights litigated under the due process clause. Failing to perceive the fact that certain guarantees of the Bill of Rights are entitled to greater weight, he mistakenly labeled Jackson's acknowledgment of this distinction as a "preferred freedoms" doctrine. Although such a doctrine would in fact be created—and exist for a short period of time—it was ironic that he attacked Jackson on this point. The author of the *Barnette* opinion would be his ally in most future attacks for a decade to come; and both ultimately would believe that the courts were not the primary resolvers of the clash when freedom was endangered. In the end, however, Frankfurter's view of constitutional guarantees, the flag-salute, free exercise, and the judicial function (as conceived in his *Barnette* dissent) did not prevail.[56]

The outcome of the *Barnette* case was never very much in doubt. Prior to its final determination several changes regarding the composition and ideology of the Court took place.[57] First, the retirement of Chief Justice Hughes, the elevation of Justice Stone to the Chief Justiceship, and the appointment of Attorney General Robert H. Jackson to fill the new vacancy. Second, the retirement of Justice Byrnes and his replacement by Wiley B. Rutledge (the former Dean of the University of Iowa Law School). Third, the announcement by Justices Black, Douglas, and Murphy in the first *Jones* case that they had changed their minds regarding their votes in *Gobitis*—and one would assume regarding the limit and meaning of the free exercise clause as well.[58] In addition, the Court already had overruled the first *Jones* decision, thus setting the stage for the subsequent development of free exercise in the area of previous restraint. Free exercise had been given more exacting judicial scrutiny (and its freedom to proselytize finally recognized) by the rulings in the *Murdock, Douglas,* and *Martin* cases. Free exercise had also been combined with the clear and present danger plus imminence test to create the preferred freedom of religion. Also, the Court in the same year had dealt with the substantive issue of free exercise and the flag salute ceremony in the *Taylor* case. By its action in *Barnette,* the Supreme Court sought greater judicial scrutiny plus reexamination and redefinition of the standing to act with respect to the practice of religious belief. It attempted to expand an individual's freedom to make his legitimate public practice of religion a totally "private" affair answerable only to his or her own conscience. A majority of the Court would not take the decision that far.

The free exercise cases that the Court decided recently in the area of public education have brought forth no new principles of constitutional adjudication, nor given any additional meaning to the individual's right to a free exercise of religion. The decisions in *Epperson v. Arkansas*[59] and *Wisconsin v. Yoder*[60] were essentially a reiteration of the passive principles enunciated by Jackson in his *Barnette* opinion: that each individual is constitutionally guaranteed the right not to believe. To be completely free in the exercise of religious belief was one thing. To qualify the principle of complete freedom in the exercise of religious belief by making it answerable to a majority infringes on the minority right to believe in other religions, or in no religion whatsoever. The minority right is just as important as that of the majority. Such was the holding of the Court in the *Epperson* case. The state of Arkansas had enacted a statute forbidding the teaching of evolution in public schools and in colleges and universities supported in whole or in part by public funds. Epperson, a public school teacher, brought action for declaratory and injunctive relief challenging the constitutionality of the anti-evolution statute. The State Chancery Court held the statute an unconstitutional abridgment of the free speech guarantee of the First and Fourteenth Amendments. The decision was overturned by the Arkansas Supreme Court, thus sustaining the statute as within the state's power to specify the public school curriculum.

The Supreme Court, speaking through Chief Justice Burger, held the Arkansas law violative of the free exercise and establishment clauses of the First Amendment for the following reasons: (1) the sole reason for its enactment was that a particular religious group considered the evolution theory in conflict with the Book of Genesis; and (2) a state's right to prescribe the public school curriculum does not include the right to prohibit teaching any subject for reasons that run counter to the First Amendment. Acknowledging that the *Engel* and *Schempp* precedents determined the Court's ruling, Burger went on to say:

The State's undoubted right to prescribe the curiculum for public schools does not carry with it the right to prohibit, on pain of criminal penalty, the teaching of a scientific theory or doctrine where that prohibition is based upon reasons that violate the First Amendment. It is much too late to argue that the State may impose upon the teachers in its schools any conditions that it chooses, however restrictive they may be of constitutional guarantees.[61]

Suggesting that coercion to conformity was used by Arkansas authorities (thus invoking a free exercise claim), the Chief Justice concluded that "'the same ideological considerations underlie the anti-evolution enactment as underlie the typical blasphemy statute. . . . [T]he purpose of these statutes is an ideological one which involves an effort to prevent (by censorship) or punish the presentation of intellectually significant matters which contradicts accepted social, moral, or religious ideas.'"[62]

We have in many ways come full circle regarding free exercise and the liberty of schools and individuals—for a state still cannot create an educational monopoly or coerce the individual to participate in practices opposed to his or her religious beliefs. Legislation that demands unreasonable requirements of teachers, parents, and students is still violative of the "liberty" guaranteed by the due process and free exercise clauses.

The Supreme Court's ruling in *Yoder,* which guaranteed the individual's right to be educationally different in the exercise of his religious belief, was a reiteration (in modern dress) of the initial holdings in the *Meyers* and *Pierce* cases. Members of the Old Order Amish religion and the Conservative Amish Mennonite Church were convicted of violating Wisconsin's compulsory school attendance law (which required a child's school attendance until age sixteen) by declining to send their children to public or private school after they had completed the eighth grade. The evidence also showed that respondents sincerely believed that high school attendance was contrary to the Amish religion and way of life and that they would endanger their own salvation and that of their children by complying with the law.

Once again speaking through Chief Justice Burger, the Supreme Court held that the state's interest in universal education was not a sufficient secular objective to override the free exercise claim guaranteed by the First Amendment.

[I]n order for Wisconsin to compel school attendance beyond the eighth grade against a claim that such attendance interferes with the practice of a legitimate religious belief, it must appear either that the State does not deny the free exercise of religious belief by its requirement, or that there is a state interest of sufficient magnitude to override the interest claiming protection under the Free Exercise Clause.

Long before there was general acknowledgment of the need for universal formal education, the Religion Clauses had specifically fixed the right to free exercise of religious beliefs, and buttressing this fundamental right was an equally firm, even if less explicit, prohibition against the establishment of any religion by government. The values underlying these two provisions relating to religion have been zealously protected, sometimes *even at the expense of other interests of admittedly high social importance.*[63]

Only those interests of the highest order can "overbalance" a legitimate claim to the free exercise of religion. Though the state's interest in universal education may be important, enforcement of a compulsory education requirement on Amish children would endanger (if not destroy) the free exercise of their religious beliefs. Indeed, without the overriding charge of criminal conduct raised in *Prince,* even the claim of the state as *parens patriae* could not be sustained in the face of the minority's judicially protected right to believe and practice a minority point of view. No secular regulation rule can be absolute to the exclusion or subordination of all other interests.

This was the Chief Justice's second free exercise case, and his opinion seemed to imply a return to the Stone Court's view that religious motives—if not to be accorded greater protection than the nonreligious (by subjecting the restrictive legislation to more exacting judicial scrutiny)—must at least be treated equally with all other paramount interests.[64] If the former was not Burger's intention (and he was certainly not an activist libertarian), it certainly was the end result of the decision. Burger then went on to create a new test for determining who was religious—a test quite different from Douglas' sincerity test in *Ballard:* the test of durability and longevity.[65] Morgan suggests that the Chief Justice was saying that if your religion has been long recognized as legitimate, and everyone has perceived your action to be religious, you must be accorded the protection of the free exercise clause.[66] What is troublesome, of course, is the distinct possibility that the Chief Justice has equated traditional and orthodox with religious. Hopefully he does not mean that it is proper to apply one interpretation of the free exercise clause to religious actions the judge finds personally acceptable—and another (and more restrictive) interpretation to unorthodox religious groups. This very point seems to trouble Lionel H. Frankel as well. He hopes that the Chief Justice's message does not mean that we may have "one rule for well established religions and a different rule for religions 'newly discovered.'"[67] Moreover, Frankel believes that "[i]t is precisely in its dynamic infancy that a new religious doctrine will seem most threatening to the old order. It is at this stage that it is most likely to be met by some form of community resistence. The First Amendment must surely apply to protect new religions as well as old from governmental restraints."[68]

SUMMARY

These cases serve to indicate a pattern of increased liberality on behalf of the Supreme Court in the area of free exercise and public education. In large measure, this liberality is based on the kind of basic convictions about individual freedom of conscience expressed by Jackson in his *Barnette* opinion. More specifically, these cases deal with the freedom of religious belief. Thomas I. Emerson defines *belief* in the following way: "[T]he right of an individual [both parent and child] to form and hold ideas and opinions whether or not communicated to others."[69] He also says that freedom of religious belief, and belief in general, "lies at the heart of a democratic society";[70] and any effort by the state "to coerce belief—to employ the powers of the state to force public expression of beliefs or to punish beliefs"[71]—no matter how valid the secular objective—the Court will look upon with hostility. This *is* the Court's responsibility under the judicial scrutiny concept of footnote four. In a free society, present (as well as future) action must not be regulated by governmental intrusion into the realm of beliefs.[72] That is what Jackson implied in his *Barnette* opinion; particularly when the believers are such a small, harmless sect. He would say many of the same things the following year in his *Ballard* "dissent."

From the "institutional" cases of *Meyers* and *Pierce* to the "individual" cases of *Barnette, Epperson,* and *Yoder* the Court—for a variety of free exercise reasons—has extended full protection to religious belief. It was quite immaterial "whether the infringement came from an attempt to compel affirmation of a belief, from an effort to force disclosure of a belief, or from any kind of sanction upon belief including disqualification from benefit or privilege."[73] The full protection extended to religious belief in *Barnette* became absolutely essential. Remember, Jackson warned that any governmentally sanctioned action designed to coerce belief would inevitably lead to the "conformity of the graveyard." This coercion of belief was simply wrong, he implied, because it would always be unnecessary. And along with this freedom of religious belief development (the increased liberality), there also developed a corresponding decline of the secular regulation rule. In effect, the rule was virtually no longer useable as a standard of adjudication, although, according to Manwarning, it would still maintain a very minimal existence from 1943 onward.[74] It would be resurrected once again with the *Smith* decision.

Freedom of religious belief deserves the full protection of the Supreme Court. It has, more often than not, received it. Almost a decade after *Barnette,* Jackson once more confronted the basic belief problem and said what should be the last word:

> I think that under our system, it is time enough for the law to lay hold of the citizen when he acts illegally, or in some rare circumstances when his thoughts are given illegal utterance. I think we must let his mind alone.[75]

CHAPTER 4

Conscientious Objection I

This chapter is concerned with two grants of congressional authority. The first is Article I, Section 8, Clause 4. It gives Congress the power "To establish a Uniform Rule of Naturalization."[1] The Naturalization Act of 1906 required applicants to answer certain questions for the court, among them: "If necessary, are you willing to take up arms in the defense of this country?" Answers to the questions were to satisfy the naturalization court concerning the individual's beliefs in the "moral and political principles" of the United States.

In the cases of *United States v. Schwimmer,*[2] and *United States v. Macintosh,*[3] the Supreme Court denied applicants the right to naturalized citizenship because of their refusal to take the prescribed oath of allegiance without reservations, particularly regarding the requirement to bear arms in defense of the country. By so doing, the Court not only set forth a rather narrow interpretation of the rights of the individual in matters of conscience, but also saw fit to question individual religious beliefs. In addition, the Court wanted to know if the pacifists and conscientious objectors involved were attached to the principles of the Constitution. In each case citizenship was ultimately denied on the ground that the defendants were found not to be so attached.

In the *Schwimmer* case, Justice Butler (speaking for a six-man majority) said that the right of an alien to become a citizen was not a natural but a statutory right. The statutes prescribing qualifications and governing procedure for admission to citizenship were to be construed in favor of the government. And the burden of proof was upon the applicant for naturalization to show that he or she had the specified qualifications. For Butler, the specified qualifications included the duty of citizens by force of arms to defend the government against all enemies whenever necessity arose. This, Rosika Schwimmer—a fifty-year-old female Hungarian educator, lecturer, and alien resident of the state of Illinois since 1921—could not accept.

> That it is the duty of citizens by force of arms to defend our government against all enemies whenever necessity arises is a fundamental principle of the Constitution. The common defense was one of the purposes for which the people ordained and established the Constitu-

tion. . . . Whatever tends to lessen the willingness of citizens to discharge their duty to bear arms in the country's defense detracts from
the strength and safety of the government.[4]

Unfortunately, as the dissenters were to point out, Butler also
attacked ideas and opinions that would probably not have resulted in
action. After using references such as "feelings of dislike and distrust,"
he said that "The record shows . . . respondent strongly desires to
become a citizen. . . . Her expressed willingness [on the other hand] to
be treated as the government dealt with conscientious objectors who
refused to take up arms in the recent war indicates that she deemed herself to belong to that class. The fact that she is an *uncompromising pacifist* with no sense of nationalism but only a cosmic sense of belonging to
the human family justifies belief that she may be opposed to the use of
military force as contemplated by our Constitution and laws. And her
testimony clearly suggests that she is disposed to exert her power to
influence others to such opposition."[5] The free exercise clause notwithstanding, the Court saw no harm in compromising the First Amendment
by inquiring into the propriety of the applicant's opinions and beliefs.

Justice Holmes, with Justices Brandeis and Sanford concurring, dissented. Holmes ridiculed the majority for ruling that a woman applicant
fifty years old must swear to bear arms in defense of the United States.
"So far as the adequacy of her oath is concerned," he observed, "I
hardly can see how that is affected by the statement, inasmuch as she is
a woman over fifty years of age, and would not be allowed to bear arms
if she wanted to."[6] Attacking the majority opinion for its emphasis on
Rosika Schwimmer's so-called "noxious doctrines," Holmes concluded:
"[I]f there is any principle of the Constitution that more imperatively
calls for attachment than any other it is the principle of free thought—
not free thought for those who agree with us *but freedom for the
thought we hate.* . . . I would suggest that the Quakers have done their
share to make the country what it is, . . . and . . . I had not supposed
hitherto that we regretted our inability to expel them because they
believed more than some of us in the teachings of the Sermon on the
Mount."[7] There was no clear and present danger, no threat to American
institutions, yet citizenship was denied to an "uncompromising pacifist." The decision, with its imposition of official orthodoxy, would
have a long-range effect on Justice Stone.[8]

Douglas Clyde Macintosh came to the United States from Canada
in 1916, and in 1925 declared for naturalized citizenship. He had served
as a chaplain with the Canadian Army in World War I, and at the time
of his application was chaplain of the Yale Graduate School and Dwight
Professor of Theology at Yale Divinity School. His application was

denied in the District Court on the ground that he would not *promise in advance* to bear arms in defense of the United States—unless he believed the war to be morally justified. He was found not to be attached to the principles of the Constitution. Speaking for the majority, Justice Sutherland viewed the naturalization process solely as an assumption of obligations rather than as a balance between obligations and privileges.

> When he speaks of putting his allegiance to the will of God above allegiance to the government, it is evident, . . . that he means to make *his own interpretation* of the will of God the decisive test which shall conclude the government and stay its hand. We are a Christian people . . . [and] a nation with the duty to survive; a nation whose Constitution contemplates war as well as peace; whose government must go forward upon the assumption, and safely can proceed with no other, that unqualified allegiance to the nation and submission and obedience to the laws of the land, as well as those made for war as those made for peace, are not inconsistent with the will of God.[9]

Sutherland believed that since the Court was bound by an act of Congress, it—as well as the naturalization authorities—was justified in determining whether citizenship applicants were honest in claiming to assume the obligations. And the Court would refuse citizenship to aliens failing to comply with its prejudged standards of political and moral righteousness.

But Sutherland was not content with rejecting Macintosh's free exercise contention. Going beyond the immediate facts of the case, he accepted the proposition that during periods of crisis the fundamental law was subject to suspension: *inter arma silent leges* (during time of war the laws are silent). In effect, government itself would set whatever limits it thought necessary.[10] There could be no significant limitations that the Court could impose on an emergency (or crisis) government with regard to its power over personal and property rights. Yet Sutherland would later refuse to accept the fact that the Great Depression was also an emergency.

Chief Justice Hughes, joined by Justices Brandeis, Holmes, and Stone, dissented. Reiterating the very grounds used by Sutherland to deny the application for naturalization,[11] Hughes attacked the Court's construction of the naturalization oath, charging that it was now an outright religious test while the one for national office was not. Yet, for the dissenters, the two oaths were the same in substance. How, then, could the majority justify an inquiry into the beliefs of citizenship seekers and hold unacceptable a search into the beliefs of officeholders?

> It goes without saying that it was not the intention of the Congress in framing the oath to impose any religious test. When we consider the

history of the struggle for religious liberty, the large number of citizens of our country from the very beginning, who have been unwilling to sacrifice their religious convictions, and in particular, those who have been conscientiously opposed to war and who would not yield what they sincerely believed to be their allegiance to the will of God, I find it impossible to conclude that such persons are to be deemed disqualified for public office in this country because of the requirement of the oath which must be taken before they enter upon their duties.[12]

The dissenters concluded that there might be for each individual a duty to a moral power higher than the nation. This put a difficult burden on the government. It meant enforcing the authority and supremacy of the law without requiring religious people to forsake their moral duties. A refusal to take the oath for conscientious reasons must be included with the guaranteed rights of religious freedom.

One additional point: Hughes also suggested a justification for a unique type of selective conscientious objector, a religious individual who might not be a total pacifist in all wars—depending upon the war's morality and justness.

Nor is there ground, . . . for the exclusion of Professor Macintosh because his conscientious scruples have particular reference to wars believed to be unjust. There is nothing new in such an attitude. Among the most eminent statesmen here and abroad have been those who condemned the action of their country in entering into wars they thought to be unjustified. Agreements for the renunciation of war presuppose a preponderant public sentiment against wars of aggression.[13]

Chapter 6 will deal with this unusual problem in greater detail.

Between 1931 and 1946, when the case of *Girouard v. United States*[14] was decided, the Supreme Court underwent a change in personnel as well as attitude toward the First Amendment generally and the free exercise clause in particular. The primary value worthy of the Court's protection ceased to be private property after 1937; and it was replaced by individual rights. The change in personnel, which began with the retirement of many of the "nine old men," created a Supreme Court that was decidedly more libertarian in nature. Speaking through Justice Douglas in *Girouard,* the Court specifically overruled the *Schwimmer, Macintosh,* and *Bland* decisions. This granted citizenship to a Seventh-Day Adventist who refused to take the oath to bear arms in defense of his country, although he was willing to perform any noncombatant duty. The decision largely cut away much of the precedent relied upon by a previous Court majority in *Hamilton,*[15] effectively leaving that decision a judicial brick without straw.

The crucial issue to Douglas (as in the previous naturalization cases) was one of statutory construction. He relied on much of the arguments advanced by Hughes in his *Macintosh* dissent and Holmes in his dissent in *Schwimmer*. After stressing that no difference existed between the oath for citizenship and that for public office, he indicated that the oath requirement did not demand bearing arms in a physical sense. There were many other ways for a citizen to support and defend our institutions. The Second War Powers Act of 1942 allowed alien noncombatants to expedite naturalization. It was supported by such a judicial interpretation.[16]

> The struggle for religious liberty has through the centuries been an effort to accommodate the demands of the State to the conscience of the individual. The victory for freedom of thought recorded in our Bill of Rights recognizes that in the domain of conscience there is a moral power higher than the State. Throughout the ages men have suffered death rather than subordinate their allegiance to God to the authority of the State. Freedom of religion guaranteed by the First Amendment is the product of that struggle. . . . The test oath is abhorrent to our Constitution. Over the years Congress has meticulously respected that tradition.[17]

The statutory requirement that an applicant for admission to citizenship must take, that is, an oath to support and defend the Constitution and laws of the United States against all enemies, did not exclude from citizenship an individual unwilling to take the oath to bear arms in the country's defense. Moreover, the majority believed that no viable distinction would—or should—be made between those serving in combatant and noncombatant capacities.

The primary problem faced by Douglas and the majority was balancing rights of the individual and the authority of the government. How was the balancing to be done? Was it the duty of the national courts or the national legislature to correct "error" in the judicial construction of the naturalization laws? In emphasizing the new understanding of the judicial scrutiny concept (as developed in the Witness cases), Douglas suggested that the duty belonged to the courts because of legislative failure to overrule these previous decisions.[18] Failure of Congress to enact proposed amendments to the naturalization laws, nullifying previous judicial construction, may not be construed to preclude judicial reconsideration of the question of construction. Subsequently, the Court granted citizenship to an individual who, unlike Girouard, would not serve in the armed forces even in a noncombatant role.[19]

Chief Justice Stone, along with Justices Reed and Frankfurter, dissented from the majority opinion. Believing that Congress had, by enactment of the Nationality Act of 1940, confirmed the Court's earlier con-

struction of the naturalization laws, Stone now believed it was the obligation of the Court to sustain congressional intent. And he believed,
contrary to the majority opinion, that Congress specifically meant what
it said.

> With three other Justices of the Court I dissented in *the Macintosh* and
> *Bland* cases, for reasons which the Court now adopts as ground for
> overruling them. Since the Court in three considered earlier opinions
> has rejected the construction of the statute for which the dissenting Jus-
> tices contended, the question, which for me is decisive of the present
> case, is whether Congress has likewise rejected that construction by its
> subsequent legislative actions, and has adopted and confirmed the
> Court's earlier construction of the statutes in question. A study of Con-
> gressional action taken with respect to proposals for amendment of the
> naturalization laws since the decision in the *Schwimmer* case, leads me
> to conclude that Congress has adopted and confirmed this Court's ear-
> lier construction of the naturalization laws. For that reason alone I
> think that the judgment should be affirmed.[20]

This was particularly true, reasoned Stone, when Congress had refused
to change its intention even after the matter had been brought to the
attention of both the public and the legislature.

Equally important, Stone once more invoked *his* conception of judicial self-restraint: "[I]t is not . . . to be implied that Congress has . . . del-
egated to this Court the responsibility of giving new content to language
deliberately adopted after this Court has construed it."[21] Indeed, the
Court's role was partially limited. Although it was free to reconsider and
correct judicial "mistakes" of constitutional doctrine,[22] the Court was
not free to revise previous (and perhaps even erroneous) interpretations
of congressional legislation. On this crucial distinction Stone broke with
Black, Douglas, Murphy, and Rutledge. For him, it was simply "not the
function of this Court to disregard the will of Congress in the exercise
of its constitutional power."[23]

The second grant of congressional authority is Article I, Section 8,
Clauses 11, 12, and 14. These grants enable the Congress to declare war,
raise armies, and make rules for the armed forces. Congress has required
compulsory military service in times of great national emergency. The
Selective Draft Act of 1917 exempted theological students and ordained
ministers of certain major religious groups. Unlike the draft act of World
War II, conscientious objectors were not exempt from the required service. This group of people, whose religious tenets prohibited engaging in
war—challenged the constitutionality of the draft act on religious
grounds by failing to register with draft boards as required by law.

In *Arver v. United States*,[24] individuals prosecuted were unable to
find relief for their religious and constitutional claims in the national

courts. Many minority sects (including Jehovah's Witnesses, Quakers, and Seventh-Day Adventists) said their members were ordained ministers entitled to the same exemption given ministers and theological students of major religious groups. The courts not only denied that military exemption to certain groups was a preference of religion but, incredibly, ruled that no infringement of free exercise was involved.

> [W]e pass without anything but statement the proposition that an establishment of a religion or an interference with the free exercise thereof, repugnant to the First Amendment, resulted from the exemption clauses of the act to which we at the outset referred because we think its unsoundness is too apparent to require us to do more.[25]

Speaking through Chief Justice White in the *Arver* case, the Court held that section 7(d) of the 1917 act—even with its emphasis on theistic beliefs—violated neither the establishment nor free exercise clauses. Almost as an afterthought, White added that the Selective Draft Act of 1917 was also not violative of the involuntary servitude clause of the Thirteenth Amendment.

Section 5(g) of the Selective Service and Training Act of 1940 established the new draft classification of IV-E (conscientious objector). It exempted those individuals who "by reason of religious training and belief" were opposed to participation in all wars. Political, moral, sociological, and philosophical grounds were specifically disallowed as grounds for exemption. The act did not consider those individuals who were not members of orthodox religions, or whose religious training was insignificant (or even nonexistent), or those with nontheistic beliefs.[26] As cases came to the federal courts different answers were given.[27] Many of the decisions accepted the substance of the *Arver* opinion, rejected all free exercise and establishment claims, and placed a very secular definition on the term "minister of religion." Others, particularly those from the Second Circuit, were far more libertarian. There would be great confusion until Congress saw fit to specify its preference toward the conflicting judicial interpretations.

A citizen who presented necessary proof and registered with the draft board as a minister of religion was classified IV-D, exempt from both combatant and noncombatant service. If the draft board believed he did not qualify under the judicial definition of the term "minister of religion" as set forth in the case of *Buttecalli v. United States*,[28] but did qualify as a conscientious objector, he was classified IV-E and made subject to noncombatant duty. The court defined the "minister of religion" as an individual

> who has followed a prescribed course of study of religious principles, has been consecrated to the service of living and teaching that religion

through an ordination ceremony under the auspicies of an established church, has been commissioned by that church as its minister in the service of God, and generally is subject to control or discipline by a council of the church by which he was ordained.[29]

The obvious flaw in applying the definition of the term "minister of religion" was the general unwillingness of local draft boards to accept many of the varied (and legitimate) meanings attached to the term by members of the particular group involved. And differences over the meaning and definition brought forth the numerous litigations.

Standards of classification established by the act were, if not preferential toward established major religions, an abridgment of religious liberty. They (the standards) failed to allow for differences in religions. Some religious groups are constituted as hierarchies, with their ministers of religion as a separate and special class of people, Other religious groups, such as Quakers and Jehovah's Witnesses, believe any individual may have true spiritual contact with a Supreme Being of his choice and become an ordained minister without full-time duty or the added trappings of ceremonial rituals. Many individuals were prosecuted by the national government for failure to report for noncombatant duty. The courts overruled their claims for exemption, saying that only a small part of their time was spent in religious duties such as distributing, soliciting, and proselytizing for their religious faiths.[30] Judicial classification of an individual as a conscientious objector rather than as a minister of religion, or limiting him to a free exercise of religion only in a conscientious objector camp, was not deemed an infringement of the religious liberty guarantee of the First Amendment.[31] Apparently the lower courts chose to disregard Douglas' opinion in the *Follette* case that the part-time itinerant preacher deserved the same constitutional protection as the minister who preached from the pulpit.

Cases arising during the Korean Conflict period presented the same problem to the national courts, that is, defining the term "minister of religion" as interpreted by draft boards and members of minority religious groups. The statute involved this time was section 6(j) of the Universal Training and Service Act of 1948. The act was revised again in 1951, but section 6(j) remained intact. Experience during World War II had taught the national government that draft board interpretation of this term according to secular meaning rather than individual religious meaning raised more problems than it solved. This experience had also taught the courts a lesson of a different nature. They would no longer refrain from questioning a "final" selective service classification.[32] In a series of decisions,[33] the Supreme Court cut much of the precedent from the earlier periods of adjudication, but ministerial exemption probably always will be a matter of legislation discretion. This new moderation in judicial thinking accepted the wisdom of Justice Murphy's dissenting opinion in *Falbo*,[34] where he proclaimed: "The law knows no finer hour than when it cuts through formal concepts and transitory emotions to protect unpopular citizens against discrimination and persecution."[35] Twenty-one years after Murphy's dissent an individual would be accepted as a conscientious objector without the secular prerequisite of holding a belief in a Supreme Being.

Congress has been generous in recognizing bona fide conscientious objectors and in exempting them from military service. Those individuals claiming such status after receiving an induction notice have not always been as successful. And in granting such exemptions the problem has always been making a distinction between the obviously bona fide claim and the questionable (and oftentimes unorthodox) one.[36] While it is a desired—I would suggest necessary—principle of a free society that no individual making a religiously motivated conscientious objector claim should even be compelled to participate in war or be jailed for refusing to do so,[37] until 1970 the Court would not grant exemption for pacifist ideals that were moral, sociological, philosophical, or political in nature.[38]

In *United States v. Seeger*,[39] a unanimous Supreme Court broadened the meaning of "religious training and belief" to include all forms of religious belief, not simply the traditional religious views founded on a relationship between man and God. In essence, the Court side-stepped the constitutional question brought about when a United States Court of Appeals ruled section 6(j) of the Universal Training and Service Act of 1948 an unconstitutional discrimination against religious beliefs not based on the existence of a Supreme Being. Creating a new definition of free exercise, at least for statutory purposes,[40] the Court held that the beliefs expressed by Seeger (even without the acceptance of a Supreme Being) entitled him to the conscientious objector exemption.

Stressing that many well-established religious sects do not teach belief in a Supreme Being or mystical force of "Godness," the Court, speaking through Justice Clark, said the test of belief was whether it was sincere and occupied a meaningful place in the life of its possessor, paralleling the orthodox belief in God held by one clearly qualified for conscientious objector exemption.

> In light of his beliefs and the unquestioned sincerity with which he held them, we think the Board, had it applied the test we propose today, would have granted him the exemption. We think it clear that the beliefs which prompted his objection occupy the same place in his life as the belief in a traditional deity holds in the lives of his friends, the Quakers. . . . It may be that Seeger did not clearly demonstrate what

his beliefs were with regard to the usual understanding of the term "Supreme Being." But as we have said Congress did not intend that to be the test.[41]

Emphasizing that neither the validity of what the defendant believed, nor the truth of his concepts can be questioned, Clark pointed out that these areas of inquiries were closed to government. Starting with Douglas' remarks in the *Ballard* case that "men may believe what they cannot prove," he continued: "They may not be put to the proof of their religious doctrines or beliefs. Religious experiences which are as real as life to some may be incomprehensible to others."[42] To Clark, local boards and courts cannot reject beliefs because they considered them "incomprehensible." Instead, their task was to decide whether beliefs professed by a registrant were sincerely held, and whether they were truly religious. But how does one test "sincerity" and "religion"?

While rejecting the orthodox belief in a Supreme Being as the only acceptable test, the Court accepted the idea that conscientious objector status would be granted to an individual without an institutional tie to a religious group or belief. The individual might even acquire his "religious training and belief" through his own study and meditation. Beyond this, however, the Court would not go. In the circumstances of the *Seeger* case it was unwilling to embrace the idea that training and belief could be based instead on moral, sociological, philosophical, or political views. The Court did not then consider the issue. Neither did it suggest with any degree of finality whether there was a constitutional or a moral obligation to conscientious exemption to military service. Both of these issues, as well as the problem of selective conscientious objection, would soon be brought to national attention by U.S. district court decisions.[43]

The *Seeger* decision accomplished several things. First, it sounded the death-knell for the older, more traditional definition of religion.[44] Instead the Court broadened the meaning of free exercise (although not yet to the point of including conscience) by negating the mandatory notion of a Supreme Being. Nevertheless, some religious motivation, whatever its origin, was still required.[45] Second, it caused an obvious reaction in the Congress. Representative L. Mendel Rivers (D.-S.C.) and Senator John Stennis (D-Miss.), aided by the "fashionable" draft card burnings and the superpatriotic backlash that followed, revised the draft law and deleted the term "Supreme Being." The new provision of the 1967 law read as follows: "Religious training and belief does not include essentially political, sociological or philosophical views, or a merely personal moral code."[46] According to Henry J. Abraham, the congressional "hawks" were unable to require a belief in an organized and recognized religion before conscientious objector status was granted to an individual.[47] Nevertheless, they at least believed (their belief was shortlived) that the new language corrected and neutralized the Court's definition of the term.

Within the framework of the conscientious objection problem, we are ultimately concerned with the meaning of the freedom of religion guarantee—and whether it can be defined broadly enough to incorporate the secular.[48] Accommodation has been reached when it is religion versus the secular, or religion and the secular. The real question is whether the Constitution, and particularly the free exercise clause, protects the nonreligious conscience? Assuming this is answered in the affirmative, will conscience replace religion as the substantive right to be protected and enlarged by a activist libertarian judiciary? In June 1970, in the case of *Welsh v. United States*,[49] the Supreme Court accepted the responsibility posed by these questions and answered both affirmatively. An individual was entitled to conscientious objector status even when he expressly rejected a religious basis for his antiwar beliefs. By going beyond the principles handed down in *Seeger*, the Court granted protection to the nonbeliever, the agnostic, and the atheist, who based their total objection on a personal moral code.

Welsh was a Los Angles commodities broker who had applied for draft exemption as a conscientious objector in 1964. In filing Form 150, he crossed out the words "religious training" (Seeger had only used quotation marks) to show his opposition to the war on grounds much broader than religion itself—that is, on the grounds of conscience. His application for exemption was denied (along with all subsequent appeals) because he could show no religious basis for his claim. He refused induction and was sentenced to a three-year prison term. The Court, speaking through Justice Black, reversed the conviction on the grounds—feared by Rivers and Stennis—that Welsh's conviction was simply inconsistent with the holding in the *Seeger* case itself. Although the draft law of 1967 barred exemptions on grounds other than "religious training and belief," Black nevertheless indicated that political, philosophic, sociological, and moral beliefs can be held so firmly as to be "religious" within the meaning of the law. Indeed, he even concluded his opinion by suggesting that the law actually exempted "from military service all those whose conscience, spurred by deeply held moral, ethical, or religious beliefs, would give them no rest or peace if they allowed themselves to become a part of an instrument of war."[50] Contrary to congressional intent, Black emphasized that section 6(j) really required no more.

Indicating that there can be no distinction between religious and ethical objections to service in war, the Court ruled that the only criterion was that the moral code be "deeply and sincerely held."

> If an individual deeply and sincerely holds beliefs that are purely ethi-
> cal or moral in source and content but that nevertheless impose upon
> him a duty of conscience to refrain from participating in any war at
> any time, those beliefs certainly occupy in the life of that individual "a
> place parallel to that filled by . . . God" in traditionally religious per-
> sons. Because his beliefs function as a religion in his life, such an indi-
> vidual is as much entitled to a "religious" conscientious objector
> exemption under section 6(j) as is someone who derives his conscien-
> tious opposition to war from traditional religious convictions.[51]

A major reason in making the majority take this unique position was
Welsh's documented belief that "the taking of life—anyone's life—[was]
morally wrong."[52] Since he held this nonreligious "religious" belief with
the strength of more traditional religious convictions (as Clark suggested in *Seeger*), he could not be denied the exemption.

The effect of the decision was to substitute the notion of "conscience" for the older standard of "religious training and belief" as the
new priority to be protected. The nonreligious believer was now covered
by the new substantive guarantee of free "nonreligious" exercise.[53]
Accepting the contention of Madison in his submitted draft of the First
Amendment—and the implications of Hughes' dissent in *Macintosh*—
Black's majority opinion held conscience "synonymous" with religion.
Both occupy the same preferred position in the hierarchy of judicially
imposed values. And the expansion of the meaning of free exercise
finally reached its outer limits; it would go no further.

Justice Harlan wrote a separate concurring opinion. Although he
grudgingly accepted the result in *Welsh*, he rejected both the continued
expansion of the *Seeger* rationale and the new linking of conscience with
religion. Attacking Black's version of the legislative history of the act,
Harlan felt that it was

> a remarkable feat of judicial surgery to remove, as did *Seeger,* the the-
> istic requirement of section 6(j). The [Court] today, however, in the
> name of interpreting the will of Congress, has performed a lobotomy
> and completely transformed the statute by reading out of it any dis-
> tinction between religiously acquired beliefs and those deriving from
> "essentially political, sociological, or philosophical views or a merely
> personal code."[54]

Nevertheless, he was still able to concur in the result of *Welsh,* but obviously for reasons different from those of Black's majority opinion.[55]

Justice White, along with Justice Stewart and Chief Justice Burger,
dissented on the ground that Welsh (contrary to the *Seeger* test) was
simply not of that class of conscientious objectors that Congress had
either provided or intended exemption.

> Whether or not *Seeger* . . . accurately reflected the intent of Congress in providing draft exemptions for religious conscientious objectors to war, I cannot join today's construction of section 6(j) extending draft exemption to those who disclaim religious objection to war and whose views about war represent a purely personal code arising not from religious training and belief as the statute requires but from readings in philosophy, history, and sociology. Our obligation in statutory construction cases is to enforce the will of Congress, not our own; and . . . construing section 6(j) to include Welsh exempts from the draft a class of persons to whom Congress has expressly denied an exemption.[56]

White believed that "[i]f it is contrary to the express will of Congress to exempt Welsh, . . . there is no warrant for saving the religious exemption and the statute by [judicially] redrafting it in this Court to include Welsh and all others like him."[57] And whether section 6(j) was constitutional or not, there could be no First Amendment excuse for Welsh not to report for induction. In other words, what the free exercise clause grants the establishment clause cannot take away, especially when the free exercise clause offers no protection to individuals like Welsh in the first place.

This, then, is the current status of the law and conscientious objection in the area of selective service. Due to the changing composition of its membership (among other reasons), the Supreme Court has not seen fit to go beyond the generous limits of *Welsh*—and confront the constitutional issue. Perhaps this current judicial status quo was reflected most clearly in a *per curiam* opinion involving the famous sports personality Muhammad Ali—in the case of *Cassius Clay v. United States.*[58]

A Louisville, Kentucky, draft board denied Ali conscientious objector status. Upon appeal to the Kentucky Appeal Board, a Justice Department hearing officer found Ali to be sincere in his objection to war in any form and recommended the exemption. However, the Justice Department itself recommended that the exemption be denied, because Ali failed to satisfy each of the three basic tests for qualification as a conscientious objector—namely, (1) he must be conscientiously opposed to war in any form,[59] (2) this opposition must be based upon religious training and belief,[60] and (3) this objection must be sincere. The Kentucky Appeals Board concurred, but without a statement of reasons. Ali refused to submit to induction and was convicted in U.S. district court; and the conviction was later affirmed by the Court of Appeals for the Fifth Circuit.

On *certiorari*, the Supreme Court reversed the conviction. In a *per curiam* opinion it held that since Ali's beliefs were based on Muslim religious doctrines as he understood them, they were religious and satisfied one of the required tests. It further held that since Judge Grauman (the hearing officer) found Ali sincere in his claim—thus meeting another test—the Justice Department erred in its advice. It was not a legitimate ground to reverse simply because Ali withheld his conscientious objector claim until military service was imminent. Lastly, the opinion held that since the Kentucky Appeals Board relied on no discernible ground in denying the claim, the conviction would not stand.

It was on this last point that the Supreme Court failed to face the constitutional issue raised by the *Seeger* and *Welsh* decisions. By suggesting that an "articulated reason of refusal might have legitimized the Appeals Board decision, the Court implied a willingness (given the proper circumstances of total war) to return to the errors of the World War II period—the secular criteria of the *Buttecalli* ruling and the continued disregard of Douglas' *Follette* opinion. At no time did the Court give its blessing to the earlier attempt to substitute conscience for the narrower concept of religion; nor did it even raise that issue. By allowing the government to concern itself with its own interpretation of the dogma of a religious sect, the Court failed to clearly command that the government be concerned with the registrant as an individual,[61] answerable only to the dictates of his own conscience.

Perhaps the Burger Court should have given greater thought to, and closer acceptance of, Clark's suggestion in *Seeger*: "[I]t must be remembered that in resolving these exemption problems one deals with the beliefs of different individuals who will articulate them in a multitude of ways. In such an intensely personal area, . . . the claim of the registrant that his belief is an essential part of a religious faith must be given great weight."[62] Like Clark (and later Black), I am convinced that pacifists and conscientious objectors are not draft evaders and traitors. And like both I am pragmatic enough to know, too, that until Congress recognizes that fact legislatively (before the next war begins and the next draft law is passed), the Supreme Court can go just so far in extending the meaning of the free exercise clause.

CHAPTER 5

Conscientious Objection II

One of the inevitable problems confronting the courts in the area of conscientious objection (taken in the broadest meaning of the term) involves the conflict between free exercise and the competing state—not federal—interest. These cases deal with situations where the state set standards for the beliefs of individuals residing in them, the free exercise of religion guarantee notwithstanding. Rules concerning admission to the bar of the state of Illinois brought to light one such instance. Others to be considered include religious oaths for public office, unemployment compensation benefits, Sunday blue laws, and the unique situation posed by the Native American Church. With the exception of the Illinois bar case, those involving the blue laws, and the use of peyote (sometimes), all free exercise claims were upheld. And each, in its own unique way, extended the meaning of free exercise beyond its original understanding. It would provide protection for otherwise proscribable action.

In the case of *In re Summers*,[1] the Supreme Court sustained the state's belief—that conscientious objectors ought to be excluded from admission to the bar—as a position that was not unreasonable.[2] In its ruling the Court relied on the naturalization case precedents of the *Schwimmer, Macintosh,* and *Bland* decisions. Justice Reed, in a 5-4 holding, suggested that the state of Illinois, like any other state with a "vital interest" at stake, had the fundamental authority to interpret the oath requirement to support the state constitution. According to the state, argued Reed, not only did petitioner refuse to take in good faith the required oath, but his conscientious belief in nonviolence (he would not use force to prevent wrong) made him a unsatisfactory candidate for the practice of law. Reed emphasized the fact (he assumed it to be a justification for his decision) that, although Congress had made provision for conscientious objection under the draft act of 1940, the state of Illinois did not make a similar exemption.[3]

Justice Black, joined by Justices Douglas, Murphy, and Rutledge, dissented. He felt that the state demanded Summers take an oath compromising his free exercise of religious beliefs; and his rejection was based solely on those beliefs.[4] The minority argued to no avail that the state cannot under *any* circumstances penalize the religious beliefs of an individual through "the circuitous method of prescribing an oath, and then barring [him] on the ground that his present belief might later prompt him to do or refrain from doing something that might violate that oath. Test oaths, designed to impose civil disabilities upon men for their beliefs rather than for unlawful conduct, were an abomination to the founders of this nation."[5] Invoking the dissents of both the *Schwimmer* and *Macintosh* decisions, Black suggested that the Illinois oath was in fact a "religious test"—and as such was prohibited by Article VI, Clause 3, of the Constitution. He concluded by suggesting that a state cannot lawfully bar from a semipublic position "a well-qualified man of good character solely because he entertains a religious belief which might prompt him at some time in the future to violate a law which has not yet been and may never be enacted."[6] For Black and the dissenters, men are punished under the Constitution for what they do or fail to do—and not for what they think and believe. "Freedom to think, to believe, and to worship has too exalted a position in our country to be penalized on such an illusory basis."[7] Clyde Summers was admitted to the bar of the state of New York several years later.

The underlying principle of the so-called Sunday closing law is the right of the state (under its police power) to decide which commercial enterprises may remain open and which must close. This power is exercised (when exercised at all) in order to protect the health, welfare, safety, and morals of all citizens—including those ultimately punished for violating the statute. More importantly, the oftentimes "insane" pattern of exceptions and exemptions has raised serious questions regarding the reasons and logic (if any) sustaining them. And this uncertainty finally brought the Sunday closing laws before the Supreme Court in 1961.[8] The cases of *Braunfeld v. Brown*[9] and *Gallagher v. Crown Kosher Super Market*[10] raised the question of free exercise, as well as the question of equal protection by an "unreasonable, arbitrary, and capricious" classification. The organizations involved were owned and operated by Orthodox Jews who, because of their religious beliefs, closed their businesses on Saturday—while the law compelled them to close on Sunday as well.

Henry J. Abraham suggests that the Court was unhappy and uncomfortable in handing down these decisions, for there was no prevailing majority opinion in either one. All that was certain in Chief Justice Warren's opinions (concurred in by enough justices to supply a numerical majority) was that no acceptable free exercise or equal protection violations were shown. Moreover, the Court simply did not wish to strike down statutes based on legislative discretion or popular referenda, and which were enforced only occasionally.[11] Consequently, Warren's two opinions, concurred in by Black, Clark, and Whittaker (with a separate concurrence by Frankfurter and Harlan), presented the general theme that, although originally of religious intent, the Sunday blue laws no longer had any religious purpose. In fact, the present legislative purpose was only to set aside "a day of community tranquility, respite and recreation, a day when the atmosphere is one of calm and relaxation rather than one of commercialism, as it is during the other six days of the week."[12] And with the state's growing preoccupation with improving the health, safety, morals, and general well-being of all its citizens, the motivation for such legislation was surely secular rather than religious.

Applying the direct-indirect effects doctrine to the free exercise clause, Warren reintroduced a modified secular regulation rule by suggesting that the present cases did not involve religious belief—only the freedom to act. And in so doing, the Chief Justice implied (as did the Frankfurter concurrence)[13] that, although an otherwise valid secular regulation that imposed a direct burden on religion would be invalid, most secular regulations imposing indirect burdens would not violate the free exercise clause.[14]

> If the purpose or effect of a law is to impede the observance of one or all religions or is to discriminate invidiously between religions, that law is constitutionally invalid even though the burden may be characterized as being only indirect. But if the State regulated conduct enacting a general law within its power, the purpose and effect of which is to advance the State's secular goals, the statute is valid despite its indirect burden on religious observance unless the State may accomplish its purpose by means which do not impose such a burden.[15]

Indeed, for the Court to strike down legislation that imposed only an indirect burden on the exercise of religion—"legislation which does not make unlawful the religious practice itself, would radically restrict the operating latitude of the legislature"[16]—would once again make the Court a legislative drafting bureau for statutes. For Warren and the others composing the majority, this was not the Court's function (although the majority during the 1940s would—and did—rule otherwise).

The Chief Justice concluded that he could neither concern himself with the wisdom of the Sunday closing laws nor compel the states to enact exemptions for Orthodox Jews. And in view of the overriding secular nature and intent of these laws (and the secular activity they regulated), *it was simply unfortunate* that such an excessive burden was attached to the Sabbatarian's religious beliefs! Yet all of these things that Warren, in 1961, believed the Court could not—or should not—do were very much in line with what Warren and the Court believed it could command states to do beginning the following year in the reapportionment cases.

Justices Brennan and Stewart dissented in *Braunfeld* and *Crown Kosher*, exclusively on free exercise grounds. Justice Douglas also dissented on both free exercise and establishment grounds.[17] Brennan believed that the Sunday closing laws could be saved (constitutionally speaking) only by granting exemption to those who in good faith observed as "Sabbath" some day other than Sunday. He rejected the distinction inherent in the majority opinion that "the law's effect does not inconvenience all members of the Orthodox Jewish faith but only those who believe it necessary to work on Sunday."[18] Rather, the issue for him in these cases was quite the contrary: "Whether a state may put an individual to a choice between his business and his religion."[19] His answer was that neither the state nor the Court has the power to compel such a choice.

> Admittedly, these laws do not compel overt affirmation of a repugnant belief, . . . nor do they prohibit outright any of appellants' religious practices. . . . But their effect is that appellants may not simultaneously practice their religion and their trade, without being hampered by a substantial competitive disadvantage. Their effect is that no one may at one and the same time be an Orthodox Jew and compete effectively with his Sunday-observing fellow tradesmen. This clog upon the exercise of religion, this state-imposed burden on Orthodox Judaism, has exactly the same economic effect as a tax levied upon the sale of religious literature. And yet, such a tax, when applied in the form of an excise or license fee, was held in valid in *Follette v. McCormick*.[20]

In his view, however, the Court "has exalted administrative convenience to a constitutional level high enough to justify making one religion economically disadvantageous."[21]

And finally going to the heart of the matter, Brennan strongly criticized the Court majority for turning its back on the tradition of religion in America, as well as on the recent development—with the Court itself in the vanguard—of the new meaning accorded free exercise. Proclaiming as an eternal verity the notion of *protected religiously motivated action*, Brennan reiterated the fact that religious freedom has been one of the highest values of our society. Even the critics of free exercise's expansion have admitted its validity in principle. Consequently, Brennan believed that the Court had incorrectly departed from the *preferred freedom status accorded free exercise* as early as the *Murdock, Martin, Follette, Ballard,* and *Marsh* decisions. Therefore, he concluded by issuing a warning to his colleagues on the majority: "The Court forgets, I think, a warning uttered during the congressional discussion of the First Amendment itself: '. . . the rights of conscience are, in their nature, of peculiar delicacy, and will little bear the gentlest touch of governmental hand.'"[22]

I am convinced that the dissenters were quite correct. The choice between religion and economics was a cruel one. Although several states have enacted Sabbatarian laws, most states continued to enforce (in oftentimes very haphazard ways) the Sunday closing laws. And the courts no longer seem concerned that substantial federal questions are still involved and remain unanswered.

In the same year the Supreme Court also handed down its ruling in *Torcaso v. Watkins*,[23] and faced the free exercise issue once again. Justice Black's opinion signaled a return to the more activist libertarian thinking about free exercise and the Court's willingness to subject legislation infringing freedom of religion to a more searching judicial scrutiny. It also set the stage for what was to follow two years later. Speaking for a unanimous Court, Black said that Article 37 of the Declaration of Rights of the Maryland constitution, which imposed as a condition for holding public office "a declaration of belief in the existence of God," was unconstitutional. Torcaso had been appointed by the Governor of Maryland to the office of notary public; but he was denied a commission because he refused to declare his belief in God, as required by Maryland law. Picking up the concluding theme of his *Summers* dissent, Black said that such a declaration was prohibited by Article VI, Clause 3, of the Constitution, as well as by the First Amendment. Neither the national nor state governments can constitutionally force people to believe or not believe in a religion based on the existence of a Supreme Being, as against a religion based on different beliefs. "The Maryland religious test for public office unconstitutionally invades the appellant's freedom of belief and religion and therefore cannot be enforced against him."[24]

Black emphasized that an oath professing belief—any religious belief—was as much a test oath as the type requiring adherence to the tenets of an established church. Such action by the state must be subjected to scrutiny and hostility by the Court. Invoking references to the Founding Fathers for added support, he declared that such a law could not be enforced. And almost as an afterthought, Black added: "[I]t is objected that the people of America may, perhaps, choose representatives who have no religion at all, and that pagans and Mahometans may be admitted into office. *But how is it possible to exclude any set of men, without taking away that principle of religious freedom which we ourselves so warmly contend for?*"[25] Two years later the implications of this point would be applied to the problem of free exercise and unemployment compensation benefits.

Adell H. Sherbert was a member of the Seventh Day Adventist Church. She was discharged[26] by her employer for refusing to work on Saturday, the sabbath day of her faith. When her religious beliefs kept her from finding other work, she applied for unemployment compensation benefits. The South Carolina Unemployment Compensation Act declared a claimant ineligible for benefits if, *without showing good cause,* available work was not accepted. The state Employment Security Commission ruled that Mrs. Sherbert's refusal to work on Saturdays, religious reasons notwithstanding, made her ineligible. The South Carolina Supreme Court upheld the Commission's finding. To borrow Warren's language in his *Braunfeld* opinion, the state court suggested, in effect, that the South Carolina law did "not make unlawful any religious practices of appellants," and as applied operated only "so as to make the practice of . . . religious beliefs more expensive."[27]

Speaking for the Court in *Sherbert v. Verner,*[28] Justice Brennan reversed the South Carolina authorities. In language that set aside the direct-indirect distinction established earlier by Warren and Frankfurter, Brennan said that the failure of the state to grant unemployment compensation to Mrs. Sherbert simply abridged her free exercise rights.

> The ruling forces her to choose between following the precepts of her religion and forfeiting benefits, on the one hand, and abandoning one of the precepts of her religion in order to accept work, on the other hand. Government imposition of such a choice puts the same kind of burden upon the free exercise of religion as would a fine imposed against appellant for her Saturday worship.[29]

Brennan's dissent in *Braunfeld* now became the "law of the land." And the free exercise clause was to receive a new, more expanded meaning so as to protect certain forms of action not covered by the other guarantees of the First Amendment.

Holding two years earlier that a religious test may not be imposed as a qualification for public office, the Court now made the logical transition and ruled that religion (or the lack of it) may not be imposed as a qualification for any public benefits. Brennan then went on to say that the state could not constitutionally claim that unemployment benefits were not a "right" but only a "privilege." At the same time it could not apply the eligibility provision of the act to an individual whose religious beliefs did not agree with those of a majority of the community. Brennan therefore suggested that the free exercise guarantee prevented a state action conditioning benefits upon the willingness of an individual to violate religious principles.

The Court majority now began to develop the concept of free exercise *and free it,* once and for all, from the belief-action distinction set out in the secular regulation rule, without rejecting the rule itself. The free exercise clause was—and is—a bar against any governmental regulation of religious beliefs. It prohibited the government from compelling affirmation of repugnant beliefs; or penalizing and discriminating against individuals and groups that held religious views abhorrent to the authorities; or employing the taxing power to inhibit the dissemination (proselytizing in many of its manifest forms) of particular religious views. Reiterating that the governmentally imposed choice between religion and welfare was a cruel and unconstitutional one, Brennan drew heavily on his line of argument in *Braunfeld:* the Court must never again forget what it previously said about free exercise in the Jehovah's Witness cases. *Cantwell, Murdock, Martin, Follette, Marsh, Tucker,* and *Suia* had suggested *explicitly* that the free exercise clause had a life and meaning all its own. Its purpose, aside from protecting religious beliefs absolutely, was to afford similar (although not absolute) protection for religiously motivated behavior—even for behavior not normally covered by the speech, press, and assembly clauses of the First Amendment.

For Brennan, it was no longer important whether the burden imposed on the free exercise of religion was direct or indirect. If its effect was "to impede the observance of one or all religions or . . . to discriminate invidiously between religions,"[30] then the law was constitutionally invalid. *The state must bear the burden of proof to show a compelling interest in the regulation at issue.*

> It is basic that no showing merely of a rational relationship to some colorable state interest would suffice; in this highly sensitive constitutional area, "[o]nly the gravest abuses, endangering paramount interests, give occasion for permissible limitation."[31]

Compelling interest, of course, was something quite different—and much more difficult to prove—than reasonable legislative purpose.[32] Only the latter had been required under the old secular regulation rule. Brennan was now suggesting, according to Morgan, that the "special tests of necessity and the unavailability of alternative means (which are applied when governmental regulation touches upon free speech) must now be applied when a regulation touches upon religiously motivated action."[33] Free exercise was no longer the "little boy on the constitutional block." By combining *compelling interest* and *alternative means* into one test, Brennan made the free exercise clause into a comprehensive formula to protect unorthodox religious behavior. Religious communication and action could now travel as far—and occasionally even further—than similar forms of secular communication and action. What began with the Witness cases two decades earlier was applicable to all bona fide believers and nonbelievers alike; and the lessons and precedents of the previous restraint cases were now available to conscientious objectors as well.

At the same time I am convinced that the decision in *Sherbert* cannot be reconciled with the holdings in *Braunfeld* and *Crown Kosher,* no matter how hard Brennan attempted to distinguish them. Justice Stewart[34] in a concurring opinion, along with Justices Harlan and White in a joint dissent,[35] believed that *Sherbert* had the specific effect of overruling Warren's judgments in the two previous cases. Indeed, Brennan's attempt to distinguish the South Carolina unemployment insurance problem from the practical difficulties and consideration of granting Sunday closing exemptions were ironic: he actually tried to bring the facts of the present case within the direct-indirect dichotomy of Warren's *Braunfeld* opinion.[36] Yet, as George W. Spicer put it: "The countervailing factor of *Braunfeld*—a strong state interest in providing one uniform day of rest for all workers—finds no equivalent in the present case."[37]

Surely the cruel choice between "following the precepts of her religion and forfeiting benefits, on the one hand, and abandoning one of the precepts of her religion in order to accept work, on the other hand," was similar to the problem confronting the Orthodox Jews in the earlier cases. In fact, the majority's suggestion that in the *Sunday Closing Law Cases* there was "less direct burden upon religious practices"[38] was questionable. If anything, there was less compelling interest and more chance to use alternative means in the Pennsylvania and Massachusetts situations than in the rather unique South Carolina case. Logic would suggest that it was easier (at least in a public policy sense) for the state to enact Sabbatarian laws than to make fundamental exceptions in a highly bureaucratic unemployment compensation system. Moreover, as Stewart stressed in his concurrence, the basic thrust of Brennan's opinion implied something more than state neutrality was required in free exercise situations—almost an understated favoritism for bona fide religious people.[39] But would such an official attitude not run into a head-on collision with the establishment clause? In truth, we do not know because Brennan never faced the complicated issue. The conclusion, as Abraham suggests, was that the majority opinion was not always logical and not completely convincing.[40]

Yet despite all of the criticism leveled at Brennan's attempt to distinguish the two cases, the result was the thing—and there were few activist libertarians to criticize the result. From this point on in the free exercise area "only the grossest abuses, endangering paramount interests, give occasion for permissible limitation." For the concept of free exercise that was surely a different standard of judicial construction; but I think an appropriate one nevertheless. And from this point on the "compelling (paramount) state interest—no alternative means" test would place the burden of proof on the state, and would in theory (at least) reverse the presumption of constitutionality. The free exercise clause was now to be given constitutional status as a specific limitation on the actions of government. The secular regulation rule—and the implications of the *Reynolds* and *Beason* holdings—was now less applicable in this highly sensitive area of individual conscience.

Or so it was believed at the time when the original draft of this study was written; and until very recently—with the exception of some frivolous free exercise claims that could not possibly emerge victorious[41]—my predictions had stood the test of time for two decades.

After *Sherbert* and *Yoder*, any government undertaking to burden or coerce persons because of their religious beliefs was considered a violation of the free exercise clause. Consequently, the courts have employed from *Sherbert* onward a two-step test. Initially the court examines the severity of the burden on the individual's religion. If the burden is significant, government must demonstrate that the law is narrowly tailored to achieve a compelling state interest. The availability of less burdensome alternatives is considered; and the doctrines employed in the freedom of expression cases (prior restraint or void for vagueness and overbredth) are usually applied in free exercise cases.

The result of employing a strict scrutiny standard has been the granting of a constitutionally mandated compelled exemption for religiously motivated behavior. For example, in *McDaniel v. Paty*,[42] *Thomas v. Indiana Employment Security Division*,[43] *Hobbie v. Unemployment Appeals Commission*,[44] and *Frazee v. Illinois Department of Employment*,[45] the Supreme Court has ruled that—in accommodating religion to a valid secular objective—the government cannot condition the receipt of public benefits on the surrender of constitutional rights, including the free exercise of one's religion. Conditioning the receipt of public benefits or the exercise of constitutional rights on the willingness to violate one's religious principles (and ultimately one's conscience as well), imposes a significant burden on free exercise. Only a compelling (paramount) government interest, which cannot be realized by means less burdensome on constitutional values, justifies such coercion.

Several recent cases merit fuller treatment here because they seem to have "scaled down" the application of the *Sherbert* precedent (if not actually calling it into question) and signalled a willingness by the Supreme Court's new majority to return to the approach of Warren's *Braunfeld* opinion and not apply the strict scrutiny (preferred freedom) standard. In *Bob Jones University v. United States*,[46] the Court rejected a challenge to IRS denials of tax-exempt status to private educational institutions who practice racial discrimination in accordance with their religious beliefs upon which they were founded.

Speaking through Chief Justice Burger, the Court held that the government can punish a nonsecular institution for its religiously divined racist policy.[47] In properly rejecting Bob Jones' free exercise claim, the majority argued that

> [t]his Court has long held the Free Exercise Clause of the First Amendment to be an absolute prohibition against governmental regulation or religious beliefs. As interpreted by this Court, moreover, the Free Exercise Clause provides substantial protection for lawful conduct grounded in religious belief. However, "[n]ot all burdens on religion are unconstitutional. . . . The state may justify a limitation on religious liberty, by showing that it is essential to accomplish an overriding governmental interest."[48]

Indeed, Burger concluded, on occasion this Court "has found certain governmental interests so compelling as to allow even regulations prohibiting religiously based conduct."[49] Although "[d]enial of tax benefits will inevitably have a substantial impact on the operation of private religious schools," it nevertheless "will not prevent those schools from observing their religious tenets."[50] Even applying a strict scrutiny test, in the face of arbitrary racial discrimination the free exercise claim had to be rejected.

Goldman v. Weinberger,[51] on the other hand, was simply not decided properly. In fact, after holding 5-4 against the religious claimant, the Court's opinion was effectively overturned the following year by an act of Congress.[52] The petitioner sought strict scrutiny under the *Sherbert* standard and argued that his religiously motivated conduct (the wearing of the headgear) should accordingly be immune from the military regulation. Justice Rehnquist's majority opinion, however, seemed to apply no standard at all—and showed total deference to the military position: "Our review of military regulations challenged on First Amendment grounds is far more deferential than constitutional review of similar . . . regulations designed for civilian society. The military need not encourage debate or tolerate protest to the extent that such tolerance is required of the civilian state by the First Amendment; to accomplish its mission the military must foster instinctive obedience, unity, commitment, and esprit de corps."[53] Indeed, continued the majority, when evaluating

> whether military needs justify a particular restriction on religiously motivated conduct, courts must give great deference to the professional judgment of military authorities concerning the relative importance of a particular military interest.[54]

More importantly, Justice Rehnquist seemed unconcerned with the religious issue. What the Court was dealing with was a form of compelled expression, although it never acknowledged that fact. When a government requires an individual to engage in practices contrary to the central tenets of his/her religion, it imposed a direct burden on the free exercise of religion. Unfortunately the majority could not bring itself to accept that only a compelling or overriding government interest justifies such a significant burden on free exercise. What, possibly, did the Court have in mind when it allowed a "clothing requirement"[55] to be substituted for a "compelling" interest?

In a series of dissents, Justices Brennan, Marshall, Blackmun, and O'Connor took exception to the majority's failure to invoke the strict scrutiny standard in light of the compelled expression involved here. What was used instead, according to the dissenters, was a "subrational-basis standard—absolute, uncritical deference to the professional judgment of military authorities."[56] And invoking language reminiscent of his *Sherbert* opinion, Brennan concluded:

> The Court and the military services have presented patriotic Orthodox Jews with a painful dilemma—the choice between fulfilling a religious obligation and serving their country. Should the draft be reinstated, compulsion will replace choice. Although the pain the services inflict on Orthodox Jewish servicemen is clearly the result of insensitivity rather than design, it is unworthy of our military because it is unnecessary. The Court and the military have refused these servicemen their constitutional rights; we must hope that Congress will correct this wrong.[57]

Lastly, we come to the two most troublesome cases of the period. In *Lyng v. Northwest Indian Cemetery Protective Association*[58] and *Department of Human Resources of Oregon v. Smith*,[59] the Supreme Court held for the first time that the strict scrutiny standard did not apply to a generally applicable and otherwise valid law, even though application of the law incidently imposed a significant burden on religion. In fact, these holdings seem to suggest a general doctrinal revision rejecting strict scrutiny review of laws having only an incidental effect of significantly burdening religious freedom. If the trend continues, however, the entire notion of a constitutionally mandated compelled exemption for proscribed religious practices may be neutralized—or even negated—and the key question will become whether the challenged government action directly, rather than indirectly, burdens free exercise. Incidental burdens on religion would be insufficient to generate strict scrutiny review.

Speaking through Justice O'Connor, the Court held in *Lyng* that the free exercise of religion clause did not prevent the national government from allowing timber harvesting in or constructing a road through the national forest area used for religious purposes by Indians. Recognizing that the governmental activity would have severe adverse effects on the specific practices of the religious beliefs, the Court nevertheless argued in an almost "desensitized" way that the free exercise clause does not prevent the government from using its land in any way it wishes. Indeed, according to O'Connor, the burden imposed on the national government was not sufficiently great enough to trigger any form of heightened scrutiny, and the government did not have to meet a "compelling interest" standard of justification for either the road project or timber harvesting. Relying heavily on Roy[60] as her major precedent, she said:

> The building of a road or the harvesting of timber on publicly owned land cannot meaningfully be distinguished from the use of a Social Security number in Roy. In both cases, the challenged Government action would interfere significantly with private persons' ability to pursue spiritual fulfillment according to their own religious beliefs. In neither case, however, would the affected individuals be coerced by the Government's action into violating their religious beliefs; nor would either governmental action penalize religious activity by denying any person an equal share of the rights, benefits, and privileges enjoyed by other citizens.[61]

Although she acknowledged the fact that "indirect coercion or penalties on the free exercise of religion, not just outright prohibitions, are subject to scrutiny under the First Amendment,"[62] O'Connor seemed unconcerned by the revelation. Indeed, she does not show hostility toward the practice of religion by the Indian tribes involved here, only a generalized lack of caring about an unorthodox religion practiced in an unorthodox way.[63] Her final argument, therefore, was not convincing at all. Invoking judicial restraint (not strict scrutiny) as the standard, O'Connor concluded that the "government simply could not operate if it were required to satisfy every citizen's religious needs and desires."[64] In fact, her argument continued, "[t]he First Amendment must apply to all citizens alike, and it can give to none of them a veto over public programs that do not prohibit the free exercise of religion."[65] In final analysis, what was controlling for the majority was not the free exercise claim but the fact that the land belonged to the government.

Justice Brennan, joined by Justices Marshall and Blackmun, dissented. Objecting strongly to the majority's distinction between the form of restriction involved in the government action challenged here and restrictions that would coerce or penalize religious activity, he said: "The constitutional guarantee we interpret today, however, draws no such fine distinctions between types of restraints on religious exercise, but rather is directed against any form of governmental action that frustrates or inhibits religious practice."[66] After describing the importance of the national forest area to the religious beliefs of the Indian tribes, Brennan criticized the majority's concept of "coercion."[67] Arguing throughout that the *Sherbert* "compelling interest" standard (remember Brennan was the author of that opinion) was appropriate to the present case,[68] he concluded with the following ominous language:

> Today, the Court holds that a federal land-use decision that promises to destroy an entire religion does not burden the practice of that faith in a manner recognized by the Free Exercise Clause. . . . I find it difficult, . . . to imagine conduct more in sensitive to religious needs than the Government's determination to build a marginally useful road in the face of uncontradicted evidence that the road will render the practice of respondents' religion impossible. Nor do I believe that respondents will derive any solace from the knowledge that although the practice of their religion will become "more difficult" as a result of the Government's actions, they remain free to maintain their religious beliefs.[69]

In the *Smith* case[70] the Court specifically ruled against the religious claimant by holding that (1) the free exercise clause permits the state to include religiously inspired use of peyote within the reach of the state's general criminal prohibition on use of that drug; (2) the free exercise clause does not prohibit the state of Oregon from denying unemployment benefits to persons dismissed from their jobs because of such religiously inspired use; and (3) generally applicable, religion-neutral criminal laws that have the effect of burdening a particular religious practice no longer need be justified by a compelling governmental interest under the free exercise clause.

Arguing that the *Sherbert* standard of strict scrutiny should not be expanded beyond its original fact situation (unemployment compensation), Justice Scalia's majority opinion lost sight of the fact that respondents in this case were looking for unemployment compensation benefits. Instead, like Justice Stevens in the first hearing of this case, he placed emphasis not on the religious claim but on the question of legality of the statute involved. Thus, he states that "[w]e have never held that an individual's religious beliefs excuse him from compliance with an otherwise valid law prohibiting conduct that the State is free to regulate. On the contrary, the record of more than a century of our free exercise jurisprudence contradicts that proposition."[71] In essence, like Chief Justice Waite in *Reynolds* and Justice Field in *Beason,* Scalia simply embraced the old secular regulation rule.

Attacking the "centrality" inquiry—the probing of the centrality of a belief or practice to a religion in assessing the significance of the burden on free exercise—as the reason courts have engaged in judgments (when applying the compelling interest test) they cannot make on a nonarbitrary basis, Scalia suggested that

[i]t is no more appropriate for judges to determine the "centrality" of
religious beliefs before applying a "compelling interest" test in the free
exercise field, than it would be for them to determine the "importance"
of ideas before applying the "compelling interest" test in the free
speech field.[72]

In other words, according to the majority, the free exercise of religion
required no special preference or consideration[73]—and certainly, under
the facts of the present case, no exemption.

Justice Blackmun, along with Justices Brennan and Marshall, dissented. Justice O'Connor wrote a separate opinion wherein she concurred in the judgment of the Court but not in its reasoning.[74] Stressing
three main points of disagreement, Blackmun argued that a state statute
that burdens the free exercise of religion may stand only if the law is
general, and the state's refusal to allow a religious exemption in particular, are justified by a compelling interest that cannot be served by less
drastic means (the *Sherbert* test). In addition, the dissenters emphasized
that Oregon's interest in refusing to make an exception for the religious
use of peyote was not sufficiently compelling to outweigh the counselors' right to the free exercise of religion. Therefore, Oregon could not,
consistent with the free exercise of religion clause, deny the counselors
unemployment benefits.

> This Court over the years painstakingly has developed a consistent and
> exacting standard to test the constitutionality of a state statute that
> burdens the free exercise of religion. Such a statute may stand only if
> the law in general, and the State's refusal to allow a religious exemp-
> tion in particular, are justified by a compelling interest that cannot be
> served by less restrictive means. Until today, I thought this was a set-
> tled and inviolate principle of this Court's First Amendment jurispru-
> dence. The majority, however, perfunctorily dismiss it as a "constitu-
> tional anomaly." . . . The Court views traditional free exercise analysis
> as somehow inapplicable to criminal prohibitions (as opposed to con-
> ditions on the receipt of benefits), and to state laws of general applica-
> bility (as opposed . . . to laws that expressly single out religious prac-
> tices). . . . The Court cites cases in which, due to various exceptional
> circumstances, we found strict scrutiny inapposite, to hint that the
> Court has repudiated that standard altogether. . . . In short, it effectu-
> ates a wholesale overturning of settled law concerning the Religion
> Clauses of our Constitution. One hopes that the Court is aware of the
> consequences and that its result is not a product of overreaction to the
> serious problems the country's drug crisis has generated.[75]

What is most troublesome with the *Smith* decision, aside from calling the strict scrutiny test of *Sherbert* into very serious question, is that
the so-called clarity of the new free exercise rule is actually not clear at

all. What we are given is a two-prong test—neutrality and general applicability—to determine whether the strict scrutiny standard should be applied. But we are given nothing to help us find answers. For example, does the majority really think that the sacramental use of peyote has ever harmed anyone (either the user or any third party)? If not harmful, how can it be forbidden? The national government exempted sacramental wine from the prohibition laws. Imagine the uproar if it had not; yet isn't the peyote situation identical, except that the Native American Church has no political power comparable to that of the Catholic Church? Isn't alcohol far more harmful to society than peyote? (Peyote is unlikely to be anyone's drug of self-indulgence.) What is at work in the majority opinion, one could argue, is at least selective religious indifference, or unconscious antireligious conduct. One could also argue, unfortunately, that the facially neutral antidrug statute of the state of Oregon had a disproportional racial effect. Because the religion disadvantaged in *Smith* is made up of a racial minority, isn't the problem presented here a serious one under the equal protection clause? As I said, the new test promulgated in *Smith* allows you to ask the questions but it supplies you with no help in finding the answers. Is this the improvement in line-drawing the Court promised?

Fortunately, Congress heeded the dissenters and tentatively overruled the *Lyng* and *Smith* decisions with passage of the Religious Freedom Restoration Act of 1993.[76] The purpose of the act was to (1) restore the compelling interest test of *Sherbert* and *Yoder* and to guarantee its application in all cases where the free exercise of religion is substantially burdened; and (2) provide a claim or defense to persons whose religious exercise is substantially burdened by government.

The "legislative history" of the 1993 statute emphasizes this nation's struggle and attainment—from persecution to toleration to freedom—of religious liberty.[77] More than a simple history lesson, however, the legislative history sets out the judicial meaning of the free exercise of religion. In the hands of the Supreme Court, since the late 1930s, free exercise had come to mean more than the right to believe and worship according to the dictates of one's own conscience. Religious freedom meant (among other things) the right to proselytize—to engage in activities designed to win converts to the faith, to distribute and sell religious literature free from license requirements and tax burdens, to refuse to participate in secular practices against one's own religious beliefs, to use public streets and parks for religious meetings, and to make door-to-door solicitations free from local restrictions. Moreover, the free exercise clause had come to mean not only protection (and sometimes even promotion) for conscience, but a right not to believe as well. In short, the free exercise of religion clause now had a *positive* (as well as the earlier passive) meaning.

The "legislative history" had been brought into serious question by the *Smith* decision. For two centuries, the guarantees of the First Amendment had proven to be the boldest and most successful experiment in religious liberty. Partly due to legislative common sense and partly because of judicial protection, the free exercise of religion clause became America's most protected (and oftentimes promoted) freedom. The majority opinion in *Smith* threatened to derail that experiment and make religious freedom a matter of legislative grace. In effect, *Smith* rejected virtually the entire legal history of religious freedom in America. It did so expansively, reaching far beyond the issue before the Court and declaring that government practices and policies that were neutrally stated and generally applicable would be upheld against constitutional attack as long as the policies were not targeted at religious practice. Thus, under the *Smith* rule, laws passed in ignorance or passed irrespective of their impact on religious freedom would be deemed constitutionally valid. And in rejecting the compelling government interest standard that previously governed such cases, the Court majority characterized the test as a "luxury" that the nation could no longer afford as a result of the country's growing religious diversity. What the rationale of the decision unfortunately did was turn the First Amendment on its head, and guaranteed free exercise judicial protection only in periods of relative religious homogeneity.

Passage of the Religious Freedom Restoration Act (RFRA) was designed to restore the level of legal protection that was previously enforced by the courts under the First Amendment. The Act simply restored the previous status quo, under which religious practices had to be accommodated unless a compelling governmental interest could be demonstrated and advanced in the least restrictive manner. This, of course, brings us to the current situation: In 1993 the San Antonio, Texas, archdiocese decided that it should enlarge St. Peter's Church in the City of Boerne to accommodate the gathering in excess of a thousand worshippers who come to the shrine each Sunday (the seventy-two-year-old church holds only 230 people, requiring it to hold several masses each Sunday in a high school gymnasium). But local officials denied the necessary permissions, asserting that the Church of St. Peter was listed as a historic place and could not be altered. Archbishop Patrick Flores sued the local authorities, claiming that the RFRA gave church officials the right to a hearing in which the government would be required to demonstrate that it had a compelling reason to keep the church at its present size.

The U.S. District Court for the Western District of Texas denied the request of the archdiocese and, in addition, declared the RFRA unconstitutional.[78] The lower court based its decision on the fact that Congress explicitly set out to overturn a Supreme Court ruling.[79] According to the court, the statute sought to overturn an interpretation of the Constitution by the Supreme Court; and the deliberate effort by Congress to overturn the *Smith* decision violated the doctrine of the separation of powers between the judicial and legislative branches. Cognizant of Congress' authority under section 5 of the Fourteenth Amendment, Judge Bunton nevertheless seemed convinced that by the use of that power Congress had intruded on power and responsibility reserved for the judicial branch. In addition, regardless of its questionable applicability on a constitutional issue, the District Court invoked the doctrine of *stare decisis* and simply proclaimed that the *Smith* decision remained the law in this area. Nowhere, of course, did the court even apply the two-prong *Smith* test of neutrality and general applicability.

The Fifth Circuit Court of Appeals unanimously reversed,[80] holding the RFRA constitutional and forcing the Supreme Court to clarify the very issues it created with the 1990 ruling. Speaking through Judge Higginbotham, the Court of Appeals argued that Congress, in passing the Religious Freedom Restoration Act, explicated textually located rights and obligations pursuant to section 5 of the Fourteenth Amendment. In so doing, Congress met the standard articulated in the three-prong *Morgan* test.[81] Therefore, the court held that RFRA (1) should be regarded as an enactment to enforce the Fourteenth Amendment; (2) is plainly adapted to that end; and (3) is consistent with the letter and spirit of the Constitution. In other words, RFRA was fully consistent with the separation of powers principle.[82] According to Higginbotham, "RFRA is also, in a sense, an assignment by Congress of a higher value to free-exercise-secured freedoms than the value assigned by the courts [under the *Smith* test]—that is, strict scrutiny versus a form of intermediate scrutiny."[83]

And now to bring the story up-to-date. Logically, the Supreme Court should have ruled RFRA constitutional, although the Court has not always been logical or, for that matter, consistent. So on June 25, 1997, a 6-3 majority of the Court reversed the Fifth Circuit and ruled RFRA unconstitutional. Speaking through Justice Kennedy, the Court emphasized two main points: (1) In imposing RFRA's requirements on the states, Congress misused its enforcement power under section 5 of the Fourteenth Amendment by enacting a law that was neither "preventive" nor "remedial." Legislation (like RFRA) that alters the meaning of the free exercise clause cannot be said to be enforcing the clause. Congress simply cannot "enforce" a constitutional right "by changing what the right is."[84] Furthermore, there must be a congruence and proportionality between the injury to be prevented or remedied and the means adopted to that end. If, on the other hand, such congruence and proportionality are lacking, the legislation may become "substantive" in operation and effect—as it did with RFRA. When that occurs, continued the Court, Congress has exceeded its power and such legislation is unconstitutional.

(2) RFRA is not a proper exercise of congressional section 5 enforcement power because it contradicts vital principles necessary to maintain separation of powers and the federal-state balance (federalism). Indeed, RFRA fails to take into account, argues Kennedy, that the "appropriateness of remedial measures must be considered in light of the evil presented."[85] According to the majority, the legislative record of RFRA "lacks examples of any instance of generally applicable laws passed because of religious bigotry"[86] in the past forty years.

> Regardless of the state of the legislative record, RFRA cannot be considered remedial, preventive legislation, if those terms are to have any meaning. RFRA is so out of proportion to a supposed remedial or preventive object that it cannot be understood as responsive to, or designed to prevent, unconstitutional behavior. It appears, instead, to attempt a substantive change in constitutional protections. Preventive measures prohibiting certain types of laws may be appropriate when there is reason to believe that many of the laws affected by the congressional enactment have a significant likelihood of being unconstitutional.[87]

What the record does show, rather, are laws that place an incidental burden on religion. Indeed, argues Kennedy, it is literally impossible to maintain that such laws are based on hostility toward religion, or that they constitute a prevailing or widespread pattern of religious discrimination in the country. RFRA's most serious shortcoming, however, is that it is out of proportion to a supposed remedial or preventive object—that is, unconstitutional behavior. The legislation is nothing more than an attempt to substantively change constitutional protections, proscribing state conduct that the Fourteenth Amendment itself does not prohibit. "When the exercise of religion has been burdened in an incidental way by a law of general application, it does not follow that the persons affected have been burdened any more than other citizens, let alone burdened because of their religious beliefs."[88] RFRA is a congressional intrusion into the traditional prerogatives and general authority of the states to regulate for the health and welfare of their citizens. What it is not, however, is legislation designed to identify and counteract state laws likely to be unconstitutional because of their treatment of religion.

What these two main points of argument by the majority boils down to is that the power to interpret the meaning of the Constitution remains with the judiciary and that Congress (unlike the British Parliament) cannot change the Constitution unilaterally. More than that, however, the *Smith* decision has been reinvigorated as the standard for free exercise review: strict scrutiny and less drastic means remain applicable when religion is burdened in a direct, substantial way, but no longer the prevailing test when the burden is only incidental. Then *Smith* enters the picture with the two-prong test of neutrality and general applicability.

Justice O'Connor wrote the primary dissenting opinion.[89] Believing that the problem stems from the fact that the *Smith* decision was—and still is— incorrect,[90] O'Connor says that because of the 1990 holding religious liberty has been greatly harmed in the United States. In particular, she argues that the *Smith* opinion misinterpreted the real meaning of the free exercise clause. It is not simply "an antidiscrimination principle that protects only against those laws that single out religious practice for unfavorable treatment."[91] On the contrary, the free exercise clause has more than a "passive" side to it; it is also an "affirmative" guarantee of the "right to participate in religious practices and conduct without impermissible governmental interference, even when such conduct conflicts with a neutral, generally applicable law."[92] Again, for O'Connor this case was unnecessary if the *Smith* decision had been rightly decided—that is, return to the free exercise meaning of *Sherbert* and grant a religious preference to the application of neutral laws. If the Court had seen the wisdom of this approach in 1990, RFRA would have been unnecessary in the first place.

Most troublesome about the *Flores* decision—aside from the fact that I believe it (like *Smith)* to be wrong both historically and legally— is the potential results for religious liberty that may be expected down the road. According to the *Smith* test (remember *Flores* was controlled by *Smith*) only blatant and clearly bigoted attempts by state and local governments to discriminate against religious practices will be illegal. But, as even Kennedy's majority opinion points out, such attempts are rare. More common, and more threatening, are laws that discriminate unintentionally. Indeed, both *Smith* and *Flores* (like *Goldman, Roy,* and *Lyng*) ignore the fact that people lose their rights just as surely by unintentional discrimination as they do by discrimination that is intentional and aimed directly at religion.

SUMMARY

It does not seem inappropriate at this point to ask two interrelated questions: Does the state (as the ultimate agent of the people) have the right to punish, and perhaps even destroy, the religious or political nonconformist in the interest of majority rule? Must the state (as an instrument of the democratic process) recognize and protect individual conscience by allowing religious or moral unorthodoxy so long as no *valid* law is broken?[93] The conflicting views of democratic theory notwithstanding, my personal bias and values (even though I am a democrat) will always suggest the latter. Such has not always been the case with the Supreme Court.

If Madison and Jefferson had been able to forecast the events that took place during this century (from persecutions of Quakers and Witnesses to our involvement in four shooting wars), they might have fought harder to have the words "or of conscience" added to the end of the First Amendment's religious clauses. This addition would have saved the nation, Congress, and the Court from much difficulty. I should add that it probably would have saved the lives of thousands of conscientious objectors as well. All of us would be better able (considering the human mind-heart conflict in such matters) to define religion and religious belief. And at the crux of such beliefs is the notion of conscience.[94] If there is one thing that all conscientious objectors have in common when they apply for citizenship, register for the draft, apply for admission to the bar, or claim other benefits—whether they be Macintosh, a Witness, Seeger, Ali, Welsh, Summers, Sherbert or Smith—it is that

> each man's conscience compels him to say to the authorities, in the words of Luther: *Hier stehe ich! Ich nicht anders.* "Here I stand. I cannot do otherwise."[95]

Now let me be more specific. Four inevitable conclusion come out of the conscientious objector cases. And each bears directly on the described development of free exercise, and finally conscience. First, conscientious objector status will probably continue to be a legislative privilege, not a constitutionally guaranteed right. Congress has yet to recognize conscience, and certainly (I hope that I am overly pessimistic here) would never recognize a consicence severed from bona fide religious beliefs. This is another way of saying that there now exists no constitutional status for nonreligious and antiestablishment conscience. Second, the Supreme Court has invented a series of tools and tests and intellectual devices to protect individual conscience by statutory interpretations and constructions. Moreover, the Court will no longer refrain from questioning a final selective service or naturalization classification. This fact, in and of itself, has been significant. One's rights do not completely disappear the moment after taking the oath of induction. Third, until recently side-tracked by *Lyng, Smith,* and *Flores,* rulings of the Court have taken a distinctively libertarian view of free exercise and conscience; and on several occasions have made them indistinguishable.

Sherbert and *Welsh* were such cases. So was *In re Jamison*.[96] Here the Court overturned a Minnesota conviction for a women who refused to serve jury duty for reasons of religion and conscience. Lastly, the *Sherbert* test itself—at least the least drastic means portion—has already had enduring significance well beyond the disposition of that case. Properly enlarged, embellished, and structured, it has proven to be a most viable standard for future free exercise adjudication.

There is another side to this analysis, however, and the picture is not necessarily as bright. Regarding the question of conscientious objection in its purest sense, the changing (as to compositon *and* ideology) Court has in many ways come full circle back to "dead-center." There are limits, both reactionary and libertarian, that a majority of the justices will not go beyond. If a parallel example to the Burger/Rehnquist Court must be used the appropriate one would be the Court under Hughes: steps ahead of the antilibertarian stance of Taft and miles behind what was to become the activism of Stone. Now we find the Nixon, Reagan, and Bush appointees moving away from the libertarianism of the Warren era and backing into the 1990s and beyond. What we have essentially is a Court without motivating direction or moral goal. What we have is a tentative willingness to return to the notion of giving to a man's possessions the same dignity and status as we give to man himself. Ultimately, we must face the possibility of state and local authority having fewer limits and judicial authority having no limits whatsoever (in spite of its recent embrace of separation of powers doctrine). It can no longer be said with any degree of assurance that the free exercise clause (now unaided by the Religious Freedom Restoration Act) will continue to be an adequate limitation on the powers of government. The effect of the recent Clinton appointees on the Court's future direction cannot yet be analyzed.

One final point: The Court has not directly addressed itself to the question of what qualifies as a religion or religious belief under the free exercise clause. Indeed, it is not even clear—after adding the establishment clause limitations to the equation—that it is appropriate for a court to probe the meaning of "religion." At the same time, however, the Court has made suggestions, among them the following from *Yoder*: "Although a determination of what is a 'religious' belief or practice entitled to constitutional protection may present a most delicate question, the very concept of ordered liberty precludes allowing every person to make his own standards on matters of conduct in which society as a whole has important interests."[97]

The Court has clearly rejected any limitation of "religion" to theistic religions. While there must be a sincerely held religious belief to qualify for free exercise protection, it is not required that the claimant be a member of an organized religion or a particular sect. Nevertheless, the Court's decisions in both *Lyng* and *Smith*—while acknowledging that the theistic cannot be favored over the nontheistic—seem to mean as well that the orthodox and traditional will be preferred over the unorthodox and nontraditional. In fact, both decisions came remarkably close to equating the orthodox and traditional with "religious." I raised this point earlier in chapter 3 and reintroduce it here. The Native American Church was hardly treated as an orthodox and traditional religion for purposes of the free exercise clause. Rather, their beliefs—and the religious practices they believed were so necessary—were dismissed as being immaterial to the process of drawing the line. Yet "[i]t is precisely in its dynamic infancy that a new religious doctrine will seem most threatening to the old order. It is at this stage that it is most likely to be met by some form of community resistence. The First Amendment must surely apply to protect new religions as well as old from governmental restraints."[98] Unfortunately, *Lyng* and *Smith* proved not to be mere aberrations. The congressional attempt to reestablish the older standard of *Sherbert* and *Yoder* was negated by the ruling in *Flores*. Free exercise is now just a little less protected than previously. And the Congress may once again attempt to reenact something like RFRA. Perhaps this time around the majority of the Court will read the handwriting on the wall.

Most of these implications for the problem of selective conscientious objection will be considered in the next chapter.

CHAPTER 6

Selective Conscientious Objection

The previous chapters of this volume have stressed many themes within the context of the overall development of the free exercise clause. The freedoms to believe, worship, and proselytize are all part of the new, expanded notion of free exercise. From a clause once thought to protect only religious opinion it has come to mean—through Supreme Court interpretation—protection for many forms of religiously motivated behavior. It has become, in its own right, a specific limitation on the actions of government. But, at least for this author, it has come to mean even more: a protection for *conscience* as well. And, hopefully, a protection for nonreligious conscience too. If the previous chapters teach us nothing of lasting importance—for the composition of the Court will change and decisions will be distinguished or modified or overturned—they should teach us at least this: "Religion may enhance or degrade man; it all depends on what it is. But without conscience, man has no dignity; without it, man is not man."[1] In other words, to completely protect religion—an essential theme of these chapters—"it is absolutely necessary to protect conscience as well, for religion is based on conscience and without it would soon perish."[2]

What has all this to do with the topic of this particular chapter? Suggesting an answer may be much more difficult than asking the question. Let me begin by arguing that two types of rights are guaranteed by the words of the First Amendment. There are enumerated rights and "peripheral rights"; and without the latter, as the Court suggested in *Griswold v. Connecticut,*[3] the former would be less secure.[4] In other words, the First Amendment has a "penumbra" in which these rights are protected: "[S]pecific guarantees in the Bill of Rights have penumbras, formed by emanations from these guarantees that help give them life and substance."[5] And in order to secure more fully the religious freedom protected by the free exercise clause, conscience must also be protected— even conscience that is nonreligious. For it is only "[t]hrough conscience [that] man transcends the state and its laws and passes judgment on them."[6] Once this is understood, we can begin the investigation of the problem of selective conscientious objection.

The issue of conscientious objection to war on a selective basis has presented a problem potentially more explosive than that in the flag salute cases; and one decidedly more difficult to resolve. The issue has touched the rights and obligations of the individual and his community. It has placed a unique burden on the religious community, the churches and synagogues that have preached the individual can never sacrifice this conscience to his political responsibilities;[7] and also upon the political community that honored the individual conscience, but refused to grant it an absolute right.[8] The issue of selective conscience objection must ultimately touch the relationship of man to man, and to the state and community, as well as raise the basic questions of authority, responsibility, philosophy, and morality. Yet the theory that one war may be preferable to another is neither new nor novel. It dates back to the writings of St. Augustine in the fourth century, and to St. Thomas Aquinas' *Summa Theologica* and Hugo Grotius' *De Jure Belli et Pacis* in the thirteenth and seventeenth centuries respectively, on the merits of the "just" and "unjust" war. Even Chief Justice Hughes raised the theory by implication in his *Macintosh* dissent. The Selective Service Act as amended in 1967 and the Congress writing it never accepted nor reflected the spirit of that theory. Until 1969, neither had the courts.

The chapter on conscientious objection and the draft ended with the *Seeger* and *Welsh* cases as the high-water mark of Supreme Court protection for the "religious believer" and "nonreligious believer" as well, in the area of selective service. This chapter begins with the important constitutional questions neither raised nor answered by the Court in those cases.

What about the individual or religious sect holding spiritual beliefs opposing military service? In other words, if the Selective Training and Service Act was construed as allowing exemption for only those whose religious beliefs include acceptance of a Supreme Being, could this be discrimination against nonbelievers? The lower courts in the *Seeger* case ruled the statute invalid on these grounds since no similar exemptions were given to atheists or agnostics.[9] Yet the Court did not hold that the state cannot grant exemptions from military service to only certain believers. More important was the question of whether a religiously oriented exemption provision could appear in the act without coming into conflict with the establishment clause of the First Amendment? The Supreme Court had never really decided the issue of possible conflict before. But U.S. District Courts faced the issue in the cases of *United States v. Sisson*,[10] *Koster v. United States*,[11] and *United States v. McFadden*.[12]

What are the criteria for the "just" war? And once these are established, what questions must the religious or nonreligious conscientious objector ask himself before he can morally and philosophically participate in such a war? St. Augustine made specific requirements for Christian participation in war. The purpose must be moral and the means proportional to the end. St. Thomas Aquinas was more specific, setting conditions more applicable to the unpleasantness encountered during the Vietnam period. His conditions for a "just" war were: (1) the authority of the state declaring it must be legitimate and the declaration "constitutional"; (2) hostilities should be caused by a crime of the enemy[13]; and (3) the war *must* be declared with rightful intention. For him, condition three was the most important; a war would still be "unjust" (even if the first two conditions were met) through failure to meet condition three.[14]

Once these criteria are established, the selective conscientious objector must then consider standards for objection set by the Selective Training and Service Act. The objection must be (1) rooted in religious belief, (2) a matter of conscience, and (3) based on a totally pacifist position. Since the objection is a matter of conscience, the objector must know that he cannot accept standards set by the act or have them changed. He must believe and claim that the morality of war is not absolute, and that factors prompting an individual to bear arms in one situation may be changed in another. Therefore, to determine his position on a particular war the selective objector must always search his conscience for answers as to whether (a) the war prevented greater evil than it caused, (b) the war was declared by proper authority, (c) the war was supported by the people, (d) the war was waged in defense against an unjust aggressor, (e) the war could be won, (f) everything short of war had been tried first, and (g) the use of nuclear weapons against population centers was contemplated.[15] He (the selective objector) cannot allow himself to forget that he is obligated, if not legally at least morally, by the Nuremberg principles of individual guilt and responsibility to judge his nation's behavior. It must always be the *sine qua non* of the democratic process that the exercise of individual conscience, even in error, should and must be encouraged. In the *Sisson* case, District Court Judge Wyzanski upheld the moral and philosophical claims of the selective objector, ruling that in balancing individual rights against the government's need to conscript men to fight in Vietnam, *the need to fight was outweighed by the demands of conscience!*

Going to the heart of the matter, the district court held that Congress lacked constitutional power to conscript men for Vietnam if they had conscientious scruples against fighting there. Also, the court ruled specifically that the Selective Service Act of 1967, as applied to the defendant, violated the free exercise of religion clause of the First Amendment and the due process clause of the Fifth Amendment. After saying this, the court took the next logical step and spoke of the status and position of the selective objector. Acknowledging that Sisson (1) was not formally a religious conscientious objector, or (2) was unable to meet the 1967 congressional definition of religion, the court said he was still entitled to his right not to believe in acceptable orthodoxy.

> The sincerely conscientious man, whose principles flow from reflection, education, practice, sensitivity to competing claims, and a search for a meaningful life, always brings impressive credentials. When he honestly believes that he will act wrongly if he kills, his claim obviously has great magnitude. That magnitude is not appreciably lessened if his belief relates not to war in general, but to a particular war or to a particular type of war. Indeed a selective conscientious objector might reflect a more discriminating study of the problem, a more sensitive conscience, and a deeper spiritual understanding.[16]

Indeed, for the first time in a conscientious objection case since *Kauton*,[17] a court equated political, sociological, philosophical, and moral views with the idea of conscience. This set the ground for the possible creation of the right of "nonreligious conscience"—which would properly require (as did the free exercise clause) a more searching judicial scrutiny.

The final question handled by the court was the one not considered in the *Seeger* and *Welsh* cases. Would a religiously-oriented provision in the act come into conflict with the establishment clause of the First Amendment? The court answered affirmatively, holding that Congress violated the clause by requiring that the only pacifism it would recognize was one based on religion. Stressing that a distinction can be made between the status accorded religious and nonreligious objectors (since the freedom not to believe was protected by the free exercise clause), the court said the only ground it could imagine for such a statutory distinction was outright religious preference. By virtue of the draft law as amended in 1967, Congress unconstitutionally discriminated against atheists, agnostics, and men like Sisson

> who, whether they be religious or not, are motivated in their objection to the draft by profound moral beliefs which constitute the central convictions of their beings. . . . This [c]ourt, therefore, concludes that in granting to the religious conscientious objector but not to Sisson a special conscientious objector status, the Act, as applied to Sisson, violates the provision of the First Amendment that "Congress shall make no law respecting an establishment of religion or prohibiting the free exercise thereof."[18]

The court did not suggest that Congress cannot exercise the applicable "war powers" granted in Article I, Section 8, Clauses 11–14. What it did say was that under the new meaning judicially accorded free exercise and conscience, substantive constitutional rights require protection even in the face of governmental authority. The task was—and still is—the judiciary's proper role in a free society. And, ultimately, this judicial protection must extend to nonreligious conscience as well.

In June 1970, the Supreme Court confronted the explosive issue of selective conscientious objection to the war in Vietnam and refused to dispose of it. Speaking through Justice Harlan, with Chief Justice Burger and Justices Douglas and White dissenting,[19] the Court in *United States v. Sisson*[20] held that by employing a procedure know as "arrest of judgment" the district court opinion had actually been a directed verdict of acquittal. Harlan suggested that Judge Wyzanski had thrown out the conviction (actually he had not) on the ground that Sisson should have been exempted from service as a conscientious objector, even though his objections were directed only at the Vietnam War, which he considered immoral. Consequently, the Court ruled that the United States government had no legal right under 19 U.S.C. sec. 3731, Criminals Appeals Act, to appeal such an acquittal; and the Supreme Court had no jurisdiction over the matter.

In the *Koster* and *McFadden* cases, the lower courts dealt with the nonreligious conscientious objector and the religiously motivated selective objector respectively. These cases were to hold that section 6(j) of the draft law was an unconstitutional infringement of the free exercise of religion, a violation of the establishment clause, and a denial of equal protection and due process. Each was to go beyond the holding in *Sisson*—that religion and conscience were indistinguishable—and suggest that no difference existed between religious and nonreligious conscience as well.

John William Koster successfully completed boot camp and was assigned advanced training at the Navy's Nuclear Power School. He reported to this school but did not enter the training program, because it was at this time that his gradually evolving beliefs of conscientious objection to war had crystallized, and he no longer felt himself capable of remaining a member of the military. Koster later submitted his formal application for a conscientious objector discharge. Captain George F. Sharp (Koster's commanding officer) concluded[21] that he was sincere in his stated beliefs, although they were not based on his religion or religious training but rather on his own selfstyled philosophy and his over-rationalization that the expressed purpose of the armed forces was for indiscriminate killing. However, since Koster was sincere in his beliefs, Sharp recommended that he be assigned to noncombatant duties. This recommendation was turned down by the Bureau of Naval Personnel. Instead, Koster was reassigned to the Amphibious Warfare School for training before being transferred to Vietnam. Koster then filed for a writ of habeas corpus and an application for a temporary restraining order. The District Court for the Eastern District of Pennsylvania issued the restraining order (and later a preliminary injunction) on the ground that immediate and irreparable harm would result if Koster were removed from the jurisdiction of the court and coerced into participating in activities to which he was fundamentally opposed by reason of his beliefs as a conscientious objector.

The court held that Koster was entitled to an inservice honorable discharge as a conscientious objector. Criticizing the Navy's conclusion that the petitioner's scruples were not based on any religious training or belief, Judge Masterson said that such a verdict (considering Koster's sincerity) constituted "the narrowest and most sectarian view of religion which has been held to be impermissible in parallel cases."[22] Accordingly, the court—following the lead of Justice Douglas in *Ballard*—reestablished the test of sincerity: whether the applicant for a conscientious objector discharge was sincere in his objection to war in any form. And conscience, not religion, must be the standard if such sincerity was to be tested. In addition, Masterson denied that the standard of section 6(j)—religious training and belief—could pass constitutional muster. Such a standard was violative of free exercise (by requiring action contrary to what the individual's conscience would allow) and the establishment clause (by preferring some beliefs over others).[23] Quoting Justice Black's opinion in *Everson*, and applying the *Everson* test itself, the court concluded by saying (and ultimately quoting Judge Wyzanski) that "'it is difficult to imagine any ground for [such] a statutory distinction except religious prejudice.'"[24]

In the *McFadden* case the issue presented was somewhat different—selective objection religiously motivated—and the opinion went well beyond the *Koster* holding. James McFadden applied for conscientious objector status on the grounds that he believed the war in Vietnam was an "unjust" war and that it would violate his conscience to submit to induction. His beliefs were based on his training and belief in the Catholic religion and his schooling at Seminary College. He was subsequently indicted for refusal to submit to induction after his selective conscientious objector appeal was denied. The District Court for the Northern District of California ruled, however, that the statute exempting from military service only those persons whose religious beliefs forbid them from participating in all wars placed such a burden on the religious beliefs of Catholic selective objectors as to be violative of the free exercise clause.

Unwilling to resolve the question of whether exemption from military service was a right or a privilege, Judge Zirpoli nevertheless suggested that once Congress granted the exemption to some (even though it may have the power to deny it to all), "it cannot deny it to others based on unconstitutional conditions."[25]

> Section 6(j) exempts from military service only those persons whose religious beliefs forbid them to participate in "war in any form" (in short, any and all wars). The defendant is therefore made to choose between violating his religious beliefs against entering an "unjust" war, or affirming those beliefs and suffering a possible five-year jail sentence and a possible $10,000 fine. The statute in question puts the most direct burden on the Catholic selective objector—a criminal penalty. . . .
>
> However, in the instant case, defendant is not being restrained from doing an affirmative act, rather, the Selective Service Act is *commanding him to perform an affirmative act*—participation in a war which his conscience tells him is unjust. . . . If the Selective Service statute does not exempt from its command the Catholic Selective objector, then it must run afoul of this prohibition against the State commanding one to act against his conscience.[26]

Indeed, inherent in the free exercise clause was—and is—the notion that one religious group cannot be favored over another. Nor can the state, *without bearing the burden of proof that a compelling interest was at stake,* coerce an individual to participate in an act that was opposed to his deepest convictions of right and wrong.

Invoking the holding of the Supreme Court in *Sherbert* as binding precedent, Judge Zirpoli said that section 6(j) forced McFadden "to choose between following the precepts of his religion and going to jail or abandoning those precepts in order to avoid jail."[27] And such an intolerable burden had no place in a free society. "[A]lthough our history is not free from religious intolerance and persecution," he continued, "it has always been the ideal of our forefathers to create a country where, . . . '[t]he liberty enjoyed by the people of these States of worshipping Almighty God agreeably to their conscience, is not only among the choicest of their blessings, but also of their rights.'"[28]

Once again, like Judge Wyzanski in *Sisson,* the court was not content to stop there, however. Reasoning that section 6(j) might serve some administrative purpose, Zirpoli nevertheless suggested that efficiency, morale of the troops, and manpower quotas were not compelling enough interests to justify refusal of selective objector status to a sincere Roman Catholic. And without a compelling interest no justification can exist for such an invidious discrimination clearly violative of equal protection and due process of law. Moreover, section 6(j) violated the specific constitutional prohibition against an establishment of religion by its preference of pacifist over nonpacifist religions. Again invoking the

Everson test as used in *Epperson,*[29] the court held that an induction order (even for a selective objector) "based upon the application of this unconstitutional statute must fall and the indictment based on such order must be and is dismissed."[30] Religion and conscience and nonreligious conscience were indistinguishable. All were entitled to equal treatment and protection under the free exercise clause.

The Supreme Court finally accepted jurisdiction in two cases involving the question of selection conscientious objection. The first case involved Louis A. Negre, a U.S. Army private from Bakersfield, California, who applied for a discharge on the basis of his Roman Catholic beliefs. He cited the Bible and teachings of Catholic theologians who have distinguished between "just" and "unjust" wars. Private Negre said that he considered the Vietnam War so unjust that he could not stay in the service. The Army turned him down and the lower courts refused to intervene. He later sought unsuccessfully to block his transfer to Vietnam. The second case involved Guy Porter Gillette, of New York City, who was given a two-year sentence for refusing to show up for induction after a court rejected his contention that he should have been given a conscientious objector exemption because he considered the Vietnam War unconstitutional and immoral. The facts as presented were difficult (if not impossible) to distinguish from those in the *Sisson, Koster,* and *McFadden* cases.

The basic issue presented to the Court was whether Gillette and Negre could claim conscientious objector status under section 6(j) of the 1967 act. Put differently, did the congressional, and judicially modified (perhaps stretched is a better word), provision for conscientious objection allow objection to only some wars, particularly those the claimant believed to be unjust? Attorneys for the petitioners argued on three interrelated grounds: (1) the statutory claim that the words "in any form" significantly modified the word "participation"; (2) the claim of unconstitutional classification or establishment—that is, section 6(j) was a *de jure* discrimination against *some* religions; and (3) the free exercise claim that an individual cannot be compelled to serve in the armed forces (even as a noncombatant) against the dictates of his conscience. In addition, petitioners suggested that it was only logical for the Court to extend its previous free exercise–conscience holdings to include selective objectors in order to save the constitutionality of section 6(j).

Speaking for an eight-man majority, Justice Marshall rejected all three claims, as well as the suggestion that the Court—by extending the *Sherbert-Seeger-Welsh* line of reasoning—create a free exercise of conscience exemption.

The initial claim, although grammatically interesting, was the weakest one advanced by the petitioners. The pertinent language of section 6(j) exempted only those individuals who were "conscientiously opposed to participation in war in any form." In order to seek inclusion under this language, according to Kent Greenawalt, petitioners argued that because of the claimed modification in sentence structure and meaning selective objectors did in fact object to participation in war—the war in which they were forced to serve.[31] Marshall rejected this new statutory construction by suggesting that the modification was inconsistent with the fact that section 6(j) applied to noncombatants who were not opposed to participation in war in any form. Moreover, he believed that such a claim must be rejected because of the legislative history of section 6(j), including a rejection by the U.S. Senate in 1917 of a selective conscientious objector exemption. Only a claim of total objection can be squared with the language and legislative intent of the statute. And the claim for the exemption was in no way enhanced if the selective objector based his claim on a bona fide religious position.

Petitioners also charged that section 6(j) violated the establishment clause because it discriminated between religious beliefs and preferred specific sectarian affiliations. Black's opinion in *Welsh* suggested that conscientious opposition to participation in war was itself a form of religious belief.[32] And if general objection was judicially classified as a religion, then selective objection must also be equally classified; otherwise, according to Greenawalt, there would be classification according to religious belief.[33] In addition, no valid neutral reasons were provided for establishing anything other than a blanket exemption. The entire argument revolved around the *Seeger, Koster, McFadden,* and *Welsh* construction of the statute. It was immaterial whether conscientious objectors had a constitutional claim for such an exemption. The fact that Congress chose to grant an exemption to general objectors precluded a denial of the exemption to any other class of claimant (in this case selective objectors).

The Court rejected all of these contentions. Holding that section 6(j) focused only on individual conscientious belief, Marshall said there was no discrimination on its face on the basis of religious affiliation and belief. For him, the critical weakness of the establishment claim arose from the fact that the statute, on its face, simply did not discriminate

> on the basis of religious affiliation or religious belief, apart of course from beliefs concerning war. The section says that anyone who is conscientiously opposed to all war shall be relieved of military service. The specified objection must have a grounding in "religious training and belief," but no particular sectarian affiliation or theological position is required. . . .

> [T]here is no occasion to consider the claim that when Congress grants a benefit expressly to adherents of one *religion*, courts must either nullify the grant or somehow extend the benefit to cover all religions. For sec. 6(j) does not single out any religious organization or religious creed for special treatment.[34]

In other words, at best section 6(j) operated as a *de facto* discrimination against some religions;[35] but petitioners must bear the burden of proof here, and they have failed to make the requisite showing. Indeed, petitioners would be hard put to prove that section 6(j) "encourages membership in putatively 'favored' religious organizations, for the painful dilemma of the sincere conscientious objector arises precisely because he feels himself bound in conscience not to compromise his beliefs or affiliations."[36]

Marshall was not content to stop there, however. He said that the purposes underlying section 6(j) were neutral and secular. The test was not whether there was some form of interference. Rather the test must be whether some valid, secular purpose existed for both the exemption of general objectors and the exclusion of particular ones. According to this test, section 6(j) was compatible with Congress' long-established policy of not favoring any religious beliefs. By implication, Marshall and the Court were also saying that previous decisions concerning the statutory construction of section 6(j) had made it valid and secular so as to satisfy the standards of neutrality.[37] That is to say, the "secular quality of the Court version of the section 6(j) exemption," according to Richard E. Morgan, "was undisturbed by holding it to principled pacifists"[38] only. Distinctions leading to a *de facto* discrimination were permissible (though not necessarily appreciated) if the discrimination was based on criteria other than religion itself.

Marshall also dealt at great length with the government's assertions that its military capacity might be severely handicapped if selective objection were recognized as a constitutional right. What was not considered, of course, was the inherent religious claims upon which the classification was based; and the very thing the majority opinion said the free exercise clause prohibited. (These will be considered later in this chapter).

> Apart from the Government's need for manpower, perhaps the central interest involved in the administration of conscription laws is the interest in maintaining a fair system for determining "who serves when not all serve." When the Government exacts so much, the importance of fair, evenhanded and uniform decision-making [sic] is obviously intensified.[39]

Moreover, the expansion of section 6(j) to include selective objectors would endanger the government's interest in fairness. The petitioner's claim to relief because of such objection was "a claim of uncertain dimensions, and that granting the claim in theory would involve a real danger of erratic or even discriminatory decision-making in administrative practice."[40] An endless variety of positions opposing this particular war would make it vitually impossible for the government to reach fair and consistent results.

Marshall picked up this theme once again in his opinion; and his justifications suggest that he was not sure he had been convincing the first time around. What would happen, he asked, if the nature of an "unpopular" war changed—that is, if a once unjust war suddenly became just? Objectors to the particular war would have to change their minds and now willingly serve. Considering the multitude of reasons for selective objection, draft boards across the nation would be faced with the impossible task of recognition: Which draftees were sincere and which ones were feigning "selective conscience" for reasons other than conscientious beliefs.[41] Marshall simply feared that exempting selective objectors would open the door to a general theory of selective disobedience to law! And he concluded that because of these considerations, combined with the central notion of fairness, Congress has the right "to have decided that the objector to all war—and all killing in war—has a claim that is distinct enough and intense enough to justify special status, while the objector to a particular war does not."[42] Justifying reasons therefore existed so that no violation of the establishment clause occurred.

The free exercise claim was also dismissed by the Court, almost before the Court considered it: "We are not faced with the question whether the Free Exercise Clause itself would require exemption of any class other than objectors to particular wars. A free exercise claim on behalf of such objectors collides with the distinct governmental interests already discussed, and, at any rate, no other claim is presented."[43] In these two sentences Marshall temporarily put aside the Court's own development of free exercise and conscience that began almost three decades earlier. Despite the fact that the free exercise clause has a specific reach of its own, Marshall reasoned that his analysis of section 6(j) for establishment purposes had revealed "sufficient governmental interests" to justify the application of the draft law against selective objectors claiming free exercise protection. For him, and the members of the majority, no claim—religious or otherwise—relieved an objector from the obligations imposed by citizenship in a democratic society. And in invoking Warren's line of argument in *Braunfeld,* Marshall said:

> The incidental burdens felt by persons in petitioners' position are strictly justified by substantial governmental interests that relate directly to the very impacts questioned. And more broadly, of course,

there is the Government's interest in procuring the manpower necessary for military purposes, pursuant to the constitutional grant of
power to Congress to raise and support armies.[44]

The free exercise clause did prohibit a wide variety of governmental
interferences with the individual's right of belief, worship, and proselytizing; in fact, it even protected various manifestations of conscience.
But what *it did not do,* concluded Marshall, was create a constitutional
right to an exemption, especially when the claim was based on grounds
previously rejected by the Congress—selective objection to particular
wars.

Justice Douglas was the sole dissenter. For him, there were four specific grounds for extending an exemption to selective objectors—particularly in light of the Court's previous holdings in the "free exercise of
conscience" cases:

1. Both Gillette and Negre were genuine and sincere objectors to the
   Vietnam War, and in basing their objection on conscience they fell
   within the statutory requirements of section 6(j).
2. The rights of conscience and belief were the prime ingredients of the
   First Amendment's guarantees of religion and speech.
3. Section 6(j), as written, was unconstitutional in light of the establishment clause prohibition against invidious discrimination.
4. Any exemption granted to general objectors must also be accorded
   to specific objectors if their objection was based on grounds of religion and conscience.

Douglas, in assuming *"that the welfare of the single human soul was
the ultimate test of the vitality of the First Amendment,"*[45] would have
denied the judicial compromise of the statutory exemption.

> It is true that the First Amendment speaks of the free exercise of reli-
> gion, not of the free exercise of conscience and belief. Yet conscience
> and belief are the main ingredients of First Amendment rights. They
> are the bedrock of free speech as well as religion. The implied First
> Amendment right of "conscience" is certainly as high as the "right of
> association" which we recognized. . . . Some indeed have thought it
> higher.[46]

For Douglas, conscience was the echo of religious faith. It was the
sphere of intellect and spirit that the Court had previously recognized in
Barnette[47]—the domain of the First Amendment.

Quoting Hughes' dissenting opinion in *Macintosh* (as he had previously done in his *Girouard* opinion),[48] Douglas suggested that once *con-*

science became the standard, section 6(j) must fall as violative of the free exercise and establishment clauses. The First Amendment prohibited the government—no matter what the Court will allow—from discriminating against some religious persons while favoring others with similar scruples. Any classification of conscience "based on a 'religion' and a 'conscience' based on more generalized, philosophical grounds is equally invidious by reason of our First Amendment standards."[49]

The decision, I believe, was an incorrect one, and the logic was certainly questionable. The Court's opinion simply failed to address itself to various considerations that should have been met headon, in order to lay them to rest once and for all. For example, the Court's denial of classification based on religion was exactly that. It was erroneous to hold that a sincere ethical objection to killing (selective or otherwise) was identical—or at least comparable—to actions of secular relevance.[50] The *Welsh* decison had equated such ethical objection with religious belief. And if total pacifism was in fact a type of religious belief then selective objection must also be included[51]—unless Marshall believed himself capable of distinguishing between one type of ethical objection and another. Failure to do so would lead to the very classification which the Court had already held violative of the First Amendment. The Court's use of the term "compelling" interest—rather than *paramount or overwhelming*—was another example. In other words, section 6(j) was simply not subjected to the more exacting judicial scrutiny test,[52] or any of the other tests previously developed. And I would hardly accept the notion that the "reasonable man" test was sufficient for what was at stake here. Gillette and Negre were required to prove that no valid, neutral, and secular basis existed to justify the actions of government. Yet just such a test was rejected as recently as *Sherbert,* when Brennan invoked Rutledge's reversal of the presumption of constitutionality test, and forced the government to bear a heavier burden of proof. In some ways, then, the opinion was simply deficient in not articulating distinctions that were indeed different!

The Court failed to accept the logic and significance of its *Sherbert* holding. Marshall's opinion not only did not apply *Sherbert* properly but also failed to distinguish it. Under the *Sherbert* test (as indicated above) the government was saddled with a heavier burden than under normal circumstances. In *Gillette* the Court simply assumed the government had met its burden, without telling us how. (Doesn't this sound remarkably similar to what the Court did in *Lyng* and *Smith?*). Yet Gillette and Negre had a much stronger case than Mrs. Sherbert. Both faced jail. Both faced the possibility of abandoning their conscience. Both were put in the position of violating the most fundamental precept of their "religious" belief—the killing of another human being in the cause of an unjust war. Equally important, the Court simply forgot about the implications of *Torcaso*. If the government cannot (so the Court said) place the "power and authority of the State . . . on the side of one particular sort of believers,"[53] the same must be true, according to Bernard Schwartz, in granting exemptions to only one particular sort of believers.[54] And since *Welsh* held religion and conscience to be identical, how can the Court (in a single case) accept distinctions among "consciences" and close its eyes to the establishment clause?

Lastly, the question of alternative means was never considered. Government may exempt as a legislative privilege (so implied the Court). But was not the government under a legal—as well as moral—obligation, by the use of alternative means, to avoid unsolvable conflict between the free exercise and establishment clauses? The selective objector should not be faced with the choice between conscience and nation, at least not in a free society. Greenawalt suggested as feasible alternatives the all-volunteer army (which has come about since the disposition of this case and the end of the war) or some form of civilian service onerous enough that only sincere objectors (selective or general) would choose it.[55] And because of the legislative failure to adequately handle the issue (raised crucially in both *Braunfeld* and *Sherbert*), the Court legitimized the treatment of selective objectors as criminals. I can think of no result more tragic than the jailing of individuals for refusing to violate their consciences or the precepts of their religious beliefs.[56]

One additional point: Henry J. Abraham tentatively agreed with the Court's majority opinion on the ground that it was the most generous and liberal one possible under realistic policy-making conditions.[57] And since Congress already (and reluctantly) accepted the current judicially defined conscientious objector standard as supreme law, Abraham believed that it would have been inadvisable for the Court to have gone any further.[58] One cannot disagree with the logic of that conclusion. The Court had gone as far as it could go without leaving itself open to serious (and perhaps even fatal) attack. Nevertheless, I personally find one difficulty with the contention. Essentially we are talking about beliefs—religious and otherwise. In *Barnette, Ballard, Woody, Seeger, Sisson, Welsh,* and numerous other decisions, courts have recognized that religious and ethical beliefs contrary to a valid law may be the basis of disobedience to the law itself.[59] The cruel and tragic choice between conscience or the state is one that citizens in a free society should never have to face. And lacking a paramount governmental interest—and in my view a draft quota during an undeclared foreign adventure may not necessarily be such an interest—the courts ought to be exceedingly generous toward the claim of conscience. From *Barnette* onward few discriminations favoring the orthodox over eccentric beliefs have been allowed. May we hope that with the return of calmer times the Court will once again view both free exercise-conscience and national honor in proper perspective.

SUMMARY

More than seventy-five years ago, Harlan Fiske Stone wrote about the problem of conscience and objection to war:

> Both morals and sound policy require that the state should not violate the conscience of the individual. All our history gives confirmation to the view that liberty of conscience has a moral and social value which makes it worthy of preservation at the hands of the state. So deep in its significance and vital, indeed, is it to the integrity of man's moral and spiritual nature that nothing short of the selfpreservation of the state should warrant its violation; and it may well be questioned whether the state which preserves its life by a settled policy of violation of the conscience of the individual will not in fact ultimately lose it by the process.[60]

We have not yet reached this point in our constitutional development. The First Amendment's penumbra has not yet been applied to protect the peripheral right of conscience, especially the conscience of the selective objector. We have not yet accepted the idea that when conscience is involved the individual owes a duty to a moral power superior to the state. We have not, even as democrats, seen the wisdom in the command that men must never be afraid to be free.

Congress can, by statute, eliminate all exemptions to the draft. Yet it has shown no inclination to go quite that far. Hypothetically, then, if there is a constitutionally protected right to conscientious objector status, what might it be? Perhaps all that legal scholars will agree on is that such a right encompasses the corresponding right (in line with the *Barnette* holding) to refuse to perform a command of the government contrary to an overriding religious or ethical belief—in this case to enter the army. In turn, this right can never be limited solely to general objectors because the legislative recognition of such a right depends upon the conflicting interests of the state and the inductee in each war where the conscientious objector claim is made.[61]

Michael E. Tigar suggested the following argument based upon this particular line of reasoning[62]: The free exercise clause protects the individual from governmental commands that violate his religious and ethical beliefs—especially from commands that require the performance of some duty inconsistent with those beliefs. If, in turn, the individual possesses beliefs that would be offended by compulsory military service, can there be any legitimate justification in forcing him to choose between his conscience and imprisonment? Bernard Schwartz even asked whether an individual, opposed to war on religious grounds, can be drafted into the military without violating the free exercise clause?[63] Granted that a state of total mobilization (during a declared war) makes such a choice more reasonable, but any other time the right of free exercise ought to be protected.

> Therefore, if there is a constitutional right to be a conscientious objector, there is a constitutional case for selective objection, in the sense that the availability of the right will turn on whether there is, in a particular conflict, a countervailing governmental interest sufficiently strong to defeat it. More than this, however, if there is a First Amendment right to refuse military service on religious grounds, that right may be exercised at the option of the holder of it, and claimed or not claimed depending upon the dictates of his conscience with respect to the acceptability of particular wars.[64]

Applying the argument directly to selective conscientious objectors, Tigar goes on to say that even if there

> is no First Amendment right to be a conscientious objector, there is still a constitutional case for selective objection. Congress cannot . . . discriminatorily grant a benefit or a privilege. The present conscientious-objector exemption, if construed or applied to deny claims of selective objection, establishes such a discrimination. Members of the Society of Friends, the Church of the Brethren, and other pacifist sects, and those registrants whose individual beliefs lead them to oppose participation in all wars, are preferred under such a test, while those whose religious training and belief leads them to distinguish "just" from "unjust" wars are the victims of it.[65]

Yet this very argument, with modifications and embellishments, was rejected—as Douglas claimed in dissent—by the *Gillette* majority. Why? If there is an argument against selective conscientious objection it seems to turn on the admitted inability (as implied by Marshall) of draft boards to properly distinguish between sincerely held religious beliefs (leading to total pacifism) and sincerely held ethical beliefs (leading to some form of selective pacifism), Yet the standards of evaluation for each type of claim should be identical. Perhaps the *Barnette-Sherbert-Seeger-Welsh* position is as far as we can ever hope to go.

Mulford Q. Sibley believes the selective conscientious objector is entitled to the exemption on grounds other than legal ones.[66] He argues that the selective objector is both an officer of society (carrying out important functions), and a dissenter with the moral right and duty to selectively object to war in order to guarantee his own integrity. Since social change requires serious challenge to the existing patterns of behavior, Sibley suggests (regarding the selective objector as an officer of society) that he may be a significant factor in the elimination of war by keeping alive the nation's moral sensitivity.

> Jehovah's Witnesses did not make most men Witnesses nor did they invent the idea of religious liberty, but through their very existence and their obstreperousness they forced the organs of society to think more clearly about the meaning of freedom. Selective conscientious objectors may remain a minority for many years and through many wars, but they compel those in charge of the war machinery to weigh questions they might not otherwise consider.[67]

By dissenting against existing norms the selective objector breaks new ground upon which later majorities may build. And even if their view of the "just" and "unjust" war never becomes accepted, its expression hopefully makes the majority (or at least its government) reassess both its public policies and conscience. Simultaneously, the selective conscientious objector is also a social being; and as such the question of personal integrity remains paramount. When he refuses induction because the war is "unjust," he is maintaining his own integrity as a human being—which is ultimately the highest expression of conscience and truth.[68]

Perhaps all that can be said about the selective conscientious objector and the "just" war position was said by John Courtney Murray:

> It [the doctrine of the just war] is not exclusively Roman Catholic; in certain forms of its presentation, it is not even Christian. It emerges in the minds of all men of reason and good will when they face two inevitable questions. First, what are the norms that govern recourse to the violence of war? Second, what are the norms that govern the measure of violence to be used in war? In other words, when is war rightful, and what is rightful in war? One may indeed refuse the questions, but this is a form of moral abdication, which would likewise be fatal to civilization.[69]

In refusing to accept this view—and in failing to heed the warning contained in the last sentence—the Supreme Court helped justify the recent criticism that our legal system is morally bankrupt. How can our system of law recognize the binding effect of the Nuremberg principles as international law during the trial of William Calley and simultaneously (in the words of William V. O'Brien) "manage to exclude most of this law from cases involving individual citizens who claim the right to invoke it as the basis of S.C.O. [selective conscientious objection]?"[70] War crimes, crimes against peace, and crimes against humanity are not political questions, no matter what the *Gillette* majority says. A reassessment of our political position, our moral values, and our basic commitment to freedom itself is necessary. I hope that it will occur before our next "foreign adventure" raises the issues once more. I trust that we will never again fail in our responsibility by allowing others—presidents, Congresses, judges, draft boards, or a numerical majority—to make our moral judgments.

CHAPTER 7

Are Standards of Adjudication Possible?

Since 1937 at least, the Supreme Court has adjudicated the substantive issues of free exercise—and the other First Amendment guarantees as well—during the most complex times and circumstances. Neither Court nor nation had the ideological preparation for such decisions. The political and social adjustment necessary to accept these new precedents (particularly the Court's protection of certain forms of actionable religious behavior) usually followed rather than preceded the decisions.[1] This inverted process of acceptance led to many of the questions raised (and decisions discussed) in preceding chapters. Some jurists and legal scholars have criticized the Court for sometimes allowing its protection of religious liberty to get out of hand because of this inversion. The same men have criticized the Court for failing to perceive the rights of others, whether individuals or the majority, in direct conflict with the practice of a religious belief.

Justices Frankfurter, Jackson, and Harlan, and occasionally Chief Justice Stone at the very end of his tenure on the Court—and more recently Chief Justices Burger and Rehnquist and Justices Scalia and Thomas, have been among the major exponents of the judicial restraint school of thought. Professors Edward S. Corwin, Henry Steele Commager, and Wallace Mendelson, as well as numerous others, have also accepted the view that the Court's handling of the Jehovah's Witness cases showed it had not studied the complicated problems completely. Otherwise it would not have acted on the belief that the right of people to resort to their own

> places of worship and listen to their chosen teachers stands on a constitutional level with the right of religious enthusiasts to solicit funds and peddle their doctrinal wares in the streets, to ring doorbells and disturb householders, and to accost passersby and insult them in their religious beliefs.[2]

The individual's right to religious freedom cannot be absolute. As pointed out in earlier chapters, religious liberty can be open to abuse by individuals and groups. Under certain extraordinary situations this liberty may (the word *must* is avoided deliberately) be subjected to restraints in the interest of the public welfare. Theoretically, this constitutional adjudication may be characterized as attempts by the Supreme Court to set forth a workable balance between religious freedom and the police power of the state, preserving the essentials of freedom without impairing the power to govern. Practically speaking, I would prefer to see the Court make the more logical conclusion and keep unequal interests from being treated as equal. The free exercise of religion guarantee is on an altogether higher substantive plane than the mere comfort of a majority of citizens within the community to be free from distasteful and contradictory forms of belief, worship, and proselytizing. This notion will be more fully discussed later in this chapter.

FREE EXERCISE AND THE HIERARCHY OF VALUES

The free exercise of religion guarantee, like other guarantees of the First Amendment, is in absolute terms. Congress, and the states (by virtue of the due process clause) "shall make no law . . . prohibiting the free exercise [of religion]." The statement is set forth in absolute language that allows no exceptions, at least on its face. Alexander Meiklejohn accepts this absolute language in the following statement: "To say that no laws of a given type shall be made means that no laws of that type shall, under any circumstances, be made. That prohibition holds good in war as in peace, in danger as in security."[3] Judicial activists (activist libertarians) believe that the words mean what they say, and that under most circumstances governments cannot enact legislation restricting the free exercise of religion. Furthermore, they believe that, save for exceptions of an extraordinary nature, infringements would allow the substantive content of the guarantee to exist in name only. Religious freedom, at least for the activist libertarians, is a relationship between the individual and his conscience, or the Supreme Being of his or her choice (if he or she has one), and not a relationship between the individual and the government. The individual, like the free society of which he/she is a member, must not be afraid to be free.

Why is the concept of the free exercise of religion considered a preferred freedom? Previous chapters have suggested that certain limitations are attached to the meaning of free exercise. Although it now protects certain forms of actionable behavior (religious proselytizing) as well as belief and worship, it is by no means absolute. Yet the free exercise decisions give a wide, adequate concept of religious freedom in a free society. They protect the right to believe and worship according to that belief, the right to proselytize a religious faith verbally and by distribution of literature, and the right to use both public and private places to do so.[4] In addition, these decisions also protect the freedom not to believe—and to act accordingly. Moreover, a religious belief and belief in a Supreme Being are no longer synonymous. Neither will be required if the Court continues to replace the concept of religion with an equally protected notion of conscience. In its entirety, according to Paul G. Kauper, free exercise guarantees every individual the right to believe or not believe, to worship and practice religion

> as he sees fit, . . . to bear public witness to his faith, to propagandize his faith and to win converts by means of the written and spoken word, to declare the relevancy of his religious insights to matters of public concern, the freedom of religious organizations to function and carry on their programs, the principle of religious voluntarism which rejects the use of political matters, and the pluralistic idea embodied in the notion of separation of church and state—all these have become familiar and accepted phases of the American concept of religious freedom.[5]

Since no absolute freedom exists, the Supreme Court's obligation in adjudicating free exercise claims is not always easily satisfied. This is particularly true when mistakes in the political process are not corrected and minority religious groups are denied free access. Under such circumstances the Court has created new tests and devices of freedom by expanding footnote four into a preferred freedom doctrine. In essence, at least until a change very recently when the process was reversed, there has been a movement away from Frankfurter's "balance of interests" test in *Gobitis* to Stone's idea of "more exacting judicial scrutiny." There has also been occasional development beyond the meaning of footnote four. Several activist libertarian justices, sometimes speaking for a majority of the Court, have attempted to reverse the presumption of constitutionality in the area of the First Amendment. They prefer not to treat unequal things as equal.

Concerning individual liberty, judges of our national courts rarely give the same degree of value preference to each constitutionally guaranteed freedom. Since no constitutional guarantee of individual liberty is absolute, whether restrictions placed upon it are unconstitutional becomes a matter of opinion among the justices. Edgar Bodenheimer has suggested that "values are essential ingredients of the mental activity of human beings and might properly be described as facts of mental life."[6] He then suggested that determining whether the values to be served by the legal order are

> realized by its institutions involves a constant evaluation and reappraisal of the normative structure, machinery, and effectiveness of the law. . . . Specific legal norms are similarly directed to the attainment of

certain goals. Thus, the First Amendment . . . is designed to *promote freedom as a value*. . . . When we ask ourselves whether . . . normative prescriptions are adequate to the task which they purport to accomplish, or by other and better prescriptions, we are appraising the efficacy of the means chosen by the legal order to realize certain social ends.[7]

Differences arise in our society between interests of the individual and of the community as an organized, collective unit. The primary function of law under such circumstances is to adjust these interests. The problem of "valuation of interests" involves the issue of relativity, concerning where the line will be drawn in a dispute. Judges oftentimes are afraid of value judgments—or at least of pronouncing them openly—because such a "nonlogically deduced" course of action always invites criticism from the interested parties.[8] Determining the relative importance of the interests and giving outright preference to one of them raises the most difficult problems confronting the law.

The religion guarantee and the other liberties of the First Amendment reflect a basic "morality of freedom"—a fundamental moral intention of the nation—to which a free society must subscribe and dedicate itself. The identification of morality and intentions means a free society intends protecting a liberty that it has agreed to protect. Morality and law are not the same thing, but they are closely related.[9] A free society no longer subscribes to the Kantian theory that the distinction between law and morality is that law regulates men's external relations while morality governs their inner lives and motivations. Morality is looked upon now as recognition of a hierarchial ranking of basic values guiding the conduct of human beings in civilized social intercourse.

Attempts by an activist libertarian majority of the Supreme Court to reexamine, redefine, and increase the meaning and scope of the free exercise clause have made the Court (as Paul A. Freund once suggested) virtually a legislative drafting bureau of municipal ordinances. Yet if the Court requires local and state governments to observe the free exercise rights of minority groups when it deals with the dissemination of ideas, it is vindicating its responsibility as guardian of our Constitution.[10] It is rearranging the hierarchy of judicially-protected values; and it is reinforcing its proper role by making sure the society remains free. Kauper suggests that

[i]n so far as free speech and free press assume their high significance as indispensable channels in the shaping of opinions and policy in a democratic society, they are relevant only in part to the problem of religious liberty. For while religion manifests itself in the expression of ideas and opinions that help to shape opinion on public issues, this is not its sole function. It is concerned preeminently with the life and soul

of the individual through the attainment of his spiritual capacities. Religious liberty finds its highest significance in a freedom of the mind and spirit that needs not depend for its vindication upon the centrality of the legislative process in a democratic society. Because it stands for the inner sanctuary of a man's life, religious freedom has its own unique equality and dimension. This is God's domain and Caesar may not trespass upon it.[11]

Here the value line separating interests is much easier to draw, for free exercise is involved. Although the Court is oftentimes charged by its critics with inconsistency in dealing in different ways with different problems, the charge (at least in the free exercise area) is unjust. Its special role as our highest court and moral voice requires constitutional adjudication that properly distinguishes between basically different things.

FREE EXERCISE AND THE JUDICIAL PROCESS

In the preface to this volume I raised the question whether the addition of free exercise to the freedoms of speech and press gives religious communication greater freedom from regulation than is enjoyed by political or commercial communication? If the judicial decision-making process is grounded upon searches for objectivity,[12] how can one right be preferred while others are merely or marginally protected? The unwillingness of legal scholars to look at decisions like *Murdock, Follette, Martin, Marsh, Tucker, Saia, Sherbert,* and *Yoder*—and compare them with *Kovacs* and *Breard*—is a way of saying there is an uncomfortable answer to this question. Nevertheless a conclusion can be drawn. Judicial decision-making is not an exercise in objectivity, but in individual subjectivity. Benjamin N. Cardozo once wrote, "We may try to see things as objectively as we please. None the less we can never see them with eyes except our own."[13] I suspect there can be nothing more subjective than that.

Judges grudgingly admit today that they make law. Precisely because judges decide cases to a large extent on the basis of "personal predilection," the Court has attempted to find the elusive ideal of objectivity by creating selflimiting formulas. In truth, this objectivity is sometimes difficult to find simply because it does not always exist. George D. Braden suggested that ultimately a judge may do one of two things:

He may admit to himself that he decides constitutional questions in the light of his own scheme of values for all to see. Or the justice may deny this concept of freedom and personal values and assert that his decisions are based entirely and objectively on external factors. Whichever course is followd, the question is: how impregnable can the justice make his position? If his is a philosophy of personal freedom, can it be set up so that in the future it is selfexecuting? If on the other hand his philosophy is one of external considerations, can a third person look at his external scheme and find the same answers?[14]

The justice may say: "I admit that [the] mechanical method of squaring the statute and the Constitution [is] nonsense. Of course, we wield power. But this is potentially dangerous. Therefore, we create a rule which is sufficiently objective to circumscribe us and our successors in our exercise of political power."[15] If this is the case, the objective standard he is attempting to formulate expresses his own values for the society and his own conceptions of the safe limits of the judicial function.[16] The judge will use his power to protect only values he believes in strongly enough. All other values and rights, substantive and otherwise, are not protected for fear of risking the charge of judicial supremacy or abuse of judicial office. The notion of preferring values is out of the question. On the other hand, the judge who wishes to tell society how he decides cases may say: "This is what I believe is important in our civilization and I shall do all I can to preserve it. This is my creed and I shall use my office to preserve it."[17] If this is the case, the judge admits his subjectivity—identical to the process of the objective judge who makes a subjective choice every time he denies that choice can be made. He is saying certain of his values—for example, the guarantees of the First Amendment—are important enough to be enforced when the opportunity arises. He believes they ought to be enforced even when society is not yet willing to have them protected. In searching for objectivity or admitting selectivity each judge must make his or her own choice. It is my belief that the subjective approach is not only honest, but (under some circumstances) preferable. The freedoms of the First Amendment have been placed at the apex of the judicial hierarchy of values. The subjective judge (assuming he is also a activist libertarian) recognizes that freedom, though it may be a potentially dangerous way of life, is our way of life.[18]

At no point have I even remotely suggested the idea that the free exercise clause should be entitled to unlimited or absolute protection by the judiciary. On the contrary, there are limits on the exercise of this freedom, as there are limits on the exercise of judicial power and the freedom of choice to be exercised by the judge. The limitations appertaining to the free exercise clause have been discussed in previous chapters. The limitations on the judge deserve at this point at least brief discussion; and they are of three types. The first are absolute (or as absolute as possible). They include the need for a possible constitutional question to be brought before him, the probability of obedience to the decision, and the fear that an extremely unpopular position will hurt the Court as an institution, or the judge as an individual.[19] Some limitations are self-imposed and based on considerations of philosophy. They may be listed as the judge's urge for consistency, the avoidance of confusion by not changing his position (or admitting his errors) too quickly, and the conception of his role, the law, and the judicial function he is willing to defend against all attack.[20] Some limitations, finally, are composed of the judge's personality traits and his psychological makeup. These are his intellectual capacity and fortitude, the sensitivity exhibited toward personal or institutional criticism, and capacity for hard work required of all judges.[21] Considering evidence presented in preceding chapters, it means that the Court (and the judge if he/she is willing) can justify almost anything done and almost every decision handed down.

Consequently I propose the following approach. It is that equal balancing of all interests (and the elusive notion of objectivity) be replaced with a system of value-weighing. Surely, if Justice Frankfurter could proclaim that "[w]ithout a free press there can be no free society,"[22] there is overwhelming justification for proclaiming that without a free exercise of religion there can be no freedom of mind and spirit—and consequently no free men. A jurisprudence treating freedom as the primary value must be—and is—based on more than mere judicial whim. It is based on a deeply-rooted historical past supplying the necessary underpinning for the commitment to freedom and free institutions. It also is based on a more comprehensive and effective theory of the First Amendment. It is a system of "freedom of expression" in a free society that is founded on four major premises.[23] The first is, "freedom of expression is essential as a means of assuring individual selffulfillment." Second, "freedom of expression is an essential process for advancing knowledge and discovering truth." The third declares, "freedom of expression is essential to provide participation in decision-making by all of society." Lastly, "freedom of expression is a method of achieving a more adaptable and hence more stable community, of maintaining the precarious balance between healthy cleavage and necessary consensus." It is based on the judge's scheme of things and his ranking of priorities within it. It is based, also, on the idea that the Court has a role to play in keeping open the channels of the democratic process. Establishing democratic institutions and freedom as primary values means there must be a healthy dialogue involving conflict and opposition: "no opposition means no democracy, no freedom."[24] In other words, what I am proposing is a return to, and acceptance of, the Murphy-Rutledge modification of Stone's footnote four. Replace the concept of greater judicial scrutiny with the long overdue notion of the reversal of the presumption of constitutionality in all free exercise cases.

In free exercise (as well as other First Amendment) cases, the Supreme Court must take into consideration, in addition to all other factors affecting adjudication, three things. First, are the means of enforcement in the statute or ordinace reasonably adapted to ends similarly set forth? Second, were there reasonable alternatives that would have raised fewer constitutional questions? Last, and most important, do the circumstances presented on record justify the means adopted for implementation? If the Court finds that the legislation restrictive of the free exercise clause is unreasonable, unwise, or contrary to a majority of the justices' ideas of what the law ought to be, it has to rule it unconstitutional. This, of course, is a version of the least restrictive means test. Failure to so rule leaves the Court open to as much, if not more, criticism as when it acts in an overactivist manner.[25] When all the facts and arguments are before it on a suitable case on suitable record, the Court must decide the constitutional issue.[26] The Court must not refuse to decide First Amendment cases because some of its current members incorrectly believe that majority rule and constitutional democracy are the same thing. The Supreme Court has the judicial power of the United States. It must never be afraid to exercise it, particularly when protecting the free exercise guarantee. The weakness of its members can hurt the Court as much as their recklessness can.[27] Whenever the Court fails to extend the preferred position to the rights of belief, worship, and proselytizing, I believe it falters in the exercise of its role. It must always remember that "[n]o case is ever finally decided until it is rightly decided."[28] This is particularly true when we are dealing with God's domain and the free exercise of religion.

FREE EXERCISE AND THE QUEST FOR STANDARDS

General standards do in fact exist with regard to First Amendment adjudication. The Supreme Court in the last seventy years has created and used various tests and intellectual devices to justify much of its decision-making. Among these generalized so-called "tests of the First Amendment" we have bad tendency, clear and present danger, and its "imminence" modification, void on its face, greater judicial scrutiny, and ad hoc balancing. Several of these tests were applied in the free exercise cases with varying results—not all of it satisfying in nature. At the same time several tests were created for exclusive use in the free exercise area— secular regulation, sincerity, durability, the *Barnette* formula of interest weighing and necessity, strict scrutiny/alternative means, and neutrality/general applicability. The problem, of course, is that—no matter what the test—we are talking about tests and devices only. We have not yet come to grips with the development of specific and viable standards. I am talking about standards to be applied in the free excercise area alone; standards that will incorporate the unique character of the free exercise clause. I am also talking about the fact that without an almost excessive toleration of religious individuality (and its corresponding protection) all other substantive guarantees become less meaningful. In essence, I am returning to the one "intention" of the framers over which there is little dispute: that the struggle for religious freedom was (and continues to be) the crux of the struggle for freedom in general.

Between 1961 and 1970 six studies on the free exercise clause—and major attempts at establishing possible guidelines and criteria—were published. To date, only one of these suggested sets of standards has been partially acceptable to any continuing majority of the Court; and none have been acceptable, as Richard E. Morgan argues, to the Court's more articulate constituency.[29] Among these proposals we have

1. The reviviscence of the old secular regulation rule (the one proposal partially accepted) because of a suggested need for a "neutral" principle of constitutional law;[30]

2. A "subject-matter" definition of protected religion in order to test the content of the religious belief;[31]

3. A balancing test in order to clarify the difference between the ancient notions of *mala prohibita* (violations of public health, safety, and welfare laws because of a free exercise claim that requires fines and imprisonments are subject to a balancing approach) and *mala in se* (moral crimes that must be penalized uniformly throughout the entire community in spite of the free exercise claim);[32]

4. A total substitution of conscience (both theistic and nontheistic) for religion—in essence, the creation of a preferred free exercise of conscience clause;[33]

5. A distinction between laws that *compel* the performance of an act and those that *prohibit* such performance;[34]

6. A modification of the test of direct and indirect effects, with even the latter being suspect if no alternative means are considered.[35]

In 1990, of course, the Supreme Court itself added an additional test (which combined several of the above) when it articulated the *Smith* two-prong argument of neutrality and general applicability—that is, the new secular regulation rule. Each of the initial studies, unfortunately, had two things in common: a failure to be comprehensive enough, and an unwillingness to come to grips with the difficult question of line drawing. At one extreme all religious behavior is not punishable, while at the other extreme not all conscience (whether theistic or nontheistic) is beyond the police power of the state.

To say this, however, is not to say that no guidelines of value exist in any of these scholarly and articulate attempts at standard making. On the contrary, there is much in these studies (when combined and occasionally altered) to suggest a realistic appraisal of what can be while we await what ought to be.

Let me therefore propose the following test: Any law that *compels* the individual to perform a duty contrary to his or her religious belief—or the dictates of his or her conscience—must be presumed unconstitutional. The burden of proof (a showing of a compelling and overwhelming interest) falls on the state.[36] As demonstrated in previous chapters, this rule devolves from footnote four. Any law that, *in its application,* is demonstrated *prima facie* to be religious in its primary effect must once again be presumed unconstitutional.[37] Once the Court distinguishes between laws that compel and those that command nonperformance of an act, the task is easier. At the same time, no distinction should be made between religion and conscience—even nontheistic conscience.

On the other hand, where criminal conduct of a sufficiently dangerous nature is involved—and I do not mean child labor laws or the ceremonial use of peyote—the law would be presumed constitutional even against a free exercise claim. A specific type of criminal enactment—for example, a command that individuals do not handle live copperhead snakes during "religious" rituals and services[38]—would not involve any presumption of unconstitutionality because of the overwhelming state interest at stake. Other laws regulating criminal conduct (such as the one present in the *Prince* case) or conscience (as seen in the *Lyng* and *Smith* cases) would not stand if (1) such conduct is believed by the individual to be an "inexcusable duty" in a bona fide cause and (2) it involves only the individual and other consenting persons.[39] In other words, even here the most important interest protected by the free exercise clause (and the one the state cannot infringe) "is the prevention of the severe psychic turmoil that can be brought about by compelled violation of conscience."[40]

Can such a standard be applied by the Court? How will it be done? I would suggest the following:

1. The Court must define religious effect. Here I propose the following definition: "State action abridging the individual's freedom to adopt, observe, or propagate his religion (or irreligion) through programs of assistance, or systems of regulation, exercises a religious effect."[41]

2. Once such a definition is agreed upon, the Court must decide whether the free exercise clause will allow such effects. To that end it must ask (*a*) whether the purpose and primary effect of the law is secular?, and (*b*) does the state have a compelling interest in declining alternative means involving no secondary religious or conscientious effect?[42]

3. [I]f the plaintiff tenders *prima facie* proof of a secondary religious effect, without alleging a religious purpose or primary religious effect, the government must rebut the inference of the secondary effect, *or prove that it has considered alternative means free of such effects and that it has overbearing reasons for not adopting them.*"[43]

4. The Court must determine whether the state has even considered alternative means.

5. The Court must judge whether the challenged statute has possible alternatives implicit within it.

6. The Court must consider the arguments put forth by the state that is attempting to justify the impracticability of alternative means. If the state has not considered less restrictive measures, the Court cannot sustain the burden (as it did in *Lyng* and *Smith*) that none exist.[44] Under these circumstances the law must be judged unconstitutional.

The Court has occasionally taken judicial notice of these standards (at least in part) and applied them to concrete fact situations. In *Sherbert* the Court said:

> An incidental burden on the free exercise of religion may be justified by a compelling interest in the regulation of a subject within the state's constitutional power to regulate . . . [but] . . . it would plainly be incumbent upon [the state] to demonstrate that no alternative forms of regulation would combat such abuses without infringing First Amendment rights.[45]

In *McGowan*, Frankfurter's concurrence suggested much the same approach, and also implied that the same standards can be used in establishment cases as well.

> If a statute furthers both secular and religious ends by means unnecessary to the effectuation of the secular ends alone—where the same ends could equally be attained by means which do not have the consequence for the promotion of religion—the statute cannot stand.[46]

And finally the California Supreme Court held in *Woody* that, notwithstanding the secular purpose and primary effect of a narcotics control law, the statute must fall because the state could not show a compelling

interest in enforcing it against the Native American Church and imposing a secondary burden: ""[T]he state's showing of 'compelling interest'
cannot lie in untested assertions that recognition of the religious immunity will interfere with the enforcement of the state statute."[47]

This is properly a generous set of standards for free exercise and
conscience interests. It is recognition that in God's domain, when Caesar is to trespass, Caesar must do so only with honesty, consideration,
and under extraordinary circumstances.

> The presumption is against rather than in favor of the validity of legis-
> lation which on its face or in its application restricts the rights of con-
> science, expression, and assembly, protected by the First Amendment.[48]

Free exercise is—and must always be—in a preferred position. To do
less would violate, in my opinion, the proper reading of the First
Amendment. And such a standard, when properly applied, would have
struck down as void on its face, or void in its application, or void in its
secondary effect, the laws upheld by the Court in *Prince, Summers,
Braunfeld, Lyng,* and *Smith.* The *Gillette* issue is now moot, considering the all-volunteer army concept. Nevertheless, I have grave doubts
that it could be decided differently. Ultimately this standard would
encircle the free exercise clause with a preferred position—as the clause
itself encircles belief, worship, and proselytizing with a corresponding
preference.

One additional point. I have suggested throughout these chapters
that the free exercise clause enjoys a preferred position (I believe only
momentarily changed by judicial decision) in the eyes of the Court.
More specifically, I mean that when a preferred position is assigned

> to a constitutional right, two results follow. The presumption of con-
> stitutionality will no longer suffice to validate a statute which invades
> such right . . . [and] moreover, as a second consequence, the preferred
> position test requires the use of reasonable alternative, a statute "nar-
> rowly drawn to prevent the supposed evil."[49]

Hence we have the clear and present danger plus imminence test, greater
and more searching judicial scrutiny, the alternative means rule,[50] and
the reversal of the pesumption of constitutionality—all attesting to the
viability of the concept of preference in free exercise cases. In other
words, preference must be accorded to the free exercise guarantee
because (1) it has substantive meaning within the context of the First
Amendment, (2) it is concerned with the life and soul of the individual
in the attainment of capacities, and (3) it is related to the interests of
minority groups. A violation of the free exercise clause does much more
than erode a basic principle. It is essentially an infringement that is real,

never abstract; and it is a wrong with injury—for severe psychic turmoil has been caused by the compelled violation of conscience. Thus, to come full circle back to Stone's original meaning of footnote four, the protection of substantive freedom is basic to the workings of the democratic process.

My own view, as I indicated earlier, was once proclaimed by a majority of the Supreme Court; and it guided judicial decision-making in the free exercise area for a brief period of time. I believe the time has come to resurrect this standard:

> The case confronts us again with the duty our system places on this Court to say where the individual's freedom ends and the State's power begins. Choice on that border, now as always delicate, is perhaps more so where the usual presumption supporting legislation is balanced by the preferred place given in our scheme to the great, the indispensable democratic freedoms secured by the First Amendment.
>
> For these reasons any attempt to restrict those liberties must be justified by clear public interest, threatened not doubtfully or remotely, but by clear and present danger. The rational connection between the remedy provided and the evil to be curbed, which in other contexts might support legislation against attack on due process grounds, will not suffice. These rights rest on firmer foundation. Accordingly, whatever occasion would restrain orderly discussion and persuasion, at appropriate time and place, must have clear support in public danger, actual or impending. *Only the gravest abuses, endangering paramount interests, give occasion for permissible limitation.*[51]

It contains none of the vices critics have raised regarding any other standard proposed; and it works. Short of some cataclysmic event that would require a suspension of all civil liberties, all that is necessary here is the belief that the free exercise of religion is as important as everyone says it is. What could be more simple than that?

CONCLUSION

The most direct, and perhaps obvious, way to begin a conclusion is to ask what can be concluded? I believe several things. First, in its more than a century of development under Supreme Court direction, the free exercise clause has enlarge its protective coverage: from protection for belief and orthodox worship to protection for religiously and conscientiously motivated behavior—particularly certain forms of behavior not covered by the other First Amendment clauses. Second, the free exercise clause has developed correspondingly to the general enlargement of the First Amendment; and it has become one of the beneficiaries of that increased protective change. Third, the free exercise clause today finds itself (in spite of the holdings in *Lyng, Smith,* and *Flores,* we are still not sure what the far reaching impact of those decisions will be) in a preferred position. Although not the same thing as a "total protection" theory, it is nevertheless quite significant—as I believe the previous chapters have demonstrated. Fourth, the tests and devices created and used by the Court in the development of the First Amendment guarantees generally have been applicable to the free exercise clause as well. Fifth, the Court's success in developing or accepting viable standards for exclusive use in the free exercise area has been minimal at best. No definitive free exercise theory has yet to win acceptance by a continuing Court majority. Sixth, the free exercise clause has received such protection because of the unique nature of its substantive content. It is concerned with more than the expression of ideas and opinions that help shape attitudes on public issues. It is ultimately concerned, as Paul G. Kauper suggests, with the "life and soul of the individual through the attainment of his spiritual capacities."[1] It "stands for the inner sanctuary of a man's life,"[2] and the state may not tamper with it. Lastly, the enlargement of the meaning of free exercise has been helped by the state's grudging acceptance of the notion that religious accommodation (in the free exercise sense of the term) is far better for democratic institutions than religious warfare.

Religious freedom is a problem for individuals and members of minority groups either denied free access to the channels of the democratic process or, as Jackson believed in *Ballard,* too small in number to be significant. And it is this ever-present fear of a "tyranny of the majority"—the danger of "extreme and suffocating social conformity"[3]—that has led the Court to concern itself with the protection of minority religious rights.

> When society itself is the tyrant—society collectively over the separate individuals who compose it—. . . it practices a social tyranny more formidable than many kinds of political oppression, since . . . it leaves fewer means of escape, penetrating much more deeply into the details of life, and enslaving the soul itself. Protection . . . against the tyranny of the magistrate is not enough: there needs to be protection also against the tyranny of prevailing opinion and feeling, against the tendency of society to impose . . . its own ideas and practices as rules of conduct on those who dissent from them . . . and to compel all characters to fashion themselves on the model of its own.[4]

The protection of minority religious rights at the expense of extreme versions of governing power and majority rules leaves the Court open to two accusations. One is that it has attempted to burden the law with tasks it cannot perform. The other is that the Court and the law cannot perform these tasks without becoming a Leviathan.[5] This is one of the most serious problems emerging from adjudication of religious liberty cases. The Court, sometimes extreme in its defense of free exercise, has failed to define concretely what it is. Nowhere is there a proper statement of "what ought to be," except that religious exercise ought to be protected (and occasionally preferred). There are rarely any guidelines, as the previous chapters have suggested. Inevitably, theory and practice come into conflict; and more questions are raised than answered.

Sometimes the Court fails to balance the competing demands of liberty and order that come before it. It deals with normative components of the law while excluding the empirical and prudential components.[6] It concerns itself with ethical or moral aspects of law to the exclusion of prudential aspects.[7] The result is oftentimes one-sided decision-making. For example, a local majority enacts a piece of legislation based on its interpretation of empirical data. The Court, considering the legislation, looks at it from the point of view of the goals, ends, purposes, and values it wishes to make permanent. As has been argued previously, the minority religious group is allowed to continue proselytizing and preaching to the unconverted on almost unlimited terms. The majority is allowed to try again in different language to enforce its social conformity. We confront only absolutes—either of the minority or the majority. The central concern is only with ethics and power. By following first one set of absolute standards, then another, the Court has occasionally destroyed the prudence of available choices. It sometimes has created an inflexibility allowing only goals that can be achieved immediately.

Giovanni Sartori indicates that the phrase "I am free to" has three different but related meanings: "It can mean I *may,* or I *can,* or I *have the power to.* In the first sense freedom is permission; in the second sense it is ability; and in the third sense it is a substantive condition."[8] The Supreme Court has given the concept of minority religious rights the same three meanings. The "freedom from" aspect has a permissive meaning. The "freedom to" aspect denotes the meaning of ability. Although both aspects are closely related they are by no means the same thing; similarly, the type of minority rights involved with each is different. When we speak of "freedom" as a substantive condition, however, we are speaking of an absolute meaning viewed solely in ethical and moral terms. We are concerned not so much with the law per se as with its moral aspects. Only a philosophy of law that recognizes that all values do not possess equal merit, that it is proper to distinguish values that are different, can give meaning to freedom as well as order in the name of justice.

The primary error committed by both the analytical positivists and the natural law theorists was the one-sided basis of their jurisprudence. The former group conceived of law only in the formalized sense of rules and commands set forth by the legislature, constitutional conventions, and administrative agencies. The latter group dealt almost exclusively with the nonformal sources of law. Only utopian standards of equality, justice, moral convictions, and customary law made up their jurisprudence. Both groups believed their chosen legal order was complete, exhaustive, and logically consistent enough to provide answers for all future generations.[9] This belief broke down for both schools in the late nineteenth and early twentieth centuries. Problems subsequently presented to the American legal system were found unanswerable by either form of legal philosophy.[10] Of course, the answer was a jurisprudence that would combine the best features of both schools, while acknowledging that the law must be made to attain and serve values in a society. Furthermore, these social ends would be both unchanging and changing. The law must protect and prefer as suggested by the Supreme Court's interpretation of our constitutional development. At the same time it must give attention to the policies and social trends that continually shift (as the general values of society change), and that make up the community interest.

In evaluating these sometimes-conflicting interests, the Court is confronted by a dual problem. It must make (1) a judicial discernment of value patterns or a judicial imposition (creation) of value judgments[11] and then (2) apply the chosen method either *praeter legem* (besides the written law) or *contra legem* (against the written law).[12] In the free exercise cases, at least since footnote four and *Murdock,* the Court has

approached this issue of conflict between religious freedom and authority through judicial imposition of moral judgments applied *contra
legem*.[13] Oftentimes the majority has enacted legislation under its police
power that infringes upon the rights of belief, worship, and proselytizing.
This conflict occurs, for example, because mistakes in the political process have not been corrected and religious minorities have been denied
free access. The Court has been forced to create new tests of freedom satisfying its view of correct social policy and proper judicial role. Yet creating such judicial tools and resorting to judicial imposition of value
judgments should not be regarded as a transgression by the judicial
authority.[14] In the life of any constitutional state there are times when the
majority will subvert the law to its own ends. The statutes it enacts are
repugnant to the most minimum standards of civilized decency when its
repression of the minority transcends the bounds of legitimate sovereign
power. But in a free society the standards are considerably higher than
minimum; and the Court's role considerably more important.

Religion is human behavior; and as such ought to be given by society the freest possible latitude to develop. William James insisted that "a
true thought is a thought that is an invaluable instrument of action."[15]
So to speak of the free exercise of religion as a negative or passive concept (and to protect it accordingly), is to fail to understand the true,
inner meaning of religion—or of its ultimate value to a free political
society. Kauper believes that the preferred status accorded the free exercise of religion clause finds its warrant in several considerations.

> In so far as free speech and free press assume their high significance as
> indispensable channels in the shaping of opinions and policy in a
> democratic society, they are relevant only in part to the problem of reli-
> gious liberty. For while religion manifests itself in the expression of
> ideas and opinions that help to shape opinion on public issues, this is
> not its sole function. It is concerned preeminently with the life and soul
> of the individual through the attainment of his spiritual capacities.
> *Religious liberty finds its highest significance in a freedom of the mind
> and spirit that needs not depend for its vindication upon the centrality
> of the legislative process in a democratic society. Because it stands for
> the inner sanctuary of a man's life, religious freedom has its own
> unique equality and dimension. This is God's domain and Caesar may
> not trespass upon it.*[16]

Failure by the state to allow an excessive toleration and latitude for free
religious exercise—and ultimately conscience as well—denies the state
its necessary cultural and political progress in order to maintain free
institutions.[17]

More than two hundred years after the framing of the free exercise
clause in the First Amendment, it is far easier for a man to exercise the

innermost thoughts of his conscience and practice his unorthodox religious beliefs than at any time during the history of the Republic. Yet, as Walter Kaufman has said, "To speak of religion without disturbing men is to be a false prophet."[18] And to allow less than a full religious exercise is, in a sense, to tolerate "religionists" while denying the true vitality of religion itself. *Religion, like truth, disturbs; and the difficulty is compounded by the fact that religious truth is always in the eye of the believer.* Yet man's right to such a free exercise must be guaranteed and protected. For the Supreme Court to now reverse its development of the meaning of religious liberty from *Cantwell* to *Welsh*—as it has attempted to do in *Lyng* and *Smith* and *Flores*—would be at once both unacceptable and disastrous. For the Supreme Court to do less than guarantee and protect the right to believe and worship and proselytize would make the words of the First Amendment, and the historical meaning they convey, empty ideals. To do less, moreover, would be to confirm what Albert Camus believed to be "the most incorrigible vice":[19] "The evil that is in the world always comes of ignorance, and good intentions may do as much harm as malevolence, if they lack understanding. On the whole, men are more good than bad; that, however, isn't the real point. But they are more or less ignorant, and it is this that we call vice or virtue."[20] And that ignorance is the willingness of the state (and its political and judicial institutions) to turn its back on or balance with other contending—but less important—interests the unique dimensions of free religious exercise.

One last point is perhaps necessary on the substantive free exercise cases covered in the preceding chapters. I do not believe, as some commentators have, that the recent free exercise decisions—somewhat less favorable than those coming from the Warren Court and the early years of the Burger Court—have signaled an end to religion's preferred status. On the contrary, even with passage of the Religious Freedom Restoration Act of 1993, I would suggest that *Roy, Lyng, Smith,* and *Flores* be looked at for what they actually did—a very obvious statement that the *Sherbert* standard of strict scrutiny will not be expanded in the immediate future. Remember, *Sherbert* was not overturned, simply distinguished. What it all comes down to, and a point missed by so many of the commentators, is that a working majority of the current Supreme Court has difficulty accepting the untraditional and unorthodox. The Court is simply insensitive toward the unfamiliar and the different. And if history is any kind of certain guide, changing the composition of the Court will change the decisions of the Court. Declaring RFRA unconstitutional has not really changed very much.

I have attempted over the previous chapters to look at, analyze, and draw conclusions from, the Supreme Court's legal development of the free exercise clause. I have admitted my subjectivity—as I would hope any honest legal commentator, analyst, or judge would do—and I have argued for the widest possible enlargement of religious freedom. *I do believe,* like the framers, that without religious freedom all other freedoms become less absolute. Yet, within the wide expanse of my arguments and analysis, there is another, darker side to the issue. When Justice Jackson warned the legal profession, as well as the nation, that no court—no matter what the extent of its power—can save a people from the evils of intolerance and hate and stupidity,[21] he spoke directly to some of the issues raised in this study. If man hates and fears and distrusts his fellow man because of religious differences, how far can the Supreme Court actually go in "civilizing" the two litigants? It can determine the legal outcome of the case, but it cannot change a man's heart and mind and soul that is filled with hate and fear and intolerance. We simply have no way as a people to convince our fellow citizens that conformity of opinion and belief and action does eventually lead to the unanimity of the graveyard.

The preface of this volume implicitly asked the question "What is religion?" In the chapters since I have attempted to piece together from the historical intentions of the framers and the oftentimes idealistic or pragmatic line-drawings of the justices themselves, some acceptable definition. In conclusion a quote from Gorden W. Allport:

> A man's religion is the audacious bid he makes to bind himself to creation and to the Creator. It is his ultimate attempt to enlarge and to complete his own personality by finding the supreme context in which he rightly belongs.[22]

This is religion *as life itself,* and it pervades the inner soul of the human spirit. It is, once again, God's domain and Caesar ought not to trespass upon it.

APPENDIX A

Footnote Four and
Greater Judicial Scrutiny

Justice Chase, in his *Calder*[1] opinion (as in his *Hylton*[2] dictum two years earlier), would rule an act of Congress unconstitutional only "in a very clear case." But what about the borderline cases? What about those questions of freedom and authority where the lines cannot be drawn with automatic precision or even certainty? Arthur E. Sutherland[3] suggests that Chase never implied nor even perceived the possibility of debate over whether a case was clear, but not very clear. Sutherland also suggests that Justice Stone was struggling with the same difficulty, when in 1938 he distinguished "specific" provisions from others in the Constitution.[4]

In distinguishing between those rights that are and those that are not implicit in the concept of ordered liberty, Justice Cardozo (in his Palko[5] opinion) explained that "we reach a different plane of social and moral values when we pass to . . . freedom of thought . . . [which] is the matrix, the indispensable condition, of nearly every other form of freedom."[6] And with this distinction firmly in mind, Stone—in the case of *United States v. Carolene Products Co.*[7]—attached to this opinion on economic regulation a footnote concerned with a special judicial responsibility in the area of civil liberties. It also included the notion that judicial protection of freedom required a much firmer base than sheer judicial enthusiasm. In fact, it was an attempt to base the Court's new responsibility on the words of the Constitution itself, thus providing "a unified and integrated theory rising above a purely individual commitment to freedom."[8]

> There may be a narrower scope for operation of the presumption of constitutionality when legislation appears on its face to be within a specific prohibition of the Constitution, such as those of the first ten amendments, which are deemed equally specific when held to be embraced within the Fourteenth. . . .
>
> It is unnecessary to consider now whether legislation which restricts those political processes which can ordinarily be expected to bring about repeal of undesirable legislation, is to be subjected to more exacting judicial scrutiny under the general prohibitions of the Fourteenth Amendment than most types of legislation. . . .

> Nor need we enquire whether similar considerations enter into review of statutes directed at particular religious . . . or national . . . or racial minorities, . . . whether prejudice against discrete and insular minorities may be a special condition, which tends seriously to curtail the operation of those political processes ordinarily to be relied upon to protect minorities, and which may call for a . . . more searching judicial inquiry.[9]

This tentative inquiry set forth by Stone suggested that the courts must be watchful of legislation (usually directed at minorities) that would tend to lessen the political process. For Stone, the ballot box was the remedy for political ills that could be cured by voting; but the Court must also act to preserve the ballot box. In fact, there was an even greater judicial role when for some reason the electoral process was altered or threatened.[10] Consequently, the three paragraphs spoke of three different, though by no means unrelated, ideas:[11]

1. When legislation, on its face, interferes with the explicit substantive guarantees of the First Amendment, the usual presumption of constitutionality may be curtailed—and such legislation more closely scrutinized.

2. The judiciary has a special responsibility to protect those liberties necessary for the health of the democratic process, *and those liberties that make all other rights possible.*

3. The Court must consider the possible role as defender of minorities and unpopular groups helpless at the polls because of discriminatory attack. Indeed, the Court may be under a special obligation to scrutinize any infringements of the political process—and ultimately to safeguard the process itself.

Stone spoke of the presumption of constitutionality concept, and recognized that a judge had to address himself to the question of a statute's constitutionality. He knew, also, that it would be assumed constitutional until a satisfactory showing to the contrary. The crucial question raised by Stone concerned the determination of the strength of the presumption and the kind of evidence to which it must yield. Every justice would attempt an answer to the question. There would be little agreement. Nevertheless, the central notion of the footnote, what was later to be labeled the "preferred freedom" doctrine, maintained that laws that abridge the guarantees of the First Amendment must be looked upon by the Court with a great deal of scrutiny.[12] And, here, according to Henry J. Abraham,[13] Stone explicitly articulated the "double standard."

According to Stone, economic rights simply were not the matrix of every other form of freedom; but the rights of the First Amendment were. In suggesting a "more exacting judicial scrutiny" for the substantive guarantees, Stone believed that he was facing squarely the problem of using the presumption of constitutionality as a means of forestalling due-process-clause attacks on economic legislation. And by distinguishing economic and civil liberty cases, he thought that a way had been found to make the presumption stick in commerce cases without being plagued by it in First Amendment cases.[14]

At this point let the reader be aware that I accept the distinction made by Stone. I find no inconsistency in treating different values and priorities differently. Commerce and human beings are not the same thing. Yet they are both guaranteed freedoms under the Constitution and laws. This is where the great difficulty lies—when and where and how does the line get drawn, and by whom? Perhaps what was finally inconsistent was Stone himself. Throughout his long and distinguished legal and judicial career, he believed that the judicial function (and the role of the judge) must remain constant. He criticized a majority of his brethren, while dissenting in *Butler*,[15] for elevating property rights over the powers of government. He dissented in *Gobitis*,[16] because freedom of belief was denied a religious minority, and again in the first *Jones*[17] case because the freedom to proselytize was withheld from a religious dissenter. But he also dissented in *Marsh*,[18] *Tucker*,[19] and *Girouard*,[20] when a activist libertarian majority took his tentative inquiry in footnote four beyond the preferred position to mean a doctrine that called for the reversal of the presumption of constitutionality itself. Judge Learned Hand, in summarizing Stone's conception of the judicial function, said that he could not understand

> how the principle which he had all along supported, could mean that, when concerned with interests other than property, the courts should have a wider latitude for enforcing their own predilections, than when they are concerned with property itself. There might be logical defects in his canon, but it deserved a consistent application or it deserved none at all; at any rate it was not to be made into an excuse for having one's way in any given case. Most of all was its evenhanded application important to the judges themselves, since only by not intervening could they hope to preserve that independence which was the condition of any successful discharge of their duties.[21]

Indeed, at no point did he ever go so far as to say that no economic legislation violated constitutional restraints.[22] Nevertheless, the Court's role must be strictly confined.

Stone ultimately set out his concept of what he believed to be the proper role of the judiciary in a free society: "to preserve the essentials of freedom without impairing the power to govern."[23] One legal scholar (a former law clerk of Stone's) described both his thought and decision-making in the following way:

> I am first of all a man of reason. I believe in reason and the power in the market place of discourse. I am also a democrat. I believe that our governments are to be run by the governed. Therefore I shall use my great power as a Supreme Court justice sparingly, but I shall use it when necessary to preserve the democratic process or to protect those injured by unreason under circumstances where political processes cannot be relied on to protect them.[24]

Hence, he was reshaping the fundamental law as he believed judges should—in accordance with that "sober second thought of the community, which is the firm base on which all law must ultimately rest."[25] The application of that standard to the free exercise of religion guarantee, and to the other liberties protected by the First Amendment, presented the Court with a commanding problem.

To the very end, Stone—unlike Chase a century and one-half earlier—remained troubled by the difficult, questionable cases.

Religious Freedom Restoration Act of 1993

Public Law 103–141, An Act to Protect the Free Exercise of Religion
  Be it enacted by the Senate and House of Representatives of the United States of America in Congress assembled,

Section 1. Short Title

This Act may be cited as the "Religious Freedom Restoration Act of 1993."

Section 2. Congressional Findings and Declaration of Purposes

  (a) Findings. The Congress finds that
    (1) the framers of the Constitution, recognizing free exercise of religion as an unalienable right, secured its protection in the First Amendment to the Constitution;
    (2) laws "neutral" toward religion may burden religious exercise as surely as laws intended to interfere with religious exercise;
    (3) governments should not substantially burden religious exercise without compelling justification;
    (4) in Employment Division v. Smith, 494 U.S. 872 (1990) the Supreme Court virtually eliminated the requirement that the government justify burdens on religious exercise imposed by laws neutral toward religion; and
    (5) the compelling interest test as set forth in prior Federal court rulings is a workable test for striking sensible balances between religious liberty and competing prior governmental interests.
  (b) Purposes. The purposes of this Act are
    (1) to restore the compelling interest test as set forth in Sherbert v. Verner, 374 U.S. 398 (1963) and Wisconsin v. Yoder, 406 U.S. 205 (1972) and to guarantee its application in all cases where free exercise of religion is substantially burdened; and

(2) to provide a claim or defense to persons whose religious exercise is substantially burdened by government.

Section 3. Free Exercise of Religion Protected.

(a) In General. Government shall not substantially burden a person's exercise of religion even if the burden results from a rule of general applicability, except as provided in subsection (b).

(b) Exception. Government may substantially burden a person's exercise of religion only if it demonstrates that application of the burden to the person
  (1) is in furtherance of a compelling governmental interest; and
  (2) is the least restrictive means of furthering that compelling governmental interest.

(c) Judicial Relief. A person whose religious exercise has been burdened in violation of this section may assert that violation as a claim or defense in a judicial proceeding and obtain appropriate relief against a government. Standing to assert a claim or defense under this section shall be governed by the general rules of standing under article III of the Constitution.

Section 5. Definitions

As used in this Act
  (1) the term "government" includes a branch, department, agency, instrumentality, and official (or other person acting under color of law) of the United States, a State, or a subdivision of a State;
  (2) the term "State" includes the District of Columbia, the Commonwealth of Puerto Rico, and each territory and possession of the United States;
  (3) the term "demonstrates" means meets the burdens of going forward with the evidence and of persuasion; and
  (4) the term "exercise of religion" means the exercise of religion under the First Amendment to the Constitution.

Section 6. Applicability

(a) In General. This Act applies to all Federal and State law, and the implementation of that law, whether statutory or otherwise, and whether adopted before or after the enactment of this Act.

(b) Rule of Construction. Federal statutory law adopted after the date of the enactment of this Act is subject to this Act unless such law explicitly excludes such application by reference to this Act.

(c) Religious Belief Unaffected. Nothing in this Act shall be construed to authorize any government to burden any religious
belief.

Section 7. Establishment Clause Unaffected.

Nothing in this Act shall be construed to affect, interpret, or in any
way address that portion of the First Amendment prohibiting laws
respecting the establishment of religion (referred to in this section as the
"Establishment Clause"). Granting government funding, benefits, or
exemptions, to the extent permissible under the Establishment Clause,
shall not constitute a violation of this Act. As used in this section, the
term "granting" used with respect to government funding, benefits, or
exemptions, does not include the denial of government funding, benefits,
or exemptions.

NOTES

PREFACE

1. E. Rostow, THE SOVEREIGN PREROGATIVE: THE SUPREME COURT AND THE QUEST FOR LAW xiii (1962).
2. H. Abraham, FREEDOM AND THE COURT: CIVIL RIGHTS AND LIBERTIES IN THE UNITED STATES 277 (5th ed. 1988).
3. E. Rostow, *supra* note 1, at 53.
4. *Ibid.*

INTRODUCTION

1. (P. Laslett ed. 1961), bk. II, ch. 6, sec. 57.
2. The Court makes law *passively* "by accepting the constitutional changes brought about by custom or practice" and *negatively* "by 'vetoing' the policy determinations of other governmental agencies." R. Hirschfield, THE CONSTITUTION AND THE COURT: THE DEVELOPMENT OF THE BASIC LAW THROUGH JUDICIAL INTERPRETATION 188 (1962).
3. *Ibid.*
4. E. Cahn, THE SENSE OF INJUSTICE 102 (1949).
5. Quoted in E. Bodenheimer, JURISPRUDENCE: THE PHILOSOPHY AND METHOD OF THE LAW 246 (1962).
6. E. Bodenheimer, *supra* note 5, at 176–77.
7. *Id.* at 262–63.
8. *See* S. Krislov, THE SUPREME COURT IN THE POLITICAL PROCESS 115 (1965): "The core of the democratic process is the preservation of the exchange of ideas and the appeal to the majority for support. Any artificial restriction of the means of communication or the isolation of a minority from the electoral process are threats to that core of democracy and must be prevented by all means, including the courts. The majority cannot artificially turn itself into a permanent majority by eliminating the right of the minority to become a majority."
9. C. Pritchett, CIVIL LIBERTIES AND THE VINSON COURT 198 (1954).
10. A. Mason, THE SUPREME COURT FROM TAFT TO WARREN 195 (1968).
11. *A New Kind of Society*, in THE GREAT RIGHTS 9 (E. Cahn ed. 1963) (emphasis added).
12. *Cf.* McCollum v. Board of Education, 333 U.S. 203 (1948) with Zorach v. Clauson, 342 U.S. 307 (1952). More recently, *cf.* Board of Education

v. Allen, 392 U.S. 236 (1968) with Lemon v. Kurtzman, 403 U.S. 602 (1971); Mueller v. Allen, 463 U.S. 388 (1983) with Texas Monthly v. Bullock, 489 U.S. 1 (1989).

13. M. Konvitz, FUNDAMENTAL LIBERTIES OF A FREE PEOPLE: RELIGION, SPEECH, PRESS, ASSEMBLY 5–6 (1957). The major historical sources relied upon in this section (in addition to those cited in notes) are listed in the bibliography.

14. 1 A. Stokes, CHURCH AND STATE IN THE UNITED STATES 194–95 (1950).

15. See L. Pfeffer, CHURCH, STATE AND FREEDOM 79–80 (1953): "The proprietary regimes permitted a considerable degree of toleration, at least in comparison with the other colonies. . . . Even in the proprietary colonies, however, the death of the idealistic founder, . . . resulted in considerable backsliding, and the imposition of restrictions on civil and religious rights, particularly on non-Protestants. . . . Perhaps the incident that most ironically illustrates the turn-about after the death of the idealistic founder is the action of a Rhode Island court which in 1762 denied the petition of two Jews for naturalization on the ground that to grant the petition would be 'inconsistent with the first principles on which the colony was founded.'" Pfeffer also explained that the limited tolerance that did exist "did not include Catholics, Jews, Unitarians, or Deists. . . . Primarily, the discrimination was political—the non-Protestants could not vote or hold office. But the restrictions were not always limited to political disabilities. Public performance of Catholic worship was prohibited almost everywhere, and as late as 1756 the colony which had been founded by the Catholic Calverts enacted a law subjecting Catholics to double taxation." Id. at 80.

16. According to Konvitz: "Contractualism came to mean constitutionalism and representative government for the state, and congregationalism for the Church. Self-reliance expressed itself in contractualism; contractualism came to mean constitutionalism; constitutionalism came to mean that the citizen reserved the right to criticize government and to show that government has, in a specific instance touching his conscience, violated the terms of the contract by transgressing upon rights reserved unto the people—rights which no man has given up or could give up without giving up, at the same time, his very humanity. Political action is, . . . subject to moral and religious judgment; conscience must be respected; and in the final contest it is conscience, and not majority vote or public authority, that must be obeyed." Supra note 13, at 15–16.

17. Quoted in id. at 14.

18. Id. at 16.

19. Its clause on religion read as follows: "That religion, or the duty which we owe our Creator, and the manner of discharging it, can be directed only by reason and conviction, not by force or violence, and therefore all men are equally entitled to the free exercise of religion, according to the dictates of conscience; and that it is the mutual duty of all to practice Christian forbearance, love, and charity towards each other." Quoted in H. Commager, DOCUMENTS OF AMERICAN HISTORY 104 (7th ed. 1963).

20. Quoted in id. at 126. In his opinion for the Supreme Court in Reynolds v. United States, 98 U.S. 145, 163 (1879), Chief Justice Waite stated that in these two sentences of Jefferson's "is found the true distinction between what properly belongs to the Church and what to the State."

The Virginia Statute of Religious Liberty also provided for the following: "[N]o man shall be compelled to frequent or support any religious worship, place, or ministrry whatsoever, nor shall be enforced, restrained, molested, or burdened in his body or goods, nor shall otherwise suffer, on account of his religious opinions or belief; but that all men shall be free to profess, and by argument to maintain, their opinions in matters of religion, and that the same shall in no wise diminish, enlarge, or affect their civil capacities." Quoted in H. Commager, *supra* note 19, at 126.

21. As the REMONSTRANCE disclosed throughout, Madison opposed every form and degree of official relation between religion and civil authority. For him, religion was a wholly private affair beyond the scope of civil power either to restrain or to support. Denial or abridgment of religious freedom was a violation of rights both of conscience and of natural equality. The realm of religious training should be kept private, not confounded with what legislatures may exercise in the public domain. *See* 1 A. Stokes, *supra* note 14, at 341–43.

22. M. Konvitz, *supra* note 13, at 25–26.

23. Quoted in 1 A. Stokes, *supra* note 14, at 541.

24. *Id.* at 544.

25. Cantwell v. Connecticut, 310 U.S. 296, 303–04 (1940) (Roberts, J.). The same distinction still exists today. *See, e.g.,* Gay Rights Coalition v. Georgetown University, 536 A.2d 1 (D.C. App. 1987); Intercommunity Center for Justice and Peace v. I.N.S., 910 F.2d 42 (2d Cir. 1990); Langlatz v. Picciano, 683 F.Supp. 1041 (E.D. Va. 1988), *aff'd*, 905 F.2d 1530 (4th Cir. 1988); United States v. Greene, 892 F.2d 453 (6th Cir. 1989), *cert. denied*, 495 U.S. 935 (1989); Vandiver v. Hardin County Bd. of Educ., 925 F.2d 927 (6th Cir. 1991).

26. *See* the basic ideas in J. Tussman, THE SUPREME COURT ON CHURCH AND STATE xiii–xiv (1962).

27. H. Abraham, FREEDOM AND THE COURT: CIVIL RIGHTS AND LIBERTIES IN THE UNITED STATES 283 (5th ed. 1988). Thus, we have those who believe in nothing, those who "believe but doubt, those who believe without questioning, those who worship the Judaeo-Christian God in innumerably different ways, those who adhere to Mohammed's creed, those who worship themselves, those who worship a cow or other animals, those who worship several gods—to mention just a few of the remarkable variety of expressions of belief that obtain." *Id.* at 284.

28. J. Tussman, *supra* note 26, at xix.

29. *Id.* at xx.

30. *Id.* at xix–xxii.

31. *Avoidance of Constitutional Issues in the Supreme Court of the United States: Liberties of the First Amendment*, 50 MICH. L. REV. 261, 268–69 (1951) (emphasis added).

32. Stone, *The Common Law of the United States*, 50 HARV. L. REV. 4, 22 (1936).

33. P. Kauper, FRONTIERS OF CONSTITUTIONAL LIBERTY 6 (1956). Kauper then explains: "Their educational, professional, religious, and political backgrounds, their sensitivity to any understanding of contemporary developments in American life, their conception of the interests and values that give enduring sig-

nificance to our constitutional system, the presuppositions implicit in their philosophy of law and of the judicial process, their appraisal of the judicial role in the process of constitutional interpretation, their readiness to probe into the policy considerations that attend the isolated cases presented for decision—these are the factors that shape the judicial mind and the stuff out of which judicial decisions are compounded." *Id.* at 7.

34. E. Bodenheimer, *supra* note 5, at 174–75.

CHAPTER 1. CRIMINAL CONDUCT/ANTISOCIAL BEHAVIOR

1. Cantwell v. Connecticut, 310 U.S. 296 (1940). The Jehovah's Witnesses' numerous conflicts with the law may be traced in large part to their literal interpretation of Exodus 20:3–5: "Thou shalt have no other Gods before me. Thou shalt not make unto thee any graven image, or any likeness of anything that is in Heaven above, or . . . in the earth, . . . or in the water under the earth. Thou shalt not bow down thyself to them, nor serve them: for I the Lord thy God am a jealous God." Any submission to governmental licensing regulations, or signs of obedience such as saluting the flag, come under the prohibition against bowing down to graven images. Thus, when one of the faithful refuses to procure a municipally required permit to distribute handbills, to hold a parade, or to solicit charitable contributions, he maintains that he is "sent by Jehovah to do His work," and that to have applied for a permit would have been "an act of disobedience to His commandment."

2. Lovell v. Griffin, 303 U.S. 444 (1938); Schneider v. Town of Irvington, 308 U.S. 147 (1939); Jamison v. Texas, 318 U.S. 413 (1943); Largent v. Texas, 318 U.S. 418 (1943); Murdock v. Pennsylvania, 319 U.S. 105 (1943); Follette v. Town of McCormick, 321 U.S. 573 (1944).

3. West Virginia State Board of Education v. Barnette, 319 U.S. 624 (1943), specifically overruling Minersville School District v. Gobitis, 310 U.S. 586 (1940).

4. Niemotko v. Maryland, 340 U.S. 268 (1951); Kunz v. New York, 340 U.S. 290 (1951); Fowler v. Rhode Island, 345 U.S. 67 (1953).

5. Martin v. City of Struthers, 319 U.S. 141 (1943); Marsh v. Alabama, 326 U.S. 501 (1946); Tucker v. Texas, 326 U.S. 517 (1946).

6. 98 U.S. 145 (1879).

7. "Every person having a husband or wife living, who marries another, whether married or single, in a Territory, or other place over which the United States have exclusive jurisdiction, is guilty of bigamy, and shall be punished by a fine of not more than $500, and by imprisonment for a term of not more than five years." Revised Statutes of the United States, sec. 5352, quoted in 98 U.S. at 146. *See* the present version in 48 U.S.C.A. sec. 1561 (1987).

8. *See* the complete text of the letter in 1 A. Stokes, CHURCH AND STATE IN THE UNITED STATES 334 (1950). It is quoted by Chief Justice Waite in 98 U.S. at 164.

9. R. Morgan, THE SUPREME COURT AND RELIGION 41 (1972). Morgan suggests Commonwealth v. Lesher, 17 Serg. & Rawle (Penna.) 155 (1828) and

Donahue v. Richards, 38 Me. 379 (1854) for the earliest articulation of the secular regulation rule.

10. Kurland, *Of Church and State and the Supreme Court,* 29 U. CHI. L. REV. 1, 7 (Autumn 1961).

11. "Polygamy has always been odious among the Northern and Western Nations of Europe and, until the establishment of the Mormon Church, was almost exclusively a feature of the life of Asiatic and African people. At common law, the second marriage was always void, . . . and from the earliest history of England polygamy has been treated as an offense against society. Marriage, while from its very nature a sacred obligation, is, . . . in most civilized nations, a civil contract, and usually regulated by law. Upon it society may be said to be built, and out of its fruits spring social relations and social obligations and duties, with which government is necessarily required to deal." 98 U.S. at 164–65.

12. *Id.* at 166–67.

13. *Id.* at 167.

14. The oath required that the prospective voter not be a polygamist or a member of an organization that advocated polygamy. *See* the complete text in Davis v. Beason, 133 U.S. 333, 336, note 1 (1890).

15. 133 U.S. 333 (1890). *See also* the earlier case of Murphy v. Ramsey, 114 U.S. 15 (1885), which upheld the denial of the right of Mormons to vote.

16. 133 U.S. at 342–43.

17. *Id.* at 354.

18. *Id.* at 342. Field then said: "Probably never before in the history of this country has it been seriously contended that the whole punitive power of the government, for acts recognized by the general consent of the Christian world in modern times as proper matters for prohibitory legislation, must be suspended in order that the tenets of a religious sect encouraging crime may be carried out without hindrance." *Id.* at 343.

19. *Id.* at 342.

20. *Id.* at 345.

21. G. Spicer, THE SUPREME COURT AND FUNDAMENTAL FREEDOMS 111 (2d ed. 1967).

22. 136 U.S. 1 (1890). The other case, decided simultaneously and similarly, was Rommey v. United States.

23. 136 U.S. at 47.

24. *Id.* at 56. It was never intended or supposed (reasoned the Court) that the First Amendment could be invoked against legislation for the punishment of religious practices inimical to peace, good order, and the morals of society.

25. 245 F. 710 (9th Cir. 1917). Postal Act of 1889, Rev. Stat. ch. 374, sec. 5480 (1989).

26. 245 F. at 712.

27. 310 U.S. 296 (1940). *See* chapter 2, *infra.*

28. R. Morgan, *supra* note 9, at 62.

29. 302 U.S. 319 (1937). Suggesting that some provisions of the first eight amendments were incorporated in the due process clause (while others were not), Cardozo set forth the following test for the inclusion of constitutional

guarantees of freedom: Would the denial of the right claimed "violate those 'fundamental principles of liberty and justice which lie at the base of all our civil and political institutions?'" *Id.* at 328. The distinction created the necessary tool for inclusion of all fundamental rights, depending on the Court's subsequent definition of the term "fundamental." Still needed, however, was a formula defining the kind of review that the Court would engage in, and a theory of the constitutionality of legislation affecting the First Amendment.

30. 304 U.S. 144, 152–53, note 4 (1938). *See* appendix A, *infra.*

31. United States v. Ballard, 35 F.Supp. 105 (N.D.Cal. 1940); *rev.* Ballard v. United States, 138 F.2d 540 (9th Cir. 1943). The assumption was that if the Ballards did not believe their own statements, they had to be guilty—not only of being religious hypocrites, but also of using the mails to defraud the public. G. Schubert, DISPASSIONATE JUSTICE: A SYNTHESIS OF THE JUDICIAL OPINIONS OF ROBERT H. JACKSON 40 (1969).

32. *Ibid.*

33. 322 U.S. 78 (1944). When the case came back to the court of appeals the second time around that court affirmed the conviction by a 2-1 vote. Ballard v. United States, 152 F.2d 941 (9th Cir. 1945). The Supreme Court again reversed the conviction, this time on the ground that women had intentionally been excluded from serving on grand and petit juries. Ballard v. United States, 329 U.S. 187 (1946).

34. 322 U.S. at 86.

35. *Id.* at 86–87.

36. *Id.* at 87.

37. *Id.* at 89.

38. *Id.* at 90.

39. *Id.* at 93.

40. 322 U.S. at 95. "The chief wrong which false prophets do to their following is not financial. The . . . real harm is on the mental and spiritual plane. There are those who hunger and thirst after higher values which they feel wanting in their humdrum lives. They live in mental confusion or moral anarchy and seek vaguely for truth and beauty and moral support. When they are deluded and then disillusioned, cynicism and confusion follow. The wrong of these things, as I see it, is not in the money the victims part with half so much as in the mental and spiritual poison they get. *But that is precisely the thing the Constitution put beyond the reach of the prosecutor, for the price of freedom of religion or of speech or of the press is that we must put up with, and even pay for, a good deal of rubbish.*" *Id.* at 94–95 (emphasis added).

41. M. Konvitz, FUNDAMENTAL LIBERTIES OF A FREE PEOPLE: RELIGION, SPEECH, PRESS, ASSEMBLY 101 (1957).

42. *Ibid.*

43. E. Smith, RELIGIOUS LIBERTY IN THE UNITED STATES: THE DEVELOPMENT OF CHURCH-STATE THOUGHT SINCE THE REVOLUTIONARY ERA 268–69 (1972).

44. *Id.* at 265.

45. 321 U.S. 158 (1944). *See* Mass. Gen. Laws sec. 69 (Ter. ed.), cited in *id.* at 160.

46. *Id.* at 166.

47. *See, e.g.,* Jacobson v. Massachusetts, 197 U.S. 11 (1904) (compulsory vaccination); Sturgess & Burn Mfg. Co. v. Beauchamp, 231 U.S. 320 (1913) (regulation of child labor); Munn v. Algee, 924 F.2d 568 (5th Cir. 1991) (blood transfusion); Hermanson v. State, 570 So.2d 322 (Fla.App. 1990) (general medical care). *Contra,* Sheri v. Northport Union Free School District, 672 F.Supp. 81 (E.D.N.Y. 1987) (mandatory inoculation); In Interest of E.G., 515 N.E.2d 286, 161 Ill.App.3d 765 (Ill. 1987) (blood transfusion).

48. *Id.* at 170.

49. *Ibid.*

50. Murdock v. Pennsylvania, 319 U.S. 105 (1943). *Accord,* Jones v. City of Opelika, 319 U.S. 103 (1943); Martin v. City of Struthers, 319 U.S. 141 (1943); Follette v. Town of McCormick, 321 U.S. 573 (1944). *See* chapter 2, *infra.*

51. 321 U.S. at 177–78.

52. "The great interest of the state in shielding minors from the evil vicissitudes of early life does not warrant every limitation on their religious training and activities. The reasonableness that justifies the prohibition of the ordinary distribution of literature in the public streets by children is not necessarily the reasonableness that justifies such a drastic restriction when the distribution is part of their religious faith. . . . If the right of a child to practice its religion in that manner is to be forbidden by constitutional means, there must be convincing proof that such a practice constitutes a grave and immediate danger to the state or to the health, morals or welfare of the child." *Id.* at 173–74.

53. *Id.* at 174–75.

54. *Id.* at 173.

55. *See, e.g.,* Chatwin v. United States, 326 U.S. 455 (1946), where a bona fide religious belief cannot absolve one from liability under the Federal Kidnapping Act, sec. 1, as amended in 1934, 18 U.S.C. sec. 1201; Cleveland v. United States, 329 U.S. 14 (1946), where the Mann Act of 1910, 18 U.S.C. sec. 2421, which forbade transportation of women in interstate commerce for prostitution or any other immoral purpose, was held to apply against the moral crime of polygamy; Bunn v. North Carolina, 336 U.S. 942 (1949), where the state, under its police power, has the authority to punish an individual who handled a live copperhead snake, even if he did so in the course of a religious or church service.

56. *See* Hardwicke v. Board of School Trustees, 54 Cal.App. 696, 205 P. 491 (1921); People v. Woody, 61 Cal.2d 716, 394 P.2d 813, 40 Cal.Rptr. 69 (1964); Kolbeck v. Kramer, 84 N.J. Super. 569, 202 A.2d 889 (1964). *Cf.* Application of the President and Directors of Georgetown College, 331 F.2d 1000 (D.C. Cir. 1964).

57. 61 Cal.2d 716, 394 P.2d 813, 40 Cal.Rptr. 69 (1964). The California Supreme Court upheld the free exercise claim of the Native American Church and its use of peyote for religious purposes. In effect, the court maintained that, notwithstanding the secular purpose and primary effect of a narcotics control law, the statute must fall because the state could not show a compelling interest in enforcing it against the Indians and imposing a secondary burden: "The state's showing of 'compelling interest' cannot lie in untested assertions that recognition of the religious immunity will interfere with the enforcement of the

state statute." 40 Cal.Rptr. at 75. *Accord,* Arizona v. Whittingham, 19 Ariz.App. 27, 504 P.2d 950 (1973), cert. denied, 417 U.S. 946 (1974).

58. 288 F.Supp. 439 (D.D.C. 1968). The U.S. District Court for the District of Columbia rejected the "religious legitimacy" of the Neo-American Church by denying its claim that psychedelic drugs were required by the practice of its religious beliefs.

59. 494 U.S. 872 (1990). The U.S. Supreme Court, in overturning the ruling of the Oregon Supreme Court, held that Oregon's prohibition of the use of peyote in religious ceremonies of the Native American Church did not violate the free exercise clause of the First Amendment. *See* chapter 5, *infra.*

60. Chief Justice Burger used just such a test in Wisconsin v. Yoder, 406 U.S. 205 (1972). Here the Court tested religion in terms of its longevity: If one's religion has been long recognized as legitimate, and everyone has perceived those actions to be religious, one must be accorded the protection of the free exercise clause. What is troublesome, of course, is the distinct possibility that courts will equate traditional and orthodox with religious. It is hoped that courts will not apply one interpretation of the free exercise clause to religious actions the judge finds personally acceptable and another (and more restrictive) interpretation to unorthodox religious groups. The creation of one rule for well established religions and a different rule for religions "newly discovered" must never be allowed. *See* chapter 3, *infra.*

61. R. Morgan, THE SUPREME COURT AND RELIGION 150 (1972).

62. *Id.* at 151.

63. *Ibid.*

64. *Id.* at 151–52.

65. *Id.* at 152.

66. *Ibid.*

67. H. Hart, LAW, LIBERTY AND MORALITY 41 (1966). *Cf. P.* Devlin, THE ENFORCEMENT OF MORALS (1959).

68. *Id.* at 45.

69. H. Hart, *supra* note 67, at 39.

70. *Id.* at 40.

71. J. Mill, ON LIBERTY 70–86 (Spitz ed. 1975).

72. *Ibid.*

73. H. Hart, *supra* note 67, at 46.

74. *Id.* at 46–47.

75. *Id.* at 57.

76. *Id.* at 60.

77. A. Meikeljohn, POLITICAL FREEDOM: THE CONSTITUTIONAL POWERS OF THE PEOPLE 28 (1965).

CHAPTER 2. PREVIOUS RESTRAINT

1. C. Pritchett, THE ROOSEVELT COURT: A STUDY IN JUDICIAL ATTITUDES AND VALUES, 1937–1947 at 93–94 (1948).

2. 302 U.S. 636 (1937).

3. 303 U.S. 444 (1938).

4. *Id.* at 451. In coming to its decision, the Court relied on Gitlow v. New York, 268 U.S. 652 (1925); Near v. Minnesota, 283 U.S. 697 (1931); Grosjean v. American Press Co., 297 U.S. 233 (1936); DeJonge v. Oregon, 299 U.S. 353 (1937). Chief Justice Hughes, in his opinion for the unanimous Court, also noted that in the previous Coleman case the federal question had not been properly presented.

5. 308 U.S. 147 (1939). The other cases, decided simultaneously and similarly, were Young v. California, Snyder v. City of Milwaukee, and Nicholas v. Massachusetts.

6. *Id.* at 164.

7. *Id.* at 163.

8. 310 U.S. 296 (1940).

9. *Id.* at 305.

10. *Id.* at 308.

11. *Ibid.*

12. *Id.* at 303–4.

13. R. Morgan, THE SUPREME COURT AND RELIGION 62 (1972).

14. Brandeis had recognized by 1927 that some amplification of the clear-and-present-danger test was needed to prevent its demotion to the "bad tendency" level of Gitlow v. New York, 268 U.S. 652 (1925). Consequently, he endeavored not only to resurrect the original concept but to strengthen it. His concurrence in Whitney v. California, 274 U.S. 357, 377 (1927), clarified, expanded, and liberalized the doctrine by joining to its basic test the requirement of imminence.

15. H. Abraham, FREEDOM AND THE COURT: CIVIL RIGHTS AND LIBERTIES IN THE UNITED STATES 299 (5th ed. 1988).

16. 310 U.S. at 307.

17. Morgan, *supra* note 13, at 63.

18. G. Spicer, THE SUPREME COURT AND FUNDAMENTAL FREEDOMS 115 (2d ed. 1967).

19. P. Freund, THE SUPREME COURT OF THE UNITED STATES: ITS BUSINESS, PURPOSES, AND PERFORMANCE 60–74 (1961).

20. C. Pritchett, *supra* note 1, at 92.

21. 312 U.S. 569 (1941).

22. 315 U.S. 568 (1942).

23. *Id.* at 571.

24. *Id.* at 572.

25. 316 U.S. 584 (1942). The other cases, decided simultaneously and similarly, were Bowden v. Fort Smith and Jobin v. Arizona.

26. *Id.* at 599.

27. "If all expression of religion or opinion . . . were subject to the discretion of authority, [it] . . . might be made only colorless and sterile ideas. To give them life and force, the Constitution protects their use. . . . [Nevertheless, such expression] may be limited by action of the proper legislative body of times, places and methods for the enlightenment of the community which, in view of existing social and economic conditions, [is] not at odds with the preservation of peace and good order." *Id.* at 594.

28. *Id.* at 596–97.

29. *Id.* at 599.

30. *Id.* at 599–600.

31. *Id.* at 601–2. Justices Black, Douglas, and Murphy joined this dissent. In addition, Black, Douglas, and Murphy issued a separate, unprecedented statement admitting a mistake in reasoning on their behalf in the *Gobitis* case: "The opinion of the Court sanctions a device which in our opinion suppresses or tends to suppress the free exercise of a religion practiced by a minority group. This is but another step in the direction which Minersville School District v. Gobitis . . . took against the same religious minority and is a logical extension of the principles upon which that decision rested. Since we joined in the opinion in the Gobitis Case, we think this is an appropriate occasion to state that we now believe that it was also wrongly decided. Certainly our democratic form of government functioning under the historic Bill of Rights has a high responsibility to accommodate itself to the religious views of minorities however unpopular and unorthodox those views may be. *The First Amendment does not put the right freely to exercise religion in a subordinate position.* We fear . . . that the oppinions in [this] and in the Gobitis Case do exactly that." *Id.* at 623–24 (emphasis added). *See* chapter 3, *infra.*

32. *Id.* at 608.

33. *Ibid.*

34. *Ibid.*

35. *Ibid.*

36. P. Freund, *supra* note 19, at 40.

37. 318 U.S. 413 (1943). Justice Black argued that the right to distribute handbills for the dissemination of religious ideas in public places within the community may not be prohibited at all times and under all circumstances. Granting the legitimacy of the local community to protect itself against disturbances to public safety and order, he nevertheless declared the municipal ordinance invalid on its face. He emphasized the point that the legal right to use a public street the state had left open concedes an individual the right of "the communication of ideas by handbills and literature as well as by the spoken word." *Id.* at 416. While the state can prohibit use of public streets for distributing purely commercial literature it may not prohibit the distribution of handbills "in the pursuit of a clearly religious activity merely because the handbills invite the purchase of books for the improved understanding of the religion or because the handbills seek in a lawful fashion to promote the raising of funds for religious purposes." *Id.* at 417.

38. 318 U.S. 418 (1943). Justice Reed (spokesman for the Court in the first *Jones* decision) handed down a ruling similar to the one in *Jamison.* He declared the local police regulation invalid as an outright censorship of the distribution of religious literature and the dissemination of religious ideas. Stating that the legislation was an extreme form of censorial power by an administrative official, Reed concluded as follows: "It is unnecessary to determine whether the distributions of the publications in question are sales or contributions. The mayor issues a permit only if after thorough investigation he 'deems it proper or advisable.' Dissemination of ideas depends upon the approval of the distributor by

the official. This is administrative censorship in an extreme form. It abridges the freedom of religion, of the press, and of speech guaranteed by the Fourteenth Amendment." *Id.* at 422.

39. 319 U.S. 103 (1943).

40. 319 U.S. 105 (1943).

41. *Id.* at 112.

42. *Id.* at 113.

43. *Id.* at 115.

44. *Id.* at 117.

45. *Id.* at 108–9 (emphasis added).

46. R. Morgan, *supra* note 13, at 65.

47. 319 U.S. 141 (1943). Justice Murphy, joined by Justices Douglas and Rutledge, issued a separate concurrence. Aside from proclaiming the preferred position for free exercise once again, Murphy *seemed to suggest* that religious freedom was entitled to special consideration. "I believe that nothing enjoys a higher estate in our society than the right given by the First and Fourteenth Amendments freely to practice and proclaim one's religious convictions." *Id.* at 149. "There can be no question but that appellant was engaged in a religious activity when she was going from house to house . . . distributing circulars advertising a meeting of those of her belief." *Id.* at 150. And finally, "[f]reedom of religion has a higher dignity under the Constitution than municipal or personal convenience." *Id.* at 151–52.

48. *Id.* at 146.

49. *Id.* at 146–47.

50. A. Mason, THE SUPREME COURT FROM TAFT TO WARREN 159 (1968).

51. 319 U.S. 157 (1943).

52. *Id.* at 178.

53. *Id.* at 179.

54. *Id.* at 180. Jackson emphasized what was to become his main point of dissent in the remainder of the free exercise cases: "This Court is forever adding new stories to the temples of constitutional law, and the temples have a way of collapsing when one story too many is added. . . . The Court is adding a new privilege to override the rights of others to what has before been regarded as religious liberty. In so doing it needlessly creates a risk of discrediting a wise provision of our Constitution which protects all . . . in the peaceful, orderly practice of the religion of their choice but which gives no right to force it upon others." *Id.* at 181–82.

55. *Id.* at 179.

56. Dissenting in Jones v. City of Opelika, 319 U.S. at 139. *See also* his dissent in Martin v. City of Struthers, 319 U.S. at 152–54, stressing the problem of discrimination.

57. Kurland, *Of Church and State and the Supreme Court,* 29 U. CHI. L. REV. 1, 50 (Autumn, 1961).

58. *Id.* at 51.

59. 319 U.S. 583 (1943).

60. "The statute as construed in these cases makes it a criminal offense to communicate to others views and opinions respecting governmental policies,

and prophecies concerning the future of our own and other nations. . . . [Yet,] what these appellants communicated were their beliefs and opinions concerning domestic measures and trends in national and world affairs. . . . Under our decisions criminal sanctions cannot be imposed for such communications." *Id.* at 589–90.

61. West Virginia State Board of Education v. Barnette, 319 U.S. 624 (1943). *See* chapter 3, *infra.*

62. 319 U.S. at 589.

63. 321 U.S. 573 (1944). *See also* the *per curiam* decision in Busey v. District of Columbia, 319 U.S. 579 (1943), in which the Court vacated a decision of the court of appeals of the District of Columbia that had upheld the conviction of members of the Witnesses who had canvassed within the District without obtaining the necessary permit or remitting the required fee on the grounds set forth in the *Murdock* decision.

64. *Id.* at 577.

65. *Id.* at 576–77 (emphasis added).

66. 326 U.S. 501 (1946). In the *Marsh* case, Justice Black said that individuals in company-owned towns were free citizens of their state and nation. Similar to other community-based individuals, their free exercise of religious belief was guaranteed against restriction by private ownership. For Black, the public has an interest "in the functioning of the community in such manner that the channels of communication remain free." *Id.* at 507. Stressing the new, expanded interpretation of the judicial scrutiny concept, he stated that when the Court must "balance the Constitutional rights of owners of property against those of the people to enjoy freedom of . . . religion, as [it] must here," it has to "remain mindful of the fact that the *latter occup[ies] a preferred position.*" *Id.* at 509 (emphasis added). *See especially* U.S. Senate, Hearings before the Senate Committee on Education and Labor pursuant to S.Res. 266, Violations of Free Speech and Rights of Labor, 74th Cong., 2d Sess. (1936), for the facts regarding wholesale violations of First Amendment rights suffered by residents of company towns and villages.

67. 326 U.S. 517 (1946). In the *Tucker* case, the Court implied that it could not distinguish between this case and the *Marsh* decision, even though a difference of ownership existed. Again, the primary interest must be that the channels of communication within the community remain open and free. Upon the Court devolved that ultimate responsibility. No authority could impose criminal punishment on individuals engaged in the religious evangelism involved here. Justice Black, once again the spokesman for the Court's majority, said that the national government, states, and local municipalities could not prohibit the distribution of religious literature on the streets. "Certainly neither Congress nor the Federal agencies acting pursuant to congressional authorization may abridge the freedom of . . . religion safeguarded by the First Amendment." *Id.* at 520. For him, a "spiritual distribution" cannot be made subject to tax or permit of any sort.

68. Justice Reed, joined by Chief Justice Stone and Justice Burton, dissented from the Marsh majority opinion. Reiterating Stone's original concept of judicial scrutiny and the limitation of the rule in the system of adjudication, Reed indicated that the majority opinion went too far in attempting to give new meaning

to the practice of a religious belief. He not only questioned the wisdom of giving individuals unlimited rights with respect to the manner and place of such religious exercises, but criticized the Court for creating a preferred freedom doctrine that would discriminate among substantive rights of the First Amendment. For Stone's actual dissent in *Tucker, see* 326 U.S. at 521. He suffered a massive cerebral hemorrhage while delivering his dissent, and died later that day.

69. 334 U.S. 558 (1948).

70. *Id.* at 560–61. Justices Frankfurter, Reed, and Burton dissented on the ground that the constitutional rights of free exercise and speech do not require the state to limit its powers to control electronic amplifying devices on its streets. And since no official was determining whether a cause was religious or not (as in the previous license fee cases), local authorities could in fact regulate the time, manner, and place of the sound so long as no arbitrary discrimination occurred. Justice Jackson also dissented. For him this was not a civil liberties case, but a case testing whether society can exercise control over sound amplification equipment that can render the life of the public at large unbearable.

71. T. Emerson, Toward a General Theory of the First Amendment 75 (1963).

72. *Id.* at 75–76.

73. *Id.* at 76.

74. *Ibid.*

75. 340 U.S. 268 (1951). The issue raised was the validity of an ordinance (in the City of Havre de Grace) allowing use of public parks for public meetings, including religious groups, by custom requiring an advance permit to be issued by city council. The Court, in a unanimous decision, held that the denial of the permit by city council was based on the Witnesses "unsatisfactory response" to questions concerning flag salutes, military service, and Roman Catholicism. The ordinance was a prior restraint and a censorship violative of the First Amendment's free exercise guarantee.

76. 340 U.S. 290 (1951). Carl Jacob Kunz was an ordained Baptist minister known for his inflammatory attacks against Catholocs and Jews. In 1946 Kunz received a permit to hold public worship meetings on the streets. A New York City ordinance forbade such meetings without first securing permission from the Police Commissioner. His permit was revoked after a hearing. In 1948 Kunz held one of his meetings without a permit and was arrested and fined $10 for violating the ordinance. In an 8-1 decision, Chief Justice Vinson overturned the conviction and said that "New York cannot vest restraining control over the right to speak on religious subjects in an administrative official where there are no appropriate standards to guide his action." *Id.* at 295. *Cf.* Feiner v. New York, 340 U.S. 315 (1951), where only the free speech claim was raised.

77. 345 U.S. 67 (1953). Involved was the application of a Pawtucket public park meeting ordinance that (by interpretation) did not forbid church service in public parks to Catholics and Protestants, but did ban Jehovah's Witnesses. The Court, once again in a unanimous decision, held that—by treating the religious services of the Witnesses differently from those of other faiths—Pawtucket had unconstitutionally abridged the free exercise clause of the First Amendment.

78. S. Krislov, The Supreme Court and Political Freedom 118 (1968).

79. R. Morgan, THE SUPREME COURT AND RELIGION 67–68 (1972).

80. 341 U.S. 622 (1951). *See also* Bunger v. Green River, 300 U.S. 638 (1937); Valentine v. Chrestensen, 316 U.S. 52 (1942); Railway Express Agency v. New York, 336 U.S. 106 (1949); and Note, *Freedom of Expression in a Commercial Context,* 78 HARV. L. REV. 1191 (1965). Simply stated, the doctrine is that communication of a commerical nature may not necessarily be protected by the speech and press clauses of the First Amendment. For an interesting discussion and analysis of this point, *see* T. Emerson, THE SYSTEM OF FREEDOM OF EXPRESSION 413–17 (1970).

81. 336 U.S. 77 (1949). *See also* the intriguing exception to the religious-speech distinction in Poulos v. New Hampshire, 345 U.S. 395 (1953). The case involved a valid permit system where the permit itself was denied for invalid reasons. T. Emerson, *supra* note 80, at 379. Poulos was a Jehovah Witness who sought a permit (required by ordinance) to hold a religious meeting in a public park. The city council refused his request; but he held his meeting nevertheless. The state supreme court upheld his conviction (using the *Cox* precedent), although it acknowledged that the permit has been "arbitrarily and unreasonably" withheld. Their only concern seemed to be that Poulos should not have violated the law; and instead should have sought the administrative relief prescribed by state law. The Supreme Court, speaking through Justice Reed in a 7-2 decision, sustained the conviction on the ground that the ordinance was only a routine police measure—and did not involve any previous restraint on First Amendment guarantees.

82. R. Morgan, *supra* note 79, at 68.

83. 341 U.S. at 642.

84. *Id.* at 644. Justices Black and Douglas dissented on First Amendment grounds: "Today's decision marks a revitalization of the judicial views which prevailed before this Court embraced the philosophy that the First Amendment gives a preferred status to the liberties it protects." *Id.* at 650. Chief Justice Vinson also dissented, but on grounds that the ordinance constituted an undue and discriminatory burden on interstate commerce.

85. R. Morgan, *supra* note 79, at 68.

86. *Ibid.*

87. G. Spicer, THE SUPREME COURT AND FUNDAMENTAL FREEDOMS 64 (2d ed. 1967).

88. 336 U.S. at 87–89 (emphasis added).

89. G. Spicer, *supra* note 87, at 64–65.

90. Justices Jackson and Frankfurter concurred, but rejected Reed's use of the "loud and raucous" test on the belief that sound amplification equipment could (and should) be constitutionally controlled up to—but not including—what the speaker actually said. Justices Black, Douglas, Murphy, and Rutledge dissented on the ground that the ordinance *on its face* and *as applied* constituted an absolute prohibition of all sound-amplifying equipment.

91. N. Dowling, INDIVIDUAL RIGHTS IN CONSTITUTIONAL LAW 566–67 (8th ed. 1970). *See also* his additional discussion and analysis of these points in *id.* at 554–59.

92. Kurland, *supra* note 58, at 59.

CHAPTER 3. PUBLIC EDUCATION

1. 262 U.S. 390 (1923).
2. S. Konefsky, THE LEGACY OF HOLMES AND BRANDEIS: A STUDY IN THE INFLUENCE OF IDEAS 259 (1957).
3. 262 U.S. at 399.
4. S. Konefsky, *supra* note 2, at 259.
5. *Ibid.*
6. *Id.* at 261.
7. Holmes' dissenting opinion appears in the case of Bartels v. Iowa, 262 U.S. 404, 412 (1923): "I cannot bring my mind to believe that, in some circumstances, and circumstances existing, it is said, in Nebraska, the statute might not be regarded as a reasonable or even necessary method of reaching the desired result. The part of the act with which we are concerned deals with the teaching of young children. Youth is the time when familiarity with a language is established, and if there are sections in the state where a child would hear only Polish or French or German spoken at home, I am not prepared to say that it is unreasonable to provide that in his early years he shall hear and speak only English in school."
8. Schenck v. United States, 249 U.S. 47 (1919) and Abrams v. United States, 250 U.S. 616 (1919). See also Brandeis' version of "grave and imminent" danger in Whitney v. California, 274 U.S. 357 (1927). However, the clear-and-present-danger test was not accepted by a Court majority as a test of constitutionality of legislation until Herndon v. Lowry, 301 U.S. 242 (1937).
9. 268 U.S. 510 (1925).
10. "The fundamental theory of liberty upon which all governments in this Union repose excludes any general [power of the state] to standardize its children by forcing them to accept instruction from public school teachers only. The child is not the . . . creature of the State; those who . . . direct his destiny have the right . . . to recognize and prepare him for additional obligations." *Id.* at 535. McReynolds indicated that no question was raised concerning the following powers of the state "reasonably to regulate all schools, to inspect, supervise, and examine them, their teachers and pupils; to require that all children of proper age attend some school, that teachers shall be of good moral character and patriotic disposition, that certain studies plainly essential to good citizenship must be taught, and that nothing be taught which is manifestly inimical to the public welfare." *Id.* at 534.
11. Gitlow v. New York, 268 U.S. 652 (1925).
12. Fiske v. Kansas, 274 U.S. 380 (1927).
13. *See* 2 A. Stokes, CHURCH AND STATE IN THE UNITED STATES 603–6 (1950) and D. Manwaring, RENDER UNTO CAESAR: THE FLAG-SALUTE CONTROVERSY 3–5 (1962), for a complete listing of the states that required such public expressions of loyalty—and the requirements contained therein.
14. Several groups other than the Witnesses were also affected by the flag salute ceremony—*e.g.*, the Mennonites, the Elijah Voice Society, and the Church of God. Manwaring, *supra* note 13, at 11–15.
15. *See, e.g.*, Gabrielli v. Knickerbocker, 82 P.2d 391 (1938); Shinn v. Bar-

row, 121 S.W.2d 450 (1938); People v. Sandstrom, 167 Misc. 436 (1938), *aff'd*, 279 N.Y. 523 (1939); State v. Board of Public Instruction, 139 Fla. 43 (1939); Johnson v. Deerfield, 25 F.Supp. 918 (1939).

An example of the reasoning set forth by these courts in upholding the compulsory expressions of loyalty may be seen in the court's opinion in the New York case: "To enjoy the benefits of freedom and the privileges offered in these United States correspondingly demands of its citizens that they support and defend a symbol of government. . . . The religious zealot, if his liberties were to be thus extended, might refuse to contribute taxes in furtherance of a school system that compelled students to salute the flag." 167 Misc. at 438–39. These courts explained that saluting the flag connoted a love and patriotic devotion to one's country while religious practice connoted a way of life, a relation to a Supreme Being, the brand of one's theology.

16. 302 U.S. 656 (1937).

17. 303 U.S. 624 (1938).

18. D. Manwaring, *supra* note 13, at 35–55.

19. *Id.* at 54–55.

20. 21 F.Supp. 581 (E.D.Pa. 1937). This initial decision, which for all intents and purposes was the crucial one, was on the motion to dismiss. The final opinion and decrees appeared in 24 F.Supp. 271 (E.D.Pa. 1938).

21. *Id.* at 584. In a letter to the Minersville, Pennsylvania, Superintendent of Schools Charles E. Rondabush, twelve-year-old Lillian Gobitis (her ten-year-old brother William was the other expelled student) explained her three reasons for not saluting the flag: "1. The Lord clearly says in Exodus 20:3–5 that you should have no gods besides Him and that we should serve Him. 2. The Constitution of [the] United States is based upon religious freedom. According to the dictates of my conscience, based on the Bible, I must give full allegiance to Jehovah God. 3. Jehovah [is] my God and the Bible is my creed. I try my best to obey the Creator." Quoted H. Abraham, FREEDOM AND THE COURT: CIVIL RIGHTS AND LIBERTIES IN THE UNITED STATES 300, note 69 (5th ed. 1988).

22. 108 F.2d 683 (3d Cir. 1939).

23. *Id.* at 692. In his opinion for the court, Circuit Judge Clark criticized "false patriotism" in the form of "flag-worship," blind and excessive adulation of the flag as an emblem or image without intelligent and sincere understanding and appreciation of the ideals and institutions it symbolizes. The dissenting opinion of Justice Stone in the Gobitis case emphasized the same feeling toward the mandatory notion of a legislative act that infringed on the individual's freedom of religious belief.

24. D. Manwaring, *supra* note 13, at 115. By distinguishing the precedents on the facts, the secular regulation rule ceased to be an "automatically" functioning formula—thus deny the flag salute statute its chief benefits. *Ibid.*

25. *Ibid.*

26. 310 U.S. 586 (1940).

27. *Id.* at 595.

28. Quoted in Commager, *Democracy in America: One Hundred Years After*, New York Times Mag., Dec. 15, 1935, at 15.

29. Felix Frankfurter to Harlan Fiske Stone, May 27, 1940, quoted in A.

Mason, HARLAN FISKE STONE: PILLAR OF THE LAW 526–27 (1956). In pursuing this line of reasoning, Frankfurter believed he was following the special role of judicial self-restraint set forth in footnote four, that is, the Court must use its power sparingly except when the democratic process must be preserved or when minorities cannot be protected by that process.

    30. 310 U.S. at 599.

    31. *Id.* at 597.

    32. G. Spicer, *The Supreme Court and Fundamental Freedoms* 116 (2d ed. 1967).

    33. "The ultimate foundation of a free society is the binding tie of cohesive sentiment. Such a sentiment is fostered by all those agencies of the mind and spirit which may serve to gather up the traditions of a people, transmit them from generation to generation, and thereby create that continuity of a treasured common life which constitutes a civilization. 'We live by symbols.' The flag is the symbol of our national unity, transcending all internal differences, however large, within the framework of the Constitution." 310 U.S. at 596.

    34. D. Manwaring, *supra* note 13, at 138.

    35. 310 U.S. at 594–95.

    36. R. Morgan, The Supreme Court and Religion 70 (1972).

    37. Stone's dissent stated clearly his conception of the relationship of the constitutional guarantee of free exercise and the problem of majority versus minority rights. He believed that by this law the state attempted to coerce the Gobitis children "to express a sentiment which, as they interpreted it, they do not entertain, and which violates their deepest religious convictions." 310 U.S. at 601. Stone then went on to say that the very essence of free exercise insured for the individual the freedom "from compulsion as to what he shall think and what he shall say, at least where the compulsion is to bear false witness to his religion. If [this guarantee is to have any meaning it must] be deemed to withhold from the state any authority to compel belief or the expression of it where that expression violates religious convictions, whatever may be the legislative view of the desirability of such compulsion." *Id.* at 604.

    38. *Id.* at 605–06.

    39. Mason, in his biography of Stone, suggests that the Chief Justice was at least partially effected by the religious claim advanced, particularly after his experience as a member of the Board of Inquiry in 1918 and his visitations to the conscientious objector camps. *Supra* note 29, at 523. *Accord*, Stone, *The Conscientious Objector*, 21 COLUM. U. Q. 253 (Oct. 1919).

    40. D. Manwaring, *supra* note 13, at 146.

    41. *Id.* at 143.

    42. G. Spicer, *supra* note 32, at 117.

    43. *The Christian Century*, June 19, 1940, at 791. *See also* the editorial from the St. Louis Post-Dispatch, June 10, 1940, quoted in A. Mason, *supra* note 29, at 533: "It would be a mistake to attribute these outbreaks of violence against religious minorities solely to the United States Supreme Court's opinion upholding the compulsory flag salute in public schools. . . . Yet there can be little doubt that [that] most unfortunate decision will be an encouragement for self-appointed guardians of patriotism and the national moralists to take the law

into their own hands." *See especially* D. Manwaring, *supra* note 13, at 148–86, for a complete review of the legal and media commentary, as well as a documentation of the persecution leveled at the Witnesses.

44. 319 U.S. 624 (1943).

45. D. Manwaring, *supra* note 13, at 71–72. For a brief analysis of the earlier ACLU and ABA positions, *see id.* at 69–70.

46. Borrowing from both the Bill of Rights Committee and ACLU briefs, Black, Douglas, and Murphy suggested that free exercise was a preferred freedom; or at bare minimum was entitled to the same protection as the freedoms of speech, press, and assembly. "Decisions as to the constitutionality of particular laws which strike at the substance of religious tenets and practices must be made by this Court. The duty is a solemn one, and in meeting it we cannot say that failure, because of religious scruples, to assume a particular physical position and to repeat the words of a patriotic formula creates a grave danger to the nation." 319 U.S. at 644. "Neither our domestic tranquillity in peace nor our martial effort in war depend on compelling little children to participate in a ceremony which ends in nothing for them but a fear of spiritual condemnation." *Ibid.* "The right of freedom of thought and of religion as guaranteed by the Constitution against State action includes *both* the right to speak freely and the right to refrain from speaking at all, except in so far as essential operations of government may require it for the preservation of an orderly society—as in the case of compulsion to give evidence in court." *Id.* at 645 (emphasis in the original). For a complete review of the briefs, *see* D. Manwaring, *supra* note 13, at 215–24.

47. Kurland, *Of Church and State and the Supreme Court*, 29 U. CHI. L. REV. 1, 31 (Autumn 1961).

48. 319 U.S. at 638.

49. 319 U.S. at 641–42.

50. *Id.* at 641 (emphasis added).

51. G. Schubert, DISPASSIONATE JUSTICE: A SYNTHESIS OF THE JUDICIAL OPINIONS OF ROBERT H. JACKSON 29–30 (1969).

52. R. Morgan, *supra* note 36, at 72.

53. D. Manwaring, *supra* note 13, at 228.

54. 319 U.S. at 642 (emphasis added).

55. *Id.* at 646–47. In reiterating much of his *Gobitis* opinion, Frankfurter also stressed again and again his philosophy of law and the judicial function. Here was a jurist who loved the Constitution but sorely misunderstood what it stood for.

56. According to Abraham, several school boards continued for a generation afterwards to reject Jackson's majority opinion in *Barnette*. Many of these same school boards have also refused to recognize the Court's ban on prayer in the public schools. *Supra* note 21, at 306. Thus in 1966, the New Jersey Supreme Court had to rule unanimously in Holden v. Board of Education, 46 N.J. 281 (1966), that children cannot be suspended from school if they refuse to salute the flag on the grounds of conscientious scruples. In 1973, Mrs. Susan Russo needed the Supreme Court to reverse her dismissal as a public school arts teacher, which had come about because of her refusal to recite the pledge of allegiance to the flag with pupils in her homeroom. Central School District v.

Russo, 411 U.S. 932 (1973). The decision, like the one in *Barnette*, was based on the freedom of speech clause.

57. *See id.* at 302–4 for a brief analysis of the personnel changes.

58. *See* note 31, chapter 2, *supra*.

59. 393 U.S. 97 (1968).

60. 406 U.S. 205 (1972). *See also* the earlier cases of Engel v. Vitale, 370 U.S. 421 (1962) and Abington School District v. Schempp, 374 U.S. 203 (1963), which, although peripherally raising the free exercise issue, were concerned with the establishment clause.

61. 393 U.S. at 107.

62. *Id.* at 107–8, n. 15, quoting Lafler, *Legal Liability for the Exercise of Free Speech*, 10 ARK. L. REV. 155 (1956).

63. 406 U.S. at 214 (emphasis added). Justices Brennan, Stewart, and White filed concurring opinions. Justice Douglas dissented in part. Justices Powell and Rehnquist took no part in the consideration or decision of the case.

64. R. Morgan, *supra* note 36, at 160. Earlier in the opinion, the Chief Justice said: "[I]f the Amish asserted their claims because of their subjective evaluation and rejection of contemporary secular values accepted by the majority, much as Thoreau rejected the social values of his time and isolated himself at Walden Pond, their claim would not rest on a religious base." 406 U.S. at 216. *Cf.* Garber v. Kansas, 389 U.S. 52 (1967).

65. R. Morgan, *supra* note 36, at 160.

66. *Ibid.*

67. L. Frankel, LAW, POWER AND PERSONAL FREEDOM 340 (1975).

68. *Ibid.*

69. T. Emerson, THE SYSTEM OF FREEDOM OF EXPRESSION 21 (1970). "Forming or holding a belief occurs prior to expression. But is is the first stage in the process of expression, and it tends to progress into expression. Hence safeguarding the right to form and hold beliefs is essential in maintaining a system of expression. Freedom of belief, therefore, must be held included within the protection of the First Amendment. This proposition has indeed been accepted consistently and without hesitation by all courts and commentators." *Id.* at 21–22.

70. *Id.* at 22.

71. *Ibid.*

72. *Id.* at 41.

73. *Id.* at 25–26. Emerson believes that such coercive legislation—aside from being an affront to individual integrity—is also an invasion of the privacy established by Griswold v. Connecticut, 381 U.S. 479 (1965).

74. D. Manwaring, RENDER UNTO CAESAR: THE FLAG-SALUTE CONTROVERSY 243–47 (1962).

75. From the concurring and dissenting opinion (each in part) of Jackson in American Communications Association v. Douds, 339 U.S. 382, 444 (1950). In T. Emerson, *supra* note 69, at 30, the same theme is stressed: Coerced belief "establishes the psychological tone of a closed society. Nothing of social value is gained. Whatever outward conformity is achieved is undoubtedly more than offset by the inward hostility engendered."

CHAPTER 4. CONSCIENTIOUS OBJECTION I

1. The Immigration Act of 1902 (32 Stat. 1214), increased the classes of aliens who were to be refused admission into the United States by including polygamists and anarchists. In United States *ex rel.* Turner v. Williams, 126 F. 253 (2d Cir. 1903), the circuit court of appeals held that an immigration board of special inquiry ruling (deciding that John Turner was an anarchist) was not open to further review. In his petititon for habeas corpus, Turner raised the issue that both his free exercise of religion and free speech guarantees were violated by the action of the immigration authorities. Regarding the free exercise contention the court said: "It is difficult to understand upon what theory of exclusion of an alien who is an anarchist can be held to be a prohibition of the free exercise of religion." 126 F. at 255. The exclusion order was affirmed, and the free exercise claim once more rejected, by the Supreme Court in 194 U.S. 279 (1903).

2. 279 U.S. 644 (1929). The U.S. District Court for the Eastern Division of the Northern District of Illinois denied Rosika Schwimmer's application for admission to citizenship. The decreee was reversed by the U.S. Court of Appeals for the Seventh Circuit, 27 F.2d 742 (7th Cir. 1928), and the United States brought *certiorari*.

3. 283 U.S. 605 (1931). The U.S. District Court for the District of Connecticut denied Macintosh's application for admission to citizenship. The decree was reversed by the U.S. Court of Appeals for the Second Circuit, 42 F.2d 842 (2d Cir. 1930), and the United States brought *certiorari*.

4. 279 U.S. at 650.

5. *Id.* at 651–52 (emphasis added).

6. *Id.* at 653–54.

7. *Id.* at 654–55 (emphasis added).

8. In an exchange of correspondence with Harlan Fiske Stone in 1930, John Bassett Moore severely criticized the *Schwimmer* decision and the political orthodoxy imposed by immigration officials. He rejected the notion that "the new patriotism" demanded an individual swear in advance to support every war, however unjust. He wrote: "By what authority can a court assume to set up, under the mere prescription of an oath, an inquisition into beliefs and to censor the thoughts and prescribe the views which persons seeking citizenship must or may not hold? . . . Pacifism has never been considered illegal or unconstitutional. . . . [These individuals] not only are qualified for citizenship in the sense of the Act of 1906, but that they also constitute the great body of those who pay to the cause of peace and its promotion more than an emotional, unthinking, shallow lip service. As such they perform a useful service in counteracting the general tendency to violence which has so ruthlessly held sway during the past fifteen years." John Bassett Moore to Harlen Fiske Stone, Oct. 18, 1930, quoted in A. Mason, HARLAN FISKE STONE: PILLAR OF THE LAW 521–22 (1956). Stone would be influenced by Moore's arguments.

9. 283 U.S. at 625 (emphasis in the original). *Accord,* United States v. Bland, 283 U.S. 636 (1931). The U.S. District Court denied Bland's application for admission to citizenship. The decree was reversed by the U.S. Court of

Appeals for the Second Circuit, 42 F.2d 842 (2d Cir. 1930), and the United States brought *certiorari*. Sutherland's opinion said: "This case is ruled by the decision just announced in United States v. Macintosh." Brandeis, Holmes, Hughes, and Stone once again dissented.

10. R. Hirschfield, THE CONSTITUTION AND THE COURT: THE DEVELOPMENT OF THE BASIC LAW THROUGH JUDICIAL INTERPRETATION 151 (1962).

11. "The principle ground for exclusion appears to relate to the terms of the oath which the applicant must take. It should be observed that the respondent was willing to take the oath, and he so stated in his petition. But, . . . he explained that he was not willing 'to promise beforehand' to take up arms, 'without knowing the cause for which my country may go to war' and that 'he would have to believe that the war was morally justified.' He declared . . . 'that he could not put allegiance to the government of any country before allegiance to the will of God.'" *Id.* at 629.

12. *Id.* at 630–31. "But the naturalization oath is in substantially the same terms as the oath of office to which I have referred. I find no ground for saying that these words are to be interpreted differently in the two cases. On the contrary, when the Congress reproduces the historic words of the oath of office in the naturalization oath, I should suppose that, according to familiar rules of interpretation, they should be deemed to carry the same significance." *Id.* at 632.

13. *Id.* at 635.

14. 328 U.S. 61 (1946).

15. Hamilton v. Regents of the University of California, 293 U.S. 245 (1934). In his opinion for the Court, Justice Butler said that the "liberty" protected by the due process clause included the right to entertain the belief and to teach the doctrine that war, training for war, and military training were immoral, wrong, and contrary to the precepts of Christianity. Of course, this was exactly what Butler would not accept when done by Rosika Schwimmer, a fifty-year-old woman applying for naturalized citizenship.

The Court held that an order of the board of regents of the state university making military training compulsory was not repugnant to the Kellog-Briand Peace Pact of 1928, the contracting parties to which declared that they condemned recourse to war for the solution of international controversies and renounced it as an instrument of national policy in their relations with one another.

16. Bischoff, *The Process of Constitutional Construction: The Role of Precedents,* in SUPREME COURT AND SUPREME LAW 80 (Cahn ed. 1954).

17. 328 U.S. at 68–69. *See also* the earlier cases that first approved of this point of view, *In re* Kinloch, 53 F. Supp. 521 (W.D. Wash. 1943); *In re* Sawyer, 59 F.Supp. 428 (D.Del. 1945).

18. Bischoff, *supra* note 16, at 80–81.

19. Cohnstaedt v. Immigration and Naturalization Service, 339 U.S. 901 (1950). In this memorandum decision, the Court relied on the *Girouard* case to continue its favorable interpretation of freedom of religion for the conscientious objector; and the decision reversed the holding of the supreme court of Kansas, 167 Kan. 451 (1951), *aff'd,* 207 P.2d 425 (1950). Chief Justice Vinson, with Justices Reed and Clark, dissented. No opinions were given on either side.

20. 328 U.S. at 72–73.
21. *Id.* at 76.
22. A. Mason, *supra* note 8, at 804.
23. 328 U.S. at 79.
24. 245 U.S. 366 (1918). *Accord,* United States v. Stephens, 245 F. 956 (3d Cir. 1917).
25. *Id.* at 389–90.
26. R. Morgan, THE SUPREME COURT AND RELIGION 166 (1972).
27. *Compare* United States v. Kauton, 133 F.2d 703 (2d Cir. 1943), United States *ex rel.* Phillips v. Downer, 135 F.2d 521 (2d Cir. 1943), and United States ex rel. Reel v. Badt, 141 F.2d 845 (2d Cir. 1943)—favoring the religious claiment against the government, with Berman v. United States, 156 F.2d 377 (9th Cir. 1946). Berman (rather than the decisions of the Second Circuit) was accepted by Congress when it rewrote the draft law in 1948.
28. 130 F.2d 172 (5th Cir. 1942).
29. *Id.* at 174. *See also* United States v. Mroz, 136 F.2d 221 (7th Cir. 1943); United States v. Pitt, 144 F.2d 169 (3d Cir. 1945); and Van Bibber v. United States, 151 F.2d 444 (8th Cir. 1945). For a discussion of the scope of the review of selective service classification as a minister of religion, *see* Gibson v. United States, 329 U.S. 174 (1947); Cox v. United States, 332 U.S. 442 (1947); and Note, *Constitutional Law—Freedom of Religion—Exemption of Conscientious Objectors from Military Service,* 43 COLUM. L. REV. 112 (1943).
30. *See, e.g., In re* Rogers, 47 F.Supp. 265 (N.D.Tex. 1942); *Ex parte* Stewart, 47 F.Supp. 415 (S.D.Cal. 1942); Rase v. United States, 129 F.2d 204 (6th Cir. 1942); Checinski v. United States, 129 F.2d 461 (6th Cir. 1942); Goodwin v. Rowe, 49 F.Supp. 703 (N.D.W.Va. 1943); and United States v. Domres, 142 F.2d 477 (7th Cir. 1944).
31. *See, e.g.,* Roodenko v. United States, 147 F.2d 752 (10th Cir. 1945), *cert. denied,* 324 U.S. 860 (1945); United States v. Brooks, 54 F.Supp. 995 (S.D.N.Y. 1944), *aff'd,* 147 F.2d 134 (2d Cir. 1945), *cert. denied,* 324 U.S. 878 (1945); and United States *ex rel.* Zucker v. Osborne, 54 F.Supp. 984 (S.D.N.Y. 1944), *aff'd,* 147 F.2d 135 (2d Cir. 1945), *cert. denied,* 325 U.S. 881 (1945). For the legality of the use of theological panels in evaluating claims of exemption, *see* Eagles v. United States *ex rel.* Samuels, 329 U.S. 304 (1946) and Eagles v. United States *ex rel.* Horowitz, 329 U.S. 317 (1946).
32. *See, e.g.,* Dickenson v. United States, 346 U.S. 389 (1955)—selective service authorities may not deny a legitimately claimed exemption merely because of suspicion and speculation; Siccurella v. United States, 348 U.S. 385 (1956)—willingness to participate in a theocratic war was not inconsistent with the statutory requirement of opposition to participation in war in any form; Simmons v. United States, 348 U.S. 397 (1956)—selective service registrant need not show prejudice from the government's failure to furnish him a resume, and that the hearing officer's vague hints as to adverse information (made at the hearing) afforded him no fair notice of the adverse information; Gonzales v. United States, 348 U.S. 407 (1956)—sustained the defendant's position on the ground that, although the act did not state so in terms, it required by implication that the registrant receive a copy of the Justice Department's recom-

mendation and be given a reasonable opportunity to reply.

33. During the Vietnam War, the Supreme Court rediscovered its authority to question a "final" selective service classification and set down definitive rules regarding the time, manner, and circumstance of allowable appeal in all draft classification cases. The Court finally came to understand that an oftentimes insurmountable barrier existed between individual interpretation of the terms "conscience," "religion," "religious training and belief," and "deeply and sincerely held" and those of draft boards. Under the new rules the individual was granted greater flexibility in applying for conscientious objector status both before and after induction, as well as during military service itself. *See, e.g.,* Ehlert v. United States, 402 U.S. 99 (1971); Parisi v. Davidson, 405 U.S. 34 (1972); Fein v. Selective Service System, 405 U.S. 365 (1972).

34. Falbo v. United States, 320 U.S. 549 (1944).

35. *Id.* at 561. The Court majority held that an individual (in failing to obey a local draft board's order to report for assignment to work of national importance) could not challenge that order in the courts before exhausting his administrative remedies. And it was immaterial, reasoned the Court, that the registrant's classification as a conscientious objector rather than a minister of religion was erroneous.

36. H. Abraham, FREEDOM AND THE COURT: CIVIL RIGHTS AND LIBERTIES IN THE UNITED STATES 286 (5th ed. 1988).

37. *Ibid.*

38. *See* Welsh v. United States, 398 U.S. 333 (1970), discussed *infra.*

39. 380 U.S. 163 (1965). Daniel A. Seeger and Arno S. Jakobson had been convicted by the U.S. District Court in New York, and Forest B. Peter by the U.S. District Court in San Francisco, of refusing to submit to induction. Both New York convictions were reversed by the U.S. Court of Appeals for the Second Circuit, but the Appeals Court for the Ninth Circuit upheld the Peter conviction. Seeger had told Selective Service Authorities that he was conscientiously opposed to participation in war in any form because of his "religious belief," but that he preferred to leave open the question of his belief in a Supreme Being rather than answer "yes" or "no." Jakobson asserted that he believed in a Supreme Being who was "Creator of Man," in the sense of being ultimately responsible for the existence of man, and who was the "Supreme Reality" of which the existence of man is the result. Peter said the source of his conviction was the democratic American culture, with its values derived from the Western religious and philosophical tradition. As to his belief in a Supreme Being, Peter acknowledged such a belief but emphasized that he preferred to use other descriptive words.

40. H. Abraham, *supra* note 36, at 288.

41. 380 U.S. at 187.

42. 322 U.S. at 86, quoted in *id.* at 184. In his concurring opinion, Douglas expressed the view that a construction of the statute contrary to the one adopted by the Court would violate the free exercise clause and would result in a denial of equal protection by preferring some religions over others. Only here was the question of possible conflict raised between the free exercise and establishment clauses.

43. United States v. Sisson, 297 F.Supp. 902 (D.Mass. 1969) and Koster v. Sharp, 303 F.Supp. 836 (N.D.Cal. 1969). *See* chapter 6, *infra.*

44. H. Abraham, *supra* note 36, at 289.

45. *Ibid.*

46. 81 Stat. 104, quoted in *ibid.*

47. *Ibid.*

48. M. Konvitz, RELIGIOUS LIBERTY AND CONSCIENCE: A CONSTITUTIONAL INQUIRY 25 (1968).

49. 398 U.S. 333 (1970). *See also* Mulloy v. United States, 398 U.S. 410 (1970).

50. *Id.* at 344.

51. *Id.* at 340. It followed logically, then, that Black (in his opinion for the Court) rejected as ineligible for exemption those individuals whose beliefs were "not deeply and sincerely held" but "rest solely upon considerations of policy, pragmatism, and expediency."

52. *Id.* at 343.

53. This decision created the inevitable problems of issuing and enforcing new guidelines. The Selective Service System's general unwillingness to accept these guidelines, in turn, and the local draft board's oftentimes erroneous enforcement of them, were continuing problems until the establishment of the all-volunteer army.

54. 398 U.S. at 351–52.

55. In stressing that the Court's decision did not go far enough, Harlan believed that the time had come to handle the explosive constitutional issue of possible establishment clause violations in conscientious objector cases. To deny petitioner an exemption would be to give outright preference to strictly religious convictions, thus violating the specific First Amendment prohibition. For him, section 6(j) was an unconstitutional establishment of religion.

56. *Id.* at 367–68.

57. *Id.* at 368. Equally important for White was the second ground for dissent. According to his reading of both the free exercise and establishment clauses, there was no restriction placed on Congress against distinguishing "religious" from "nonreligious" views. As a matter of fact, he went on to say, the government need not even be "neutral" in making its distinction. *See* his argument in *id.* at 372–73.

58. 403 U.S. 698 (1971).

59. Technically, the Koran 61:10–13 teaches participation only in religious wars against nonbelievers. This point was the basis of Douglas' concurring opinion.

60. The Justice Department and the Selective Service System (as well as some of the lower federal courts) failed to perceive the modification explicit in Welsh—that is, as an acceptable substitution for "religious training and belief" the new criteria of a "moral code deeply and sincerely held."

61. *See, e.g.,* Theriault v. Carlson, 339 F. Supp. 375 (N.D. Ga. 1973)— right of federal prisoners who share a common religion to gather for prayer meetings and study the tenets of that faith; Rose v. Blackledge, 477 F.2d 616 (4th Cir. 1973) and United States v. Kahane, 396 F.Supp. 687 (E.D.N.Y.

1975)—right to have meals prepared according to religious dietary laws; Brown v. Peyton, 437 F.2d 1228 (4th Cir. 1971)—right to have religious literature. *Contra,* Brown v. Wainwright, 419 F.2d 1376 (5th Cir. 1970)—no right to beards because of religious reasons; Kennedy v. Meacham, 382 F.Supp. 996 (D.Wyo. 1974)—no right to practice "Satanic" religious beliefs.

62. 380 U.S. at 184. *Cf.* Johnson v. Robinson, 415 U.S. 361 (1974), where the Court ruled that the withholding of educational benefits involved only an incidental burden upon the individual's free exercise of religion. The irony was that Justice Brennan's majority opinion overlooked the thrust of his own argument in *Sherbert. See* chapter 5, *infra.*

CHAPTER 5. CONSCIENTIOUS OBJECTION II

1. 325 U.S. 561 (1945). Clyde Summers, a law school instructor, had passed his bar examination for admission to the state of Illinois bar. He had been classified by his local draft board as a conscientious objector during World War II; and because of physical reasons had not been required to perform noncombatant duty. His application for admission to the bar was rejected, however, by the Committee on Character and Fitness (an examining committee of the Illinois bar). That committee questioned his good faith in swearing to support the Illinois constitution because he entertained conscientious scruples against participation in war; and Article 12 of the Illinois constitution in fact required service in the state militia in time of war. And in rejecting Summers' free exercise claim, the committee was later upheld by the Illinois Supreme Court on the ground of incompatibility between conscientious objection to military service and the capacity to practice law.

2. *Cf.* the following statement by Milton R. Konvitz: "Illinois had not drafted men into the militia since 1864; and the state constitution prohibited the draft of conscientious objectors except in time of war, and also permitted conscientious objectors to substitute for active military service non-war-work of national importance. Notwithstanding these facts, the state maintained that Summers, though he was willing to take an oath to support the state constitution, ought not to be permitted to take an oath because his beliefs would make it impossible for him to observe that oath." M. Konvitz, FUNDAMENTAL LIBERTIES OF A FREE PEOPLE: RELIGION, SPEECH, PRESS, ASSEMBLY 224 (1957).

3. The majority was not content to stop there, however. Reviewing Summers' petititon to the Illinois supreme court, Reed characterized him as a "religionist" and rejected his contention that the only misconduct for which he could be reproached was taking the New Testament too seriously and practicing—instead of merely reading—the Sermon on the Mount. *See* Reed's argument on this point at 325 U.S. at 571. In essence, the majority gave its blessing to the notion that a license to practice law could be withheld on the premise (according to Edward S. Corwin) "that a conscientious belief in nonviolence to the extent that the believer would not use force to prevent wrong, no matter how aggravated, made it impossible for him to swear in good faith to support the State Constitution." E. Corwin, THE CONSTITUTION OF THE

UNITED STATES OF AMERICA: ANALYSIS AND INTERPRETATION 861 (1964).

4. On this point Black argued: "I cannot believe that a state statute would be consistent with our constitutional guarantee of freedom of religion if it specifically denied the right to practice law to all members of one of our great religious groups, Protestant, Catholic, or Jewish. Yet the Quakers have had a long and honorable part in the growth of our nation, and an amicus curiae brief filed in their behalf informs us that under the test applied to this petitioner, not one of them, if true to the tenets of their faith, could qualify for the bar of Illinois. And it is obvious that the same disqualification would exist as to every conscientious objector to the use of force, even though the Congress of the United States should continue its practice of absolving them from military service. The conclusion seems to me inescapable that if Illinois can bar this petitioner from the practice of law it can bar every person from every public occupation solely because he believes in nonresistance rather than in force." 325 U.S. at 575.

5. *Id.* at 576.

6. 325 U.S. at 578.

7. *Ibid.* In this 5-4 decision, Chief Justice Stone (the original activist libertarian in the religion cases) ironically proved to be the deciding anti–free exercise vote. His reasons for voting with the majority are nowhere recorded. And it is interesting to note that his major biographer—Mason—does not make mention of his participation.

8. Two of these cases, McGowan v. Maryland, 366 U.S. 420 (1961) and Two Guys from Harrison v. McGinley, 366 U.S. 582 (1961), dealt with the establishment question and involved major discount stores open for business seven days a week.

9. 366 U.S. 599 (1961).

10. 366 U.S. 617 (1961).

11. *See* H. Abraham, FREEDOM AND THE COURT: CIVIL RIGHTS AND LIBERTIES IN THE UNITED STATES 320 (5th ed. 1988) for a discussion of the issues involved. *See also* M. Stedman, RELIGION AND POLITICS IN AMERICA (1964), esp. ch. 2.

12. 366 U.S. at 602.

13. "If the primary end achieved by a form of regulation is the affirmation or promotion of religious doctrine—primary, in the sense that all secular ends which it purportedly serves are derivative from, not wholly independent of, the advancement of religion—the regulation is beyond the power of the state. . . . Or if the statute furthers both secular and religious ends by means unnecessary to the effectuation of the secular ends alone—where the same secular ends could equally be attained by means which do not have consequences for promotion of religion—the statute cannot stand." From Frankfurter's concurrence in McGowan v. Maryland, 366 U.S. at 467. In the same opinion Frankfurter later added: "A legislature might in reason find that the alternative of exempting Sabbatarians would impede the effective operation of the Sunday statutes, produces harmful collateral effects, and entail itself, a not inconsiderable intrusion into matters of religious faith. However preferable, personally, one might deem such an exception, I cannot find that the Constitution compels it." *Id.* at 520. This concurrence applied to all four Sunday blue law cases.

14. R. Morgan, SUPREME COURT AND RELIGION 146 (1972).

15. 366 U.S. at 607. Earlier Warren suggested the continuing acceptance of the belief-action distinction: "Certain aspects of religious exercise cannot, in any way, be restricted or burdened by either federal or state legislation. Compulsion by law of the acceptance of any creed or the practice of any form of worship is strictly forbidden. The freedom to hold religious beliefs and opinions is absolute." *Id.* at 603–4. "However, the freedom to act, even when the action is in accord with one's religious convictions, is not totally free from legislative restrictions. . . . [L]egislative power over mere opinion is forbidden but it may reach people's actions when they are found to be in violation of important social duties or subversive of good order, even when the actions are demanded by one's religion." *Id.* at 604.

16. *Id.* at 606.

17. Douglas rejected the valid secular purposes that the majority believed significant enough to allow the law to stand. "If the Sunday laws are constitutional, kosher markets are on a five-day week. Thus those laws put an economic penalty on those who observe Saturday rather than Sunday as the Sabbath. For the economic pressures on these minorities, created by the fact that our communities are predominantly Sunday-minded, there is no recourse. When, however, the State uses its coercive powers—here the criminal law—to compel minorities to observe a second Sabbath, not their own, the State undertakes to aid and 'prefer one religion over another'—contrary to the command of the Constitution." 366 U.S. at 577. For him, no matter what the secular justification, such laws would always be religious in purpose and meaning.

18. 366 U.S. at 605.

19. *Id.* at 611.

20. *Id.* at 613.

21. *Id.* at 616.

22. *Id.* at 616, note 5. Justice Stewart agreed with Brennan's dissent. Nevertheless, he filed the following statement: "Pennsylvania has passed a law which compels an Orthodox Jew to choose between his religious faith and his economic survival. That is a cruel choice. It is a choice which I think no State can constitutionally demand. For me this is not something that can be swept under the rug and forgotten in the interest of enforced Sunday togetherness." *Ibid.* For him, as for Brennan, the effect of such a law upon Orthodox Jews simply violated their constitutional right to a free exercise of religion. There could not be any valid secular objectives so compelling as to prevent the Court from calling both the constitutionality and the wisdom of such laws into question.

23. 367 U.S. 488 (1961).

24. *Id.* at 496.

25. *Id.* at 495, note 10 (emphasis added).

26. For thirty-five years Mrs. Sherbert was an employee of the Spartan Mills, a textile mill in Spartanberg, South Carolina. She was on a five-day work week when she formally joined the Seventh Day Adventist Church in 1957, thus enabling her to have her sabbath on Saturdays in accordance with the tenets of the Church. In 1959, however, her employer changed the work week to six days for all three shifts that operated in his mill. When she refused to work on Saturdays she was fired.

27. 366 U.S. at 605.

28. 374 U.S. 398 (1963).

29. 374 U.S. at 404.

30. *Ibid.*, quoting himself in Braunfeld, 366 U.S. at 607.

31. *Id.* at 406 (emphasis added). Brennan was quoting Justice Rutledge's majority opinion in Thomas v. Collins, 323 U.S. 516, 530 (1945). A discussion of the implications of that opinion will be reserved for the concluding chapter.

32. R. Morgan, *supra* note 14, at 148.

33. *Ibid.* This point is especially clear under headnotes 9 and 10, section III of Brennan's opinion at 407.

34. Justice Stewart agreed with the result reached in Sherbert, but disagreed with the majority reasoning because the inherent violation of the establishment clause that the Court now forced upon South Carolina, and the failure of the majority to specifically overrule the holding in Braunfeld.

35. Justices Harlan and White, not believing that the earlier establishment cases had been wrongly decided, dissented on the following grounds: (1) Mrs. Sherbert, no matter what her religious convictions, was simply unavailable to work on Saturdays; (2) the South Carolina Supreme Court fairly decided the case without resort to the religious issue; (3) the majority opinion would require the state to violate the establishment clause by making an exception to state law that would *favor* certain religious beliefs; and (4) the Court's failure to specifically overrule *Braunfeld*, since its opinion virtually destroys the holding. *See id.* at 418–22.

36. H. Abraham, *supra* note 11, at 322–23.

37. G. Spicer, THE SUPREME COURT AND FUNDAMENTAL FREEDOMS 126 (2d ed. 1967).

38. 374 U.S. at 408.

39. R. Morgan, *supra* note 14, at 148–49.

40. "It is quite obvious that what the Court did here was try to draw a line: to balance considerations of public policy against infringement on religious liberty. In the Sunday closing law cases the Court was not willing to make exemptions in laws of general application on grounds of claims of religious liberty versus economic hardship—in the *Sherbert* case it was. And this distinction was emphatically not due to changes in personnel since Justices White and Goldberg, the successors to retired Justices Whittaker and Frankfurter, did not numerically or substantively affect the different results in the 1963 decision. Although the facts in settings of the two cases differed, the difference was surely one of kind rather than of substance." H. Abraham, *supra* note 12, at 323.

41. *See, e.g.,* United States v. Lee, 455 U.S. 252 (1982)—refusal to pay social security taxes by a member of the Amish faith; Tony & Susan Alamo Foundation v. Secretary of Labor, 471 U.S. 290 (1985)—application of the Fair Labor Standards Act to workers receiving wages from a religious organization; Bowen v. Roy, 476 U.S. 693 (1986)—use of social security numbers in administering federal assistance programs; O'Lone v. Estate of Shabazz, 482 U.S. 342 (1987)—complaint by Islamic prisoners that time and place of work regulations prevented them from attending Junu'ah, a Friday midday service; and Jimmy Swaggart Ministries v. Board of Equalization, 493 U.S. 378 (1990)—imposition

of sales and use tax liability (not a flat license fee imposed as a precondition for evangelical activity) on religious materials. The fact that a religion-neutral, generally applicable law imposes a burden on a religious group does not, without more, require an exemption under the free exercise clause. Absent a significant burden on the claimant's free exercise beliefs (a uniquely religious impact), strict scrutiny is not appropriate. This line of reasoning, of course, was the underpinning for the Supreme Court's forthcoming decision in Department of Human Services v. Smith, 494 U.S. 872 (1990).

42. 435 U.S. 618 (1978). A Tennessee law prohibiting clergymen from being legislators or delegates to the state constitutional convention violates the free exercise of religion guarantee. Treating the law as directed at conduct rather than beliefs, the Court still found no state interest of sufficient magnitude to justify the significant burden on religion. Only Justices Brennan and Marshall, concurring, applied the strict scrutiny test of *Torcaso* and *Sherbert* and found the disqualification absolutely prohibited and not subject to a balance of interests.

43. 450 U.S. 707 (1981). A state denial of unemployment benefits to a Jehovah's Witness who terminates his job because his religious beliefs forbade participation in production of armaments violates the free exercise clause. As long as the person terminates employment because of an honest conviction that such work was forbidden by his religion, the state's interest in avoiding widespread unemployment and detailed probing by employers of a job applicant's religious beliefs were not sufficiently compelling to justify the substantial burden placed on the employee's free exercise of religion.

44. 480 U.S. 136 (1987). A Florida law denying unemployment benefits because of the "misconduct" of a Seventh Day Adventist who, because of religious objections, refused to work on the Sabbath of her faith, violates the free exercise of religion. Even though her religious objections developed after she commenced employment, the Court applied the strict scrutiny test and found *Sherbert* and *Thomas* controlling.

45. 489 U.S. 829 (1989). The denial of state unemployment benefits to a worker (belonging to no sect) who refused a job because of his sincere belief that as a Christian he could not work on Sunday as the job required, violates the religious freedom guaranteed by the First Amendment. A person cannot be made to choose between fidelity to religious belief and employment absent compelling justification.

46. 461 U.S. 574 (1983). The companion case, decided simultaneously and similarly, was Goldsboro Christian Schools v. United States. The Internal Revenue Service claimed that the schools were disqualified as "charities" because their racial policies were contrary to settled public policy. A lower federal court held for the school, 468 F.Supp. 890 (1978), accepting the argument that the IRS action punished the practice of religious beliefs. When the U.S. Court of Appeals for the Fourth Circuit reversed, 639 F.2d 147 (4th Cir. 1983), the Supreme Court granted *certiorari*.

47. Although it was not affiliated with any specific denomination, Bob Jones University was dedicated to the teaching and propagation of its fundamentalist Christian beliefs, which included strong prohibitions against interracial dating and marriage. To enforce this particular tenet, the school excluded

blacks until 1971, when it accepted applications from married blacks only. After litigation, in 1976 it began to admit unmarried blacks, but only if they adhered to a strict set of rules—such as interracial dating or marriage would lead to expulsion; and the school continued to deny admission to individuals in interracial marriages. Based on its belief that Bob Jones' policies amounted to racism, the IRS revoked its tax-exempt status.

48. 461 U.S. at 603.

49. *Ibid.*

50. *Id.* at 603–04.

51. 475 U.S. 503 (1986). An Air Force regulation relating to uniforms prohibited members of the service from wearing headgear while indoors, except for headgear for armed security police in the performance of their duties. Goldman was an Air Force officer serving as a clinical psychologist at a mental health clinic on the Air Force base; and he was also an Orthodox Jew and an ordained rabbi. He had been wearing a yarmulke (skullcap) while he was on duty indoors, and wearing a service cap over his yarmulke while he was outdoors. After being warned by his hospital commander that failure to obey the regulation could subject him to a court martial, Captain Goldman brought suit against the Secretary of Defense in U.S. District Court for the District of Columbia, claiming that the regulation infringed his free exercise of religious beliefs. The district court granted him injunctive relief, 530 F.Supp. 12, but the U.S. Court of Appeals for the District of Columbia reversed, 734 F.2d 1531. The U.S. Supreme Court granted certiorari.

52. Pub. L. No. 100–180, 101 Stat. 1086–1087, sec. 508 (1987).

53. 475 U.S. at 507.

54. *Ibid.*

55. "The desirability of dress regulations in the military is decided by the appropriate military officials, and they are under no constitutional mandate to abandon their considered professional judgment. . . . [T]he First Amendment does not require the military to accommodate such practices in the face of its view that they would detract from the uniformity sought by the dress regulations." *Id.* at 509–10.

56. *Id.* at 515.

57. *Id.* at 524.

58. 485 U.S. 439 (1988). The U.S. Forest Service planned to complete a seventy-five-mile road between two California towns by building a six-mile connecting segment through an area within a national forest. The area had historically been used by members of three Indian tribes to conduct a wide variety of specific religious rituals for the purpose of personal spiritual development. A study commissioned by the Forest Service found that specific sites within the area were used for certain rituals, and that the area as a whole had religious significance to the Indians. According to the study, constructing a road along any of the available routes would cause serious and irreparable damage to the sanctity of the area. Nevertheless, the Forest Service decided to proceed with the construction, and simultaneously adopted a plan allowing for the harvesting of timber in the area. An Indian organization challenged the policy decisions. The district court, finding that both decisions violated the free exercise clause, the

Federal Water Pollution Control Act, and the National Environment Policy Act of 1969, 565 F.Supp. 586, issued an injunction forbidding timber harvesting or road building. While an appeal was pending, Congress enacted a statute under which commercial activities, including timber harvesting, were forbidden in the area except for the proposed road route itself. The U.S. Court of Appeals for the Ninth Circuit affirmed the lower court's decision, 795 F.2d 688, concluding that the government had failed to demonstrate a compelling interest in the completion of the road.

59. 494 U.S. 872 (1990). Two drug rehabilitation counselors, both members of the Native American Church, were fired from their jobs with a private corporation in Oregon because they had ingested peyote, a hallucinogenic drug, for sacramental purposes at a ceremony of the Church. The counselors applied to the Employment Division of Oregon's Department of Human Resources for unemployment compensation, but the department's Employment Appeals Board denied their application on the ground that the counselors had been discharged for misconduct connected with work. The Oregon Court of Appeals, 707 P.2d 1274 and 709 P.2d 246, reversed the board's decisions. The Supreme Court of Oregon, 721 P.2d 445, 451, affirmed both judgments, holding that such further findings were unnecessary and that the counselors were entitled to payment of unemployment benefits. The U.S. Supreme Court granted *certiorari*.

To an extent applicable as well in chapter 1 (criminal conduct/antisocial behavior), I have chosen to include the *Smith* case here for reasons of clarity and consistency. Since the decision challenges the validity of the *Sherbert* test, it should logically follow—not precede—the analysis of that case. Hence, it has been included in chapter 5 rather than chapter 1.

60. Bowen v. Roy, 476 U.S. 693 (1986). The Court rejected the Native American Church's religion-based claim that the government not make internal use of social security numbers. Three members of the majority (Burger, Powell, and Rehnquist) wrote: "Absent proof of an intent to discriminate against particular beliefs or against religion in general, the Government meets its burden when it demonstrates that a challenged requirement for governmental benefits, neutral and uniform in its application, is a reasonable means of promoting a legitimate public interest." *Id.* at 702. In other words, denial of benefits is constitutionally less serious than an imposition of direct burdens, and therefore courts ought to measure indirect burdens differently from direct burdens. This argument became the rationale of the Court in *Lyng*, *Smith*, and *Flores*.

61. 485 U.S. at 449.

62. *Id.* at 450.

63. "This does not and cannot imply that incidental effects of government programs, which may make it more difficult to practice certain religions but which have no tendency to coerce individuals into acting contrary to their religious beliefs, require government to bring forward a compelling justification for its otherwise lawful actions. The crucial word in the constitutional text is 'prohibit.'" *Id.* at 450–51. "Nothing in our opinion should be read to encourage governmental insensitivity to the religious needs of any citizen." *Id.* at 453. This is an example of language being completely devoid of meaning!

64. *Id.* at 452.

65. *Ibid.* "The Constitution does not, and courts cannot, offer to reconcile the various competing demands on government, many of them rooted in sincere religious belief, that inevitably arise in so diverse a society as ours. That task, to the extent that it is feasible, is for legislatures and other institutions." *Ibid.*

66. *Id.* at 459.

67. "Ultimately, the Court's coercion test turns on a distinction between governmental actions that prevent conduct consistent with religious belief. In my view, such a distinction is without constitutional significance. The crucial word in the constitutional text, as the Court itself acknowledges, is "prohibit," . . . a comprehensive term that in no way suggests that the intended protection is aimed only at governmental actions that coerce affirmative conduct." *Id.* at 467–68.

68. Was *Lyng* inconsistent with *Sherbert?* Or, in light of the refusal to apply strict scrutiny despite the acknowledged burden on free exercise, did *Lyng* by implication abandon *Sherbert,* even before what seemed to be explicit abandonment by the *Smith* decision in 1990?

69. 485 U.S. at 476–77. Suggesting that the majority ruling in *Lyng* allowed the respondents to know that their religion was about to be destroyed, Brennan went on to say: "The safeguarding of such a hollow freedom not only makes a mockery of the policy of the United States to protect and preserve for American Indians their inherent right of freedom to believe, express, and exercise the[ir] traditional religions, it fails utterly to accord with the dictates of the First Amendment." *Id.* at 477.

70. In Department of Human Resources of Oregon v. Smith, 485 U.S. 660 (1988)—the first time the case was argued before the Supreme Court, Justice Stevens' majority opinion limited the reach of *Sherbert* by drawing for the first time, a distinction between lawful and unlawful conduct under state law. "If a State has prohibited through its criminal laws certain kinds of religiously motivated conduct without violating the First Amendment, it certainly follows that it may impose the lesser burden of denying unemployment compensation benefits to persons who engage in that conduct." *Id.* at 670. Justice Brennan's dissent viewed the majority's emphasis on illegality as an inappropriate deference to state characterization of the strength of the governmental interest, a defense inconsistent with strict scrutiny cases. The case was remanded to the Oregon Supreme Court for specific consideration of the illegality issue, and that court held that the religious claimants were still entitled to free exercise protection.

71. 494 U.S. at 878–79. *See* chapter 1, *supra.* Scalia, of course, is simply wrong about this. He cites to Frankfurter's opinion in *Gobitis* at 310 U.S. 594–95, but never acknowledges that the opinion was a historical curiosity ever since 1843, when it was specifically overruled in *Barnette.* Even a cursory inquiry into the history and development of the free exercise clause would have shown that the notion of compelling interest had substance; the free exercise exemption doctrine was not a constitutional anomaly but rather was parallel to doctrines under the free speech and press provisions. At most, the Court could have said that there are two constitutional traditions, both with impressive pedigrees. Scalia was guilty, here, of not doing his judicial homework or of not doing it very well or very honestly.

72. *Id.* at 886–87. For an analysis generally supportive of the *Smith* opinion, *see* Marshall, *In Defense of Smith and Free Exercise Revisionism*, 58 U. Chi. L. Rev. 308 (1990) and Sullivan, *Religion and Liberal Democracy*, 59 U. Chi. L. Rev. 195 (1992).

73. "It may fairly be said that leaving accommodation to the political process will place at a relative disadvantage those religious practices that are not widely engaged in; but that unavoidable consequence of democratic government must be preferred to a system in which each conscience is a law unto itself or in which judges weigh the social importance of all laws against the centrality of all religious beliefs." *Id.* at 890. *See also* Scalia, *The Rule of Law as a Law of Rules*, 56 U. Chi. L. Rev. 1175 (1989). *Cf.* McConnell, *Free Exercise Revisionism and the Smith Decision*, 57 U. Chi. L. Rev. 1109 (1990). The McConnell article is one of the most articulate attacks on the illogical and erroneous position taken by Scalia.

74. "Although I agree with the result the Court reaches in this case, I cannot join its opinion. In my view, today's holding dramatically departs from well-settled First Amendment jurisprudence, appears unnecessary to resolve the question presented, and is incompatible with our Nation's fundamental commitment to individual religious liberty." 494 U.S. at 891. O'Connor then continued: "The Court today . . . interprets the [Free Exercise] Clause to permit the government to prohibit, without justification, conduct mandated by an individual's religious beliefs, so long as that prohibition is generally applicable. . . . But a law that prohibits certain conduct—conduct that happens to be an act of worship for someone—manifestly does prohibit that person's free exercise of his religion. A person who is barred from engaging in religiously motivated conduct is barred from freely exercising his religion. Moreover, that person is barred from freely exercising his religion regardless of whether the law prohibits the conduct only when engaged in for religious reasons, only by members of that religion, or by all persons. It is difficult to deny that a law that prohibits religiously motivated conduct, even if the law is generally applicable, does not at least implicate First Amendment concerns." *Id.* at 893–94.

75. *Id.* at 907–08. The dissenters then concluded: "This distorted view of our precedents leads the majority to conclude that strict scrutiny of a state law burdening the free exercise of religion is a 'luxury' that a well-ordered society cannot afford, . . . and that the repression of minority religion is an 'unavoidable consequence of democratic government.' . . . I do not believe the Founders thought their dearly bought freedom from religious persecution a 'luxury,' but an essential element of liberty—and they could not have thought religious intolerance 'unavoidable,' for they drafted the Religion Clauses precisely in order to avoid that intolerance." *Id.* at 908–9. *See* Church of the Lukumi Babalu Aye v. City of Hialeah, 508 U.S. 520 (1993), where the Court struck down, 9-0, the Hialeah, Florida, ordinance prohibiting animal sacrifices for religious purposes on the basis of the Smith two-prong test of neutrality and general applicability.

76. Pub. L. No. 103–141, 107 Stat. 1488 (1993). *See* appendix B, *infra*.

77. S.Rep. No. 111, 103d Cong., 2d Sess. 1892–1912 (1993).

78. Flores v. City of Boerne, 877 F.Supp. 355 (W.D.Tex. 1995). The district court argued that RFRA unconstitutionally changed the burden of proof

established under the *Smith* decision for free exercise cases, and further argued that the First Amendment did not empower Congress to regulate all federal law in order to achieve religious liberty, unless it was done pursuant to an enumerated power. In reaching this conclusion, Judge Bunton—like Justice Scalia in the *Smith* decision—failed to do his judicial homework. He cites to dissenting opinions as though they were the precedent, passes over a contrary ruling by another district court, and takes his conclusion from a single law review article—*i.e.,* Hamilton, *The Religious Freedom Restoration Act: Letting the Fox into the Henhouse Under Cover of Section 5 of the Fourteenth Amendment,* 16 CARDOZO L. REV. 357 (1994). More importantly, he erroneously categorizes the First Amendment as a limitation on Congress, not as a enumerated power. Consequently Katenbach v. Morgan and its progeny are held not to be applicable. *Contra,* Belgard v. State of Hawaii, 883 F.Supp. 510 (D.Haw. 1996). *See* notes 82 and 85, *infra.*

79. Congress, of course, has done this on several specific occasions through the use of constitutional amendments. Chisholm v. Georgia, 2 U.S. (2 Dall.) 419 (1793), holding that citizens of one state could sue in federal courts another state, was reversed by the Eleventh Amendment, guaranteeing sovereign immunity for states from suits by citizens of another state. The Thirteenth a:id Fourteenth Amendments, abolishing slavery and making blacks citizens of the United States, technically overturned the ruling in Dred Scott v. Sanford, 60 U.S. (19 How.) 393 (1857), that blacks were not persons under the Constitution. The Sixteenth Amendment reversed Pollock v. Farmers' Loan & Trust, 157 U.S. 429 (1895), which had invalidated a federal income tax.

80. Flores v. City of Boerne, 73 F.3d 1352 (5th Cir. 1996). The court of appeals in reversing the district court verdict, argued that (1) Congress had authority to enact RFRA under the enforcement clause of the Fourteenth Amendment; (2) Congress' authority under the enforcement clause of the Fourteenth Amendment is not more limited when it acts to enforce provisions other than the equal protection clause; (3) Congress' constitutional power to legislate pursuant to the enforcement clause is tied to its superior ability to find and redress nascent or disguised violations; (4) RFRA, which restored the strict scrutiny standard, does not violate separation of powers even though it imposes a stricter standard than set forth in *Smith*; (5) by enacting RFRA, Congress did not usurp the judiciary's authority to determine when a statute impermissibly burdens a person's free exercise of religion, but rather exercised its remedial power to reach conduct that only threatens free exercise.

81. Katzenbach v. Morgan, 384 U.S. 641, 651 (1966): "[T]he inquiry into what is 'appropriate legislation' under Section 5 is whether the statute may be regarded as an enactment to enforce [the Fourteenth Amendment], whether it is plainly adapted to that end, and whether it is not prohibited by but consistent with the letter and spirit of the Constitution." The same year the Court had held that the Thirteenth, Fifteenth, Eighteenth, Twenty-Third, and Twenty-Fourth (the Twenty-Sixth would be added later) Amendments contained parallel grants of enforcement power to Congress. *See* South Carolina v. Katzenbach, 383 U.S. 301, 326 (1966).

82. The major purpose of the doctrine of separation of powers is main-

taining the constitutional allocation of powers. Consequently, its chief concerns are whether some branch is improperly exercising powers the Constitution has assigned to another branch; whether one branch is improperly inhibiting another branch's legitimate exercise of its powers; and whether one or another branch is improperly aggrandizing power at the expense of another branch.

It is a question of whether the separation of powers doctrine bars corrective legislation. The answer, at least until 1997, seemed to be that it does not. The Voting Rights Act, Pub. L. No. 89–110, 79 Stat. 437 (1965), banned the use of literacy test upheld in Lassiter v. Northampton County, 360 U.S. 45 (1959). The VRA was amended, Pub. L. No. 97–205, 96 Stat. 131 (1982), to ban *de facto* electoral discrimination upheld by the Court in City of Mobile v. Bolden, 446 U.S. 55 (1980). The Privacy Protection Act, Pub. L. No. 96–440, 94 Stat. 1879 (1980), created a new statutory right against searches of newspaper offices for evidence and overturned Zucher v. Stanford Daily, 436 U.S. 547 (1978). G. Goodpaster, CONSTITUTIONAL LAW, sec. 10–6(c) (1990). In handing down its decision in *Flores* (so contrary to its own prior precedent), the Court argued that there was no religious discrimination significant enough to warrant remedial or preventive legislation.

83. 73 F.3d at 1361.

84. City of Boerne v. Flores, 138 L. Ed. 2d 624, 638 (1997).

85. *Id*. at 645.

86. *Ibid*.

87. *Id*. at 646.

88. *Id*. at 648. Kennedy then says: "[T]he Act imposed in every case a least restrictive means requirement—a requirement that was not used in the pre-Smith jurisprudence RFRA purported to codify—which also indicates that the legislation is broader than is appropriate if the goal is to prevent and remedy constitutional violations." *Ibid*.

89. Justices Breyer and Souter also wrote dissenting opinions. Both believe—as does O'Connor—that *Smith* was wrongly decided, and Souter (in addition) believes that Congress has sufficient Fourteenth Amendment enforcement authority to enact RFRA. Of the three dissenters, he alone supported this view.

90. O'Connor, like the majority of the Court, believes Congress does not possess "substantive" power under sec. 5 of the Fourteenth Amendment.

91. 138 L. Ed. 2d at 655.

92. *Ibid*. The major thrust of her dissent can be seen most clearly in the following passage: "I dissent from the Court's disposition of this case. I agree with the Court that the issue before us is whether the Religious Freedom Restoration Act (RFRA) is a proper exercise of Congress' power to enforce sec. 5 of the Fourteenth Amendment. But as a yardstick for measuring the constitutionality of RFRA, the Court uses its holding in . . . Smith, . . . the decision that prompted Congress to enact RFRA as a means of more rigorously enforcing the Free Exercise Clause. I remain of the view that Smith was wrongly decided, and I would use this case to reexamine the Court's holding there. Therefore, I would direct the parties to brief the question whether Smith represents the correct understanding of the Free Exercise Clause and set the case for reargument. If the Court

were to correct the misinterpretation of the Free Exercise Clause set forth in Smith, it would simultaneously put our First Amendment jurisprudence back on course and allay the legitimate concerns of a majority in Congress who believed that Smith improperly restricted religious liberty. We would then be in a position to review RFRA in light of a proper interpretation of the Free Exercise Clause." *Id.* at 654–55.

93. R. Morgan, THE SUPREME COURT AND RELIGION 246 (1972).

94. M. Konvitz, RELIGIOUS LIBERTY AND CONSCIENCE: A CONSTITUTIONAL INQUIRY 99 (1968). Konvitz is convinced, correctly I believe, that religious people do not possess a monopoly on conscience.

95. Quoted in *ibid.*

96. 375 U.S. 14 (1963). On petition for writ of *certiorari* to the Supreme Court of Minnesota, the Court in a *per curiam* decision said: "The judgment is vacated and the case is remanded to the Supreme Court of Minnesota for further consideration in light of Sherbert v. Verner," 265 Minn. 96, 120 N.W.2d 515.

97. 406 U.S. at 315–16.

98. L. Frankel, LAW, POWER AND PERSONAL FREEDOM 340 (1975).

CHAPTER 6. SELECTIVE CONSCIENTIOUS OBJECTION

1. M. Konvitz, RELIGIOUS LIBERTY AND CONSCIENCE: A CONSTITUTIONAL INQUIRY 104 (1968).

2. *Ibid.*

3. 381 U.S. 479 (1965). Here the constitutionality of Connecticut's birth control law was involved. The statute provided that "any person who uses any drug, medical article or instrument for the purpose of preventing conception" was to be subject to fine or imprisonment or both. The statute further specified that a person who assisted another in committing any offense could be prosecuted and punished as if he or she were the principal offender. Estelle Griswold, executive director of the Planned Parenthood League of Connecticut, was convicted of being an accessory. The Supreme Court held, 7-2, the statute unconstitutional.

4. M. Konvitz, *supra* note 1, at 105.

5. From the majority opinion by Justice Douglas, 381 U.S. at 484.

6. M. Konvitz, *supra* note 1, at 103.

7. Finn, *Introduction*, in A CONFLICT OF LOYALTIES: THE CASE FOR SELECTIVE CONSCIENTIOUS OBJECTION vii (J. Finn ed. 1968).

8. *Ibid.*

9. 2 B. Schwartz, A COMMENTARY ON THE CONSTITUTION OF THE UNITED STATES, PART III, RIGHTS OF THE PERSON: EQUALITY, BELIEF, AND DIGNITY 703 (1968).

10. 297 F. Supp. 902 (D.Mass. 1969), *appeal dismissed*, 399 U.S. 267 (1970).

11. 303 F. Supp. 837 (N.D.Cal. 1969). There was no appeal to a higher court.

12. 309 F. Supp. 502 (N.D.Cal. 1970), *aff'd*, 423 F.2d 1291 (9th Cir. 1970). *Contra*, United States v. Bowen, 415 F.2d 1140 (9th Cir. 1969).

13. By crime, Aquinas specifically meant an enemy state's refusal to make amends for injuries done by its people, or to restore anything seized unjustly.

14. For Aquinas, a war declared by legitimate authority for just cause may be unlawful through wicked intentions. These would include a passion for inflicting harm, the cruel thirst for vengeance, and the lust for power. *See generally* J. Tooke, THE JUST WAR IN AQUINAS AND GROTIUS 21–30 (1965) and M. Walzer, JUST AND UNJUST WARS (2d ed. 1992).

15. *Id.* at 195–231.

16. 297 F.Supp. at 908.

17. United States v. Kauton, 133 F.2d 703 (2d Cir. 1943). Judge Augustus Hand, writing for the court of appeals, interpreted "religious training and belief" to have the broadest possible meaning. He said: "Religious belief arises from a sense of the inadequacy of reason as a means of relating the individual to his fellow men and to his universe—a sense common to men in the most primative and in the most highly civilized societies. It accepts the aid of logic but refuses to be limited by it. It is a belief finding expression in a conscience which categorically requires the believer to disregard elementary selfinterest and to accept martyrdom in preference to transgressing its tenets." *Id.* at 708. Judge Hand then went on to say that a conscientious objection to participate in war in any form "may justly be regarded as a response of the individual to an inward mentor, call it conscience or God, that is for many persons at the present time the equivalent of what has always been thought a religious impulse." *Ibid.* Ironically, the defendant in the case did not qualify for the exemption even under this very favorable judicial language.

18. 297 F.Supp. at 911.

19. The grounds for the dissent were two: (1) The evidence adduced at trial can be considered by a district court as the basis for a motion in arrest of judgment when that evidence was used solely for the purpose of testing the constitutionality of the charging statute as applied. (2) Congress did not mean to limit "motion in arest" to its commonlaw meaning. If it had, on the other hand, it must have also believed that decisions such as this one would have been appealable under some other provisions, such as the "motion in bar," as long as there was no danger of encroaching on the defendant's jeopardy interests.

20. 399 U.S. 267 (1970).

21. Captain Sharp reached this conclusion on the basis of reports submitted by a Navy psychiatrist, a J.A.G. officer, and a Navy chaplain. Each suggested that Koster, although sincere in his pacifist beliefs, based his objection to war on grounds other than religious conviction.

22. 303 F.Supp. at 844.

23. The court also held sec. 6(j), and its standard of religious training and belief, violative of the Fifth Amendment's guarantee of due process of law. "[A] standard which exempts a religiously motivated conscientious objector from military service and denies the same relief to a person whose beliefs are just as sincere but which are not motivated by any relationship to any religion is constitutionally defective under the Fifth Amendment's guarantee of due process of law." *Id.* at 845.

24. *Ibid.*, quoting 297 F.Supp. at 911.

25. 309 F.Supp. at 505, note 10.

26. *Id.* at 505–06 (emphasis in the original).

27. *Id.* at 506. "Indeed, the case of defendant McFadden is stronger than Sherbert's, for not only is he faced with jail, but if he abandons his conscience he will be put in the position of possibly violating the fundamental precept of his religious belief—the killing of another human being in the cause of an unjust war." *Ibid.*

28. *Ibid.*

29. "Neither a state nor the Federal Government can set up a church. Neither can pass laws which aid one religion, aid all religions, or prefer one religion over another." Everson v. Board of Education, 330 U.S. 1, 15 (1947). "Government in our democracy, state and national, must be neutral in matters of religious theory, doctrine, and practice. . . . [I]t may not aid, foster, or promote one religion or religious theory against another." Epperson v. Arkansas, 393 U.S. 97, 103–4 (1968). Both quoted in *id.* at 508.

30. *Id.* at 508.

31. *All or Nothing at All: The Defeat of Selective Conscientious Objection,* 1971 SUP. CT. REV. 31, 68.

32. *See* 398 U.S. at 340: "If an individual deeply and sincerely holds beliefs that are purely ethical or moral on source and content but that nevertheless impose upon him a duty of conscience to refrain from participating in any war at any time, those beliefs certainly occupy in the life of that individual 'a place parallel to that filled by . . . God' in traditionally religious persons. Because his beliefs function as a religion in his life, such an individual is as much entitled to a religious conscientious objector exemption under sec. 6(j) as is someone who derives his conscientious opposition to war from traditional religious convictions."

33. Greenawalt, *supra* note 31, at 72.

34. Gillette v. United States, 401 U.S. 437, 450–51 (emphasis in the original).

35. Greenawalt, *supra* note 31, at 69.

36. 401 U.S. at 454.

37. *See* Marshall's argument on "neutrality" at 407 U.S. 453–54.

38. R. Morgan, THE SUPREME COURT AND RELIGION 175 (1972).

39. 401 U.S. at 455.

40. *Ibid.*

41. H. Abraham, FREEDOM AND THE COURT: CIVIL RIGHTS AND LIBERTIES IN THE UNITED STATES 294–95 (5th ed. 1988).

42. 401 U.S. at 460.

43. *Id.* at 461, note 23.

44. *Id.* at 462.

45. *Id.* at 469 (emphasis added).

46. *Id.* at 465–66. "Free expression and the right of personal conscientious belief are closely intertwined. At the core of the First Amendment's protection of individual expression, is the recognition that such expression represents the oral or written manifestation of conscience. The performance of certain acts, under certain circumstances, involves such a crisis of conscience as to invoke the

protection which the First Amendment provides for similar manifestations of conscience when expressed in verbal or written expressions of thought. The most awesome act which any society can demand of a citizen's conscience is the taking of a human life." Redlich & Feinberg, *Individual Conscience and the Selective Conscientious Objector: The Right Not to Kill,* 44 N.Y.U. L. REV. 875, 891 (1969).

47. "Freedom to differ is not limited to things that do not matter much. . . . The test of its substance is the right to differ as to things that touch the heart of the existing order." 319 U.S. at 642, quoted in *id.* at 469–70.

48. "But, in the forum of conscience, duty to a moral power higher than the State has always been maintained. The reservation of that supreme obligation, as a matter of principle, would unquestionably be made by many of our conscientious and law-abiding citizens. The essence of religion is belief in a relation to God involving duties superior to those arising from any human relations." 283 U.S. at 633–34, quoted in *id.* at 468.

49. *Id.* at 469.

50. Greenawalt, *supra* note 31, at 73.

51. *Id.* at 73–74.

52. *See* Marshall's willingness to apply the "strict scrutiny" standard to blacks, women, and the indigent in the *new* equal protection cases, *e.g.,* Levy v. Louisiana, 391 U.S. 68 (1968); Shapiro v. Thompson, 394 U.S. 618 (1969); Dandridge v. Williams, 397 U.S. 471 (1970); San Antonio Independent School District v. Rodriguez, 411 U.S. 1 (1973). But not to a sincere, religiously motivated selective objector!

53. Torcaso v. Watkins, 367 U.S. 488, 490 (1961).

54. 2 B. Schwartz, A COMMENTARY ON THE CONSTITUTION OF THE UNITED STATES, PART III, RIGHTS OF THE PERSON: EQUALITY, BELIEF, AND DIGNITY 703 (1968).

55. Greenawalt, *supra* note 31, at 90.

56. *Id.* at 92, and H. Abraham, *supra* note 41, at 293–94.

57. H. Abraham, *supra* note 41, at 295.

58. *Ibid.*

59. Tigar, *The Rights of Selective Service Registrants,* in THE RIGHTS OF AMERICANS 512 (N. Dorsen ed. 1971). For the best single discussion of the philosophical implications and moral responsibilities involved, *see* C. Cohen, CIVIL DISOBEDIENCE: CONSCIENCE, TACTICS, AND THE LAW (1971).

60. *The Conscientious Objector,* 21 COLUM. U. Q. 253, 269 (Oct. 1919). *See also* and along the same lines, M. Sibley & P. Jacob, CONSCRIPTION OF CONSCIENCE: THE AMERICAN STATE AND THE CONSCIENTIOUS OBJECTOR, 1940–1947 (1952). This volume was once regarded as the definitive work in the field.

61. Tigar, *supra* note 59, at 512.

62. *Ibid.*

63. B. Schwartz, *supra* note 54, at 701. To an extent this problem has never really occurred in the United States since some types of exemption (for some sects) have usually been allowed.

64. Tigar, *supra* note 59, at 513.

65. *Ibid.*

66. Sibley, *Dissent: The Tradition and its Implications,* in A CONFLICT OF LOYALTIES: THE CASE FOR SELECTIVE CONSCIENTIOUS OBJECTION 133–36 (J. Finn ed. 1971).

67. *Id.* at 134. Regarding the dissenter and his personal integrity, Sibley writes: "When Eugene V. Debs goes to prison for denouncing World War I, we need not defend him solely in terms of his social role; we can also suggest—as many did indeed suggest—that there is something of the good, the true, and the beautiful in his act. When the selective conscientious objector resists the draft and formulates his reasons for doing so, he is fulfilling a duty to himself and whatever his social service may be, he is justified in his objection." *Id.* at 135.

68. *Ibid.*

69. Quoted in Harrington, POLITICS, MORALITY, AND SELECTIVE DISSENT, in J. Finn, *supra* note 66, at 224.

70. O'Brien, THE NUREMBERG PRINCIPLES, in *id.* at 184.

CHAPTER 7. ARE STANDARDS OF ADJUDICATION POSSIBLE?

1. C. Pritchett, THE ROOSEVELT COURT: A STUDY IN JUDICIAL POLITICS AND VALUES, 1937–1947 at 14 (1948).

2. E. Corwin, THE CONSTITUTION AND WHAT IT MEANS TODAY 260–61 (12th ed. 1958).

3. A. Meiklejohn, POLITICAL FREEDOM: CONSTITUTIONAL POWERS OF THE PEOPLE 20 (1965). This so-called "literal meaning of words" test is not really as absolute as it seems. According to Thomas I. Emerson, the test actually involves two components: (1) "It insists on focusing the inquiry upon the definition of 'abridge,' 'freedom of speech,' and if necessary 'law,' rather than on a general de novo balancing of interests in each case." (2) "It is intended to bring a broader area of expression within the protection of the First Amendment than the other tests do. It does this by including a wider sector of governmental activity within the definition of 'abridge,' a more extensive area of governmental activity within 'the freedom of speech,' and at times a broader notion of state action within the term 'law.'" T. Emerson, TOWARD A GENERAL THEORY OF THE FIRST AMENDMENT 57 (1966).

4. P. Kauper, FRONTIERS OF CONSTITUTIONAL LIBERTY 110 (1956).

5. *Id.* at 100.

6. E. Bodenheimer, JURISPRUDENCE: THE PHILOSOPHY AND METHOD OF THE LAW 339 (1962) (emphasis added).

7. *Ibid.*

8. M. Rumelin, THE JURISPRUDENCE OF INTERESTS 14 (1948).

9. "Law falls in behind the advance of ethical reflection, attempting to make unanimous in behavior what ethical sense has made almost unanimous in motive, and in so doing (a) to make the motivation itself more clearly unanimous, and (b) to transfer the released ethical energy to a new level of issues, which in turn will eventually become material for new law. Law is the great civilizing agency it is, not because it throws conduct into artificial uniformity and order, but because it is a working partner with the advancing ethical sense of the

community." 2 Hocking, *Ways of Thinking About Rights: A New Theory of the Relation Between Law and Morals,* in LAW: A CENTURY OF PROGRESS 258 (W. Hocking ed. 1937).

10. P. Freund, THE SUPREME COURT OF THE UNITED STATES: ITS BUSINESS, PURPOSES, AND PERFORMANCE 86–87 (1961).

11. P. Kauper, *supra* note 4, at 111–12.

12. George D. Braden defines objectivity as that "quality of a rule of law which enables it to be applied to similar situations with similar results regardless of the identity of the judges who apply it." For the purposes of this study, I accept the above as a workable definition. *The Search for Objectivity in Constitutional Law,* 57 YALE L. J. 571, note 5 (1948).

13. B. Cardozo, THE NATURE OF THE JUDICIAL PROCESS 13 (1921).

14. Braden, *supra* note 12, at 579–80.

15. *Id.* at 579.

16. *Id.* at 588.

17. *Id.* at 594.

18. A. Mason, THE SUPREME COURT FROM TAFT TO WARREN 281 (1968).

19. Braden, *supra* note 12, at 578–80.

20. *Id.* at 579.

21. *Id.* at 580.

22. Concurring opinion in Pennekamp v. Florida, 328 U.S. 331, 334 (1946).

23. The quoted material in the text comes from T. Emerson, THE SYSTEM OF FREEDOM OF EXPRESSION 6–7 (1970). *See also* his earlier work on the topic, listed in note 3, *supra,* and originally published in 72 YALE L. J. 877 (1963).

24. A. Mason, *supra* note 18, at 282.

25. "The Court's power has been exercised differently at different times: sometimes with reckless and doctrinaire enthusiasm; sometimes with great deference to the status and responsibilities of other branches of government; sometimes with a degree of weakness and timidity that comes close to the betrayal of trust. But the power exists, as an integral part of the process of American government. The Court has the duty of interpreting the Constitution in many of its most important aspects, and especially in those which concern the relation of the individual and the state. The political proposition underlying the survival of the power is that *there are some phases of American life which should be beyond the reach of any majority, save by constitutional amendment.*" E. Rostow, THE SUPREME PREROGATIVE: THE SUPREME COURT AND THE QUEST FOR LAW 151–52 (1962).

26. *Id.* at 177.

27. *Id.* at 178.

28. *Id.* at 191.

29. R. Morgan, THE SUPREME COURT AND RELIGION 201 (1972).

30. Kurland, *Of Church and State and the Supreme Court,* 29 U. CHI. L. REV. 1 (1961) and RELIGION AND THE LAW (1962). If the basis for the secular regulation (and the subsequent classification) is not religion—thus neutralizing the First Amendment—the government may enact its legislation and the free exercise clause is not taken into account. Regarding the neutrality point,

Kurland says: "The utilization or application of these clauses in conjunction is difficult. For if the command is that inhibitions not be placed by the state on religious activity, it is equally forbidden that the state confer favors upon religious activity. These commands would be impossible of effectuation unless they are read together as creating a doctrine more akin to the reading of the equal protection clause, *i.e.*, they must be read to mean that religion may not be used as a basis for classification for purposes of governmental action, whether that action be the conferring of rights or privileges or the imposition of obligations." *Id.* at 5. Under this proposal religion will not be taken into account when government acts to secure its valid secular objective. And only when legislation actually classifies "in terms of religion," *i.e.*, aimed specifically at a religious belief, will the First Amendment prohibition begin to operate.

31. Mansfield, *Conscientious Objection—1964 Term*, 1965 RELIGION & THE PUB. ORD. 3. "A religious belief is . . . the affirmation of some truth, reality or value. [I]t addresses . . . the . . . questions to which man has always sought an answer, . . . the meaning of human existence, the origin of being, the meaning of suffering and death, and the existence of a spiritual reality." *Id.* at 10. Mansfield's subject-matter approach suggests, in defining the type of belief protected by the free exercise clause, that a basic distinction can be made between belief itself and the so-called psychological role it plays for the believer; and that only the former is subject to protection. At the same time his definition is so open-ended and general that any belief that "is right" seems to qualify. This approach—to borrow the notion of Marshall's majority opinion in *Gillette*— believes it proper for government to practice a *de facto* discrimination in favor of the familiar over the novel.

32. Giannella, *Religious Liberty, Non-Establishment, and Doctrinal Development: Part I. The Religious Liberty Guaranty*, 80 HARV. L. REV. 1381 (1967). Giannella's free exercise balancing test reads as follows: "A thoroughgoing balancing test would measure three elements of the competing governmental interest: first, the importance of the secular value underlying the governmental regulation; second, the degree of proximity and necessity that the chosen regulatory means bears to the underlying value; and third, the impact that an exemption for religious reasons would have on the overall regulatory program. This assessment of the state's interest would then have to be balanced against the claim for religious liberty, which would require calculation of two factors: first, the sincerity and importance of the religious practice for which special protection is claimed; and second, the degree to which the governmental regulation interferes with that practice." *Id.* at 1390. The test boils down to the following: religious claims can exempt individuals from certain health, welfare, and safety ordinances, but no free exercise claim can prevent the imposition of society's moral judgments. What Giannella does not specify, however, is how are individuals (as well as judges) to distinguish with any degree of certainty between the two?

33. M. Konvitz, RELIGIOUS LIBERTY AND CONSCIENCE: A CONSTITUTIONAL INQUIRY (1968). "Since every man, believer or nonbeliever, is made in the image of God, every man has human dignity, and a conscience that purports to him, rightly or wrongly, to be the voice of God. This at least is how the believer reads the facts. Everyone, therefore, believer or nonbeliever, has a conscience that has

the power to impose on him duties 'superior to those arising from any human relation.' He owes supreme allegiance to the commands of his conscience. It is not, therefore, a question of 'religion' or 'religious belief' or belief in any relation to a Supreme Being or God. It is entirely a matter of human dignity and conscience. A believer, then, must affirm of his nonbelieving neighbor that he, too, is made in the image of God, and that he, too, has a conscience, which has its rights and duties." *Id.* at 102–3. Konvitz later concludes that "if the religious person believes that religion is always rooted in conscience, it is conscience that is primary and religion that is derivative." *Id.* at 104. In effect, *conscience must be protected,* for without it religion could not exist.

34. Clark, *Guidelines for the Free Exercise Clause,* 83 HARV. L. REV. 327 (1969).

35. S. Shapiro, *Toward a Uniform Valuation of the Religion Guaranties,* 80 YALE L. J. 77 (1970).

36. When the situation warrants the Court may be forced to reverse the presumption of constitutionality concept, forcing governments to supply the overwhelming burden of proof for the validity of an enactment. Presumptions are reversed upon a proper showing in all other fields of law. "Working lawyers are very familiar with the shifting of presumptions to fit the case as it develops; it is something they borrowed from common sense. It is the general rule that the ship carrying goods by sea must pay for the damage if the goods are received in good condition and delivered in bad condition; once these two things are shown, a presumption arises that the ship is liable. But another rule says that the ship is not liable for damage by fire, unless caused by actual fault of the shipowner; if the ship's lawyers can show that the bad condition of the goods resulted from fire, then the presumption shifts, and the ship is presumed *not* liable until the requisite fault is shown." C. Black, THE PEOPLE AND THE COURT: JUDICIAL REVIEW IN A DEMOCRACY 217 (1960) (emphasis in the original).

37. S. Shapiro, *supra* note 35, at 99–100.

38. *See, e g.,* Harden v. State, 188 Tenn. 17, 216 S.W.2d 708 (1948); State v. Massey, 229 N.C. 734, 51 S.E.2d 179 (1949), appeal dismissed *sub nom.* Bunn v. North Carolina, 336 U.S. 942 (1949); Hill v. State, 38 Ala. App. 404, 88 So.2d 880 (1956).

39. Clark, *supra* note 34, at 345.

40. *Id.* at 342.

41. S. Shapiro, *supra* note 35, at 98.

42. *Id.* at 99.

43. *Id.* at 100 (emphasis in the original).

44. *Id.* at 100–101.

45. Sherbert v. Verner, 374 U.S. 398, 407 (1963). *See also* Warren's use of the test in Braunfeld v. Brown, 366 U.S. 599, 607 (1961): "But if the state regulates conduct by enacting a general law within its power, the purpose and effect of which is to advance the state's secular goals, the statute is valid despite the indirect burden on religious observance unless the state may acomplish its purpose by means which do not impose such burdens." *See* chapter 5, *supra,* for a discussion of the incorrect application of the test by the Chief Justice.

46. McGowan v. Maryland, 366 U.S. 420, 466–67 (1961).

47. People v. Woody, 394 P.2d 813, 819 (1964). One cannot help but wonder why the *Woody* decision, and the logic sustaining it, was never considered by Scalia's majority opinion in *Smith*. Fortunately, Congress did pass the Religious Freedom Restoration Act of 1993, 107 Stat. 1488. Unfortunately, on the other hand, *Smith* has been restored by the *Flores* decision.

48. From the concurring opinion by Justices Black, Douglas, Murphy, and Rutledge in United States v. C.I.O., 335 U.S. 106, 140 (1947).

49. Wormuth & Mirkin, *The Doctrine of the Reasonable Alternative*, 9 UTAH L. REV. 254, 301 (1964). *See also* a similar analysis by M. Shapiro, FREEDOM OF SPEECH: THE SUPREME COURT AND JUDICIAL REVIEW (1966) and Note, *A Braunfeld v. Brown Test for Indirect Burdens on the Free Exercise of Religion*, 48 MINN. L. REV. 1166 (1964).

50. The alternative means rule accomplishes two things: the individual (rather than the state) becomes the prime beneficiary of the test because the balance struck is narrowed considerably. S. Krislov, THE SUPREME COURT AND POLITICAL FREEDOM 125 (1968). Moreover, the individual "need not so much show that his interests outweigh all conceivable governmental concern with the subject, but only its concern expressed in this unique way, with all the weaknesses of the specified regulation. At its most favorable, then, the device clearly protects rights and virtually reverses the presumption of constitutionality by requiring a showing that there was no other way to achieve the governmental purpose." *Id*. at 125–26.

51. Thomas v. Collins, 323 U.S. 516, 529–30 (1945).

CONCLUSION

1. P. Kauper, FRONTIERS OF CONSTITUTIONAL LIBERTY 112 (1956).

2. *Ibid*.

3. G. Sartori, DEMOCRATIC LIBERTY 99 (1965).

4. J. Mill, ON LIBERTY 4 (Oxford ed. 1947).

5. THE SUPREME PREROGATIVE: THE SUPREME COURT AND THE QUEST FOR LAW 53 (1962).

6. *Id*. at 79, 128.

7. L. Fuller, THE MORALITY OF LAW 18–19 (1963).

8. G. Sartori, *supra* note 3, at 281 (emphasis in the original).

9. E. Bodenheimer, JURISPRUDENCE: THE PHILOSOPHY AND METHOD OF THE LAW 193 (1962). The "what ought to be" recognizes the need for change, and the reform suggested is utopian—logically feasible but not politically (or judicially) acceptable. The "what is" recognizes the perfection of the system or acknowledges that the problem is inevitable and immune to change. The difficulty, of course, is agreeing on "what can be."

10. "The truly great systems of law are those which are characterized by a peculiar and paradoxical blending of rigidity and elasticity. In their principles, institutions, and techniques they combine the virtue of stable continuity with the advantages of evolutionary change, thereby attaining the capacity for longevity and survival under adverse conditions." *Id*. at 266.

11. *Id.* at 340.

12. *Id.* at 296–303.

13. The *Lyng*, *Smith*, and *Flores* decisions, on the other hand, seem to suggest a return to the approach prevalent before footnote four and *Murdock*—i.e., a judicial discernment of value patterns applied *praeter legem*.

14. E. Bodenheimer, *supra* note 9, at 303.

15. Quoted in G. Allport, THE INDIVIDUAL AND HIS RELIGION 140 (1959).

16. P. Kauper, *supra* note 1, at 111–12 (emphasis added).

17. J. Stone, THE PROVINCE AND FUNCTION OF LAW: LAW AS LOGIC, JUSTICE, AND SOCIAL CONTROL 519 (1950).

18. *Introduction,* in RELIGION FROM TOLSTOY TO CAMUS 44 (W. Kaufman ed. 1961).

19. Quoted in *id.* at 41.

20. *Ibid.*

21. "I know of no modern instance in which any judiciary has saved a whole people from the great currents of intolerance, passion, usurpation, and tyranny which have threatened liberty and free institutions. The Dred Scott decision did not settle the question of the power to end slavery, and I very much doubt that had Mr. Justice McLean not dissented in that case it would have done any more to avoid war. No court can support a reactionary regime and no court can innovate or implement a new one. I doubt that any court, whatever its powers, could have saved Louis XVI or Marie Antoinette. None could have avoided the French Revolution, none could have prevented its culmination in the dictatorship of Napoleon. In Germany a courageous court refused to convict those whom the Nazi government sought to make the scapegoats for the Reichstag fire, clandestinely set by the Nazis themselves, and other courts decreed both the Nazi and Communist parties to be illegal under German law. Those judgments fell on deaf ears and became dead letters because the political forces at the time were against them." R. Jackson, *The Supreme Court in the American System of Government* 80–81 (1955).

22. G. Allport, *supra* note 15, at 142.

APPENDIX A

1. Calder v. Bull, 3 U.S. (3 Dall.) 386 (1798).

2. Hylton v. United States, 3 U.S. (3 Dall.) 171 (1796). The Supreme Court overruled this decision in Pollock v. Farmers Loan & Trust Co., 158 U.S. 601 (1895), thus precipitating the Sixteenth Amendment.

3. A. Sutherland, CONSTITUTIONALISM IN AMERICA: ORIGIN AND EVOLUTION OF ITS FUNDAMENTAL IDEAS 241 (1965).

4. *Ibid.*

5. Palko v. Connecticut, 302 U.S. 319 (1937).

6. *Id.* at 326–27.

7. 304 U.S. 144 (1938).

8. S. Krislov, THE SUPREME COURT AND THE POLITICAL PROCESS 114 (1965).

9. 304 U.S. at 152–53, note 4. *See* Braden, *The Search for Objectivity in Constitutional Law*, 57 YALE L. J. 571 (1948) and Lusky, *Minority Rights and the Public Interest*, 52 YALE L. J. 1 (1942), for an analysis of the footnote and additional confusion over the first paragraph's disputed authorship. *Cf.* L. Lusky, By What Rights? A Commentary on the Supreme Court's Power to Revise the Constitution (1975). Almost four decades after he "wrote" paragraph one of footnote four, Lusky modified his view.

10. S. Krislov, *supra* note 8, at 114–16.

11. *See* A. Mason, Harlan Fiske Stone: Pillar of the Law 514–15 (1956).

12. Stone was not invoking a presumption of unconstitutionality of legislation that interferred with the First Amendment's freedoms. All that he meant, contrary to Frankfurter's later interpretation in Kovacs v. Cooper, 336 U.S. 77, 91–97 (1949), was that legislation that interferred with the First Amendment should be subjected to "more searching judicial scrutiny" than that regulating ordinary commercial relations. On this particular point he said no more until his *Gobitis* dissent.

13. H. Abraham, Freedom and the Court: Civil Rights and Liberties in the United States 22 (5th ed. 1988).

14. Braden, *supra* note 9, at 580–82. Stone's written note to Chief Justice Hughes explained this new constitutional atitude and the reasons for relegating it into a footnote: "I wish to avoid the possibility of having what I have written in the body of the opinion about the presumption of constitutionality in the ordinary run of due process cases applied as a matter of course in these other more exceptional cases. For that reason it seemed to me desirable to file a caveat in the note—without, however, committing the Court to any proposition contained in it. The notion that the Court should be more alert to protect constitutional rights in those cases where there is danger that the ordinary political processes for the correction of undesirable legislation may not operate has been announced for the Court by many judges, notably Chief Justice Marshall in McCulloch v. Maryland, with reference to taxation of governmental instrumentalities." Note dated Apr. 19, 1938, and quoted in A. Mason, *supra* note 11, at 514.

15. United States v. Butler, 297 U.S. 1 (1936).

16. Minersville School District v. Gobitis, 310 U.S. 586 (1940).

17. Jones v. City of Opelika, 316 U.S. 584 (1942).

18. Marsh v. Alabama, 326 U.S. 517 (1946).

19. Tucker v. Texas, 326 U.S. 517 (1946).

20. Girouard v. United States, 328 U.S. 61 (1946).

21. Hand, *Chief Justice Stone's Conception of the Judicial Function*, 46 COLUM. L. REV. 696, 698–99 (1946).

22. A. Mason, *supra* note 11, at 513.

23. Wechsler, Mr. Justice Stone and the Constitution, in Principles, Politics, and Fundamental Law 138 (H. Wechsler ed. 1961). This essay originally appeared in 46 COLUM. L. REV. 764 (1946).

24. Braden, *supra* note 9, at 580–81.

25. H. Stone, *The Common Law of the United States*, 50 HARV. L. REV. 4, 25 (1936).

TABLE OF CASES

The cases listed here constitute the bulk of the free exercise litigation applicable to belief, worship, and proselytizing. Only the cases that appear in *italics*, however, are discussed in the pages and notes of this volume.

BIBLIOGRAPHY

GOVERNMENT DOCUMENTS

U.S. Congress, *Annals of Congress*, 1st Cong., 1st–3d Sess., 1834.

————, Hearings before the House Armed Services Committee, *Extension of the Universal and Training Act* , 90th Cong., 1st Sess., 1967.

U.S. Senate, Hearings before the Committee on Education and Labor pursuant to S.Res. 266, *Violations of Free Speech and Rights of Labor*, 74th Cong., 2d Sess. 1937.

————, Hearings before the Committee on the Judiciary, *Limitations of Appellate Jurisdiction of the United States Supreme Court* , 85th Cong., 2d Sess., 1958.

————, Hearings before the Subcommittee of the Committee on the Judiciary, *Reorganization of the Federal Judiciary*, 75th Cong., 1st Sess., 1937.

————, S.Rep. No. 111, 103d Cong., 1st Sess., 1892–1912 (1993).

Selective Service System, *Background of Selective Service*, Special Monograph No. 1.

————, *Criteria for Classification of Conscientious Objectors*, 1972.

PRIMARY SOURCES

J. Elliott, *Debates in the Several State Conventions on the Adoption of the Federal Convention* (5 vols., Elliott ed. 1881).

M. Farrand, *The Records of the Federal Convention of 1787* (4 vols., 3d ed. 1966).

A. Hamilton, et al., *The Federalist: A Commentary on the Constitution of the United States* (Rossiter ed. 1961).

F. Thorpe, *American Charters, Constitutions and Organic Laws, 1492–1908* (7 vols., Thorp ed. 1909).

SECONDARY SOURCES

H. Abraham, *Freedom and the Court: Civil Rights and Liberties in the United States* (5th ed. 1988).

————, *The Judicial Process* (6th ed. 1992).

G. Allport, *The Individual and His Religion* (1959).

R. Berger, *Congress v. the Supreme Court* (1969).

I. Berlin, *Four Essays on Liberty* (1969)

A. Bickel, *The Supreme Court and the Idea of Progress* (1970).

C. Black, *The People and the Court: Judicial Review in a Democracy* (1960).

E. Bodenheimer, *Jurisprudence: The Philosophy and Method of the Law* (1962).

I. Brant, *The Bill of Rights: Its Origin and Meaning* (1965).

E. Cahn, *Supreme Court and Supreme Law* (E. Cahn ed. 1954).

———, *The Great Rights* (Cahn ed. 1963).

———, *The Sense of Injustice* (1949).

B. Cardozo, *The Nature of the Judicial Process* (1921).

Z. Chafee, *Free Speech in the United States* (1941).

C. Cohn, *Communism, Fascism and Democracy* (1962).

H. Commager, *Majority Rule and Minority Rights* (1943).

E. Corwin, *The Constitution and What It Means Today* (8th and 12th eds. 1946, 1958).

———, *The Constitution of the United States of America: Analysis and Interpretation* (1964).

A. Cox, *The Warren Court: Constitutional Decision as an Instrument of Reform* (1968).

W. Crosskey, *Politics and the Constitution in the History of the United States* (3 vols. 1953).

P. Devlin, *The Enforcement of Morals* (1959).

N. Dorsen, *The Rights of Americans* (Dorsen ed. 1971).

N. Dowling & G. Gunther, *Individual Rights in Constitutional Law* (8th ed. 1970).

T. Emerson, *The System of Freedom of Expression* (1970).

———, *Toward a General Theory of the First Amendment* (1963).

J. Finn, *A Conflict of Loyalties: The Case for Selective Conscientious Objection* (J. Finn, ed. 1968).

———, *Protest: Pacifism and Politics* (1967).

D. Ford, *New England's Struggles for Religious Freedom* (1896).

L. Frankel, *Law, Power and Personal Freedom* (1975).

P. Freund, *The Supreme Court of the United States: Its Business, Purposes, and Performance* (1961).

L. Fuller, *The Morality of Law* (1964).

H. Hart, *Law, Liberty and Morality* (1963).

R. Hirschfield, *The Constitution and the Court: The Development of the Basic Law Through Judicial Interpretation* (1962).

R. Jackson, *The Supreme Court in the American System of Government* (1955).

W. James, *Varieties of Religious Experience* (1902).

W. Kaufman, *Religion from Tolstoy to Camus* (Kaufman ed. 1961).

P. Kauper, *Frontiers of Constitutional Liberty* (1956).

———, *Religion and the Constitution* (1964).

M. Konvitz, *Fundamental Liberties of a Free People: Religion, Speech, Press, Assembly* (1957).

———, *Religious Liberty and Conscience: A Constitutional Inquiry* (1968).

S. Krislov, *The Supreme Court and Political Freedom* (1968).

———, *The Supreme Court in the Political Process* (1965).

P. Kurland, *Religion and the Law* (1962).

L. Levy, *Judgments: Essays on American Constitutional History* (1972).

L. Lusky, *By What Right? A Commentary on the Supreme Court's Power to Revise the Constitution* (1975).

D. Manwaring, *Render unto Caesar: The Flag-Salute Controversy* (1962).

A. Mason, *Harlen Fiske Stone: Pillar of the Law* (1956).

———, *The Supreme Court from Taft to Warren* (1968).

A. Meiklejohn, *Political Freedom: The Constitutional Powers of the People* (1965).

R. Morgan, *The Supreme Court and Religion* (1972).

A. Nevins, *The American States During and After the Revolution, 1775–1789* (1924).

R. Niebuhr, *Christian Realism and Political Problems* (1953).

F. O'Brien, *Justice Reed and the First Amendment: The Religion Clauses* (1958).

L. Pfeffer, *Church, State and Freedom* (1953).

T. Powell, *Vagaries and Varieties in Constitutional Interpretation* (1956).

C. Pritchett, *Civil Liberties and the Vinson Court* (1954).

———, *The Roosevelt Court: A Study in Judicial Politics and Values, 1937–1947* (1948).

N. Reimer, *The Revival of Democratic Theory* (1962).

F. Rodell, *Nine Men: A Political History of the Supreme Court from 1789 to 1955* (1955).

E. Rostow, *The Sovereign Prerogative: The Supreme Court and the Quest for Law* (1962).

M. Rumlin, *The Jurisprudence of Interests* (1948).

G. Sartori, *Democratic Theory* (1965).

G. Schubert, *Dispassionate Justice: A Synthesis of the Judicial Opinions of Robert H. Jackson* (1969).

B. Schwartz, *A Commentary on the Constitution of the United States: Rights of the Person* (2 vols. 1968).

M. Shapiro, *Freedom of Speech: The Supreme Court and Judicial Review* (1966).

M. Sibley & P. Jacob, *Conscription of Conscience: The American State and the Conscientious Objector, 1940–1947* (1952).

E. Smith, *Religious Liberty in the United States: The Development of Church-State Thought Since the Revolutionary Era* (1972).

G. Spicer, *The Supreme Court and Fundamental Freedoms* (2d ed. 1967).

M. Stedman, *Religion and Politics in America* (1964).

A. Stokes, *Church and State in the United States* (3 vols. 1950).

J. Stone, *The Province and Function of Law: Law as Logic, Justice, and Social Control* (1950).

J. Story, *Commentaries on the Constitution of the United States* (2 vols., Bigelow ed. 1891).

A. Sutherland, *Constitutionalism in America: Origin and Evolution of its Fundamental Ideas* (1965).

J. Tooke, *The Just War in Aquinas and Grotius* (1965).

W. Torpey, *Judicial Doctrines of Religious Rights in America* (1948).

M. Walzer, *Just and Unjust Wars* (2d ed. 1992).

C. Warren, *Congress, Court and Constitution* (1925).

——, *The Making of the Constitution* (1937).

H. Wechsler, *Principles, Politics, and Fundamental Law* (Wechsler ed. 1961).

LEGAL ARTICLES

Adams & Gordon, *The Doctrine of Accommodation in the Jurisprudence of the Religion Clauses*, 37 DePAUL L. REV. 317 (1988).

Adams & Hanlon, *Jones v. Wolf: Church Autonomy and the Religion Clauses of the First Amendment*, 128 U. PA. L. REV. 1291 (1980).

Barber, *Religious Liberty v. Police Power: Jehovah's Witnesses*, 41 AMER. POL. SCI. REV. 226 (1947).

Barnette, *Constitutional Interpretation and Judicial Self-Restraint*, 39 MICH. L. REV. 213 (1940).

——, *Mr. Justice Murphy, Civil Liberties, and the Holmes Tradition*, 32 CORNELL L. Q. 177 (1946).

Bernard, *Avoidance of Constitutional Issues in the United States Supreme Court: Liberties of the First Amendment*, 50 MICH. L. REV. 261 (1951).

H. L. Black, *The Bill of Rights*, 35 N.Y.U. L. REV. 865 (1960).

Boudin, *Freedom of Thought and Religious Liberty Under the Constitution*, 4 LAW. GUILD REV. 9 (1944).

Bowser, *Delimiting Religion in the Constitution: A Classification Problem*, 11 VAL. U. L. REV. 163 (1977)

Boyan, *Defining Religion in Operational and Institutional Terms*, 116 U. PA. L. REV. 479 (1968).

Braden, *The Search for Objectivity in Constitutional Law*, 57 YALE L.J. 571 (1948).

Chafee, *Do Judges Make or Discover Law?* 35 A.B.A.J. 8 (1947).

Choper, *Defining Religion in the First Amendment*, 1982 U. ILL. L. REV. 579.

Clark, *Guidelines for the Free Exercise Clause*, 83 HARV. L. REV. 327 (1969).

Corwin, *The Establishment of Judicial Review*, 9 MICH. L. REV. 102 (1909).

——, *The Higher Law Background of American Constitutional Law*, 42 HARV. L. REV. 365 (1928).

Crosskey, *Charles Fairman, Legislative History, and the Constitutional Limitations on State Authority*, 22 U. CHI. L. REV. 1 (1954).

Delgardo, *When Religious Exercise Is Not Free: Deprogramming and the Constitutional Status of Coercively Induced Religious Belief*, 37 VAND. L. REV. 1071 (1984).

Dodge, *The Free Exercise of Religion: A Sociological Approach*, 67 MICH. L. REV. 679 (1969).

Douglas, *On Misconception of the Judicial Function and Responsibiity*, 59 COLUM. L. REV. 227 (1959).

Epstein, *Unconstitutional Conditions, State Power, and the Limits of Consent*, 102 HARV. L. REV. 4 (1988).

Fairman, *The Supreme Court and the Constitutional Limitations on State Authority*, 21 U. CHI. L. REV. 40 (1953).

Fennel, *The Reconstructed Court and Religious Freedom: The Gobitis Case* in Retrospect, 19 N.Y.U. L. REV. 31 (1941).

Fernandez, *The Free Exercise of Religion*, 36 S. CAL. L. REV. 546 (1963).

Frank, *Justice Murphy: The Goals Attempted*, 59 YALE L.J. 1 (1949).

Frantz, *The First Amendment in the Balance*, 71 YALE L.J. 1424 (1962).

Freed & Polsby, *Race, Religion, and Public Policy: Bob Jones University v. United States*, 1983 SUP. CT. REV. 1.

Freeman, *The Misguided Search for the Constitutional Definition of Religion*, 71 GEO. L.J. 1519 (1983).

Freund, *The Supreme Court and Civil Liberties*, 4 VAND. L. REV. 533 (1951).

Fried, *Two Concepts of Interests: Some Reflections on the Supreme Court's Balancing Test*, 76 HARV. L. REV. 755 (1963).

Fuller, *Freedom—A Suggested Analysis*, 68 HARV. L. REV. 1305 (1955).

Galanter, *Religious Freedoms in the United States: A Turning Point?* 1966 WISC. L. REV. 217.

Garvey, *A Comment on Religious Convictions and Lawmaking*, 84 MICH. L. REV. 1288 (1986).

——, *Freedom and Equality in the Religion Clauses*, 1981 SUP. CT. REV. 193.

Giannella, *Religious Liberty, Non-Establishment, and Doctrinal Development: Part I. The Religious Liberty Guaranty*, 80 HARV. L. REV. 1381 (1967).

Green, *Book Review*, 32 CALIF. L. REV. 111 (1944).

——, *The Bill of Rights, the Fourteenth Amendment, and the Supreme Court*, 46 MICH. L. REV. 869 (1948).

Greenawalt, *All or Nothing at All: The Defeat of Selective Conscientious Objection*, 1971 SUP. CT. REV. 31.

——, *Book Review*, 70 COLUM. L. REV. 1133 (1970).

——, *Religion as a Concept in Constitutional Law*, 72 CALIF. L. REV. 53 (1984).

Hand, *Chief Justice Stone's Conception of the Judicial Function*, 46 COLUM. L. REV. 696 (1946).

Hart, *Positivism and the Separation of Law and Morals*, 71 HARV. L. REV. 593 (1958).

Hollingsworth, *Constitutional Religious Protection: Antiquated Oddity or Vital Reality?* 34 OHIO ST. L.J. 15 (1973).

Johnson, *Concepts and Compromise in First Amendment Religious Doctrine*, 72 CALIF. L. REV. 817 (1984).

Katz, *Freedom of Religion and State Authority*, 20 U. CHI. L. REV. 426 (1953).

Killilea, *Standards for Expanding Freedom of Conscience*, 34 U. PITT. L. REV. 531 (1973).

Kurland, *Of Church and State and the Supreme Court*, 29 U. CHI. L. REV. 1 (1961).

Lacock, *Towards a General Theory of the Religion Clauses: The Case of Church Labor Relations and the Right to Church Autonomy*, 81 COLO. L. REV. 1373 (1981).

Lacock & Waelbroeck, *Academic Freedom and the Free Exercise of Religion*, 66 TEX. L. REV. 1455 (1988).

Lupu, *Where Rights Begin: The Problem of Burdens on the Free Exercise of Religion*, 102 HARV. L. REV. 933 (1988).

McConnell, *Accommodation of Religion*, 1985 SUP. CT. REV. 1.

———, *Free Exercise Revisionism and the Smith Decision*, 57 U. CHI. L. REV. 1109 (1990).

———, *Neutrality Under the Religion Clauses*, 81 NW. U. L. REV. 168 (1986).

———, *The Origins and Historical Understanding of Free Exercise of Religion*, 103 HARV. L. REV. 1409 (1990).

McWhinney, *The Supreme Court and the Dilemma of Judicial Policy-Making*, 39 MINN. L. REV. 837 (1958).

Mansfield, *Conscientious Objection—1964 Term*, 1965 REL. & PUB. ORD. 3.

———, *The Religion Clauses of the First Amendment and the Philosophy of the Constitution*, 72 CALIF. L. REV. 847 (1984).

Marcus, *Applying Standards Under the Free Exercise Clause*, 1973 DUKE L.J. 1217.

Marshall, *In Defense of Smith and Free Exercise Revisionism*, 58 U. CHI. L. REV. 308 (1990).

Meikeljohn, *What Does the First Amendment Mean?* 20 U. CHI. L. REV. 461 (1953).

Mendelson, *On the Meaning of the First Amendment: Absolutes in the Balance*, 50 CALIF. L. REV. 821 (1962).

———, *Mr. Justice Rutledge's Mark upon the Bill of Rights*, 50 COLUM. L. REV. 48 (1950).

Merel, *The Protection of Individual Choice: A Consistent Understanding of Religion Under the First Amendment*, 45 U. CHI. L. REV. 805 (1978).

Miller, *A Critique of the Reynolds Decision*, 11 W. ST. U. L. REV. 165 (1984).

Miller & Howell, *The Myth of Neutrality in Constitutional Adjudication*, 27 U. CHI. L. REV. 666 (1960).

Noone, *Rendering unto Caesar: Legal Responses to Religious Nonconformity in the Armed Forces*, 18 ST. MARY'S L. REV. 1233 (1987).

Pound, *A Survey of Social Interests*, 57 HARV. L. REV. 1 (1943).

Rabin, *When Is a Religious Belief Religious? United States v. Seeger and the Scope of Free Exercise*, 51 CORNELL L.Q. 231 (1966).

Redlich & Feinberg, *Individual Conscience and the Selective Service Objector: The Right Not to Kill*, 44 N.Y.U. L. REV. 875 (1969).

Reynolds, *Zoning the Church: The Police Power Versus the First Amendment*, 64 *Boston* U. L. REV. 767 (1984).

Rostow, *The Democratic Character of Judicial Review*, 66 HARV. L. REV. 193 (1952).

Rutledge, *Religious Liberty and the Fourteenth Amendment*, 9 GA. L. REV. 141 (1946).

Scalia, *The Rule of Law as a Law of Rules*, 56 U. CHI. L. REV. 1175 (1989).

S. Shapiro, *Toward a Uniform Valuation of the Religion Guaranties*, 80 YALE L.J. 77 (1970).

Sheffer, *Antisocial Behavior as Criminal Conduct: The Belief-Action Distinction Revisited*, 2 COOLEY L. REV. 115 (1982).

———, *Conscientious Objection and the Draft: The Free Exercise Clause Revisited*, 4 WOODROW WILSON L.J. 27 (1982).

————, *The Free Exercise of Religion and Selective Conscientious Objection*, 9 CAP. U. L. REV. 7 (1979).

————, *The Supreme Court and the Free Exercise Clause: Are Standards of Adjudication Possible?* 23 J. CHURCH & S. 533 (1981).

Smith, *The Special Place of Religion in the Constitution*, 1983 SUP. CT. REV. 83.

H. Stone, *The Common Law in the United States*, 50 HARV. L. REV. 4 (1936).

————, *The Conscientious Objector*, 21 COLUM. U. Q. 253 (1919).

Sullivan, *The Congressional Response to Goldman v. Weinberger*, 121 MIL. L. REV. 125 (1988).

————, *Religion and Liberal Democracy*, 59 U. CHI. L. REV. 195 (1992).

Tushnet, *The Constitution of Religion*, 18 CONN. L. REV. 701 (1986).

Vinet, *Goldman v. Weinberger: Judicial Deference to Military Judgment in Matters of Religious Accommodation of Servicemembers*, 36 NAVAL L. REV. 257 (1986).

Warren, *The New Liberty Under the Fourteenth Amendment*, 39 HARV. L. REV. 431 (1926).

Wormuth & Mirkin, *The Doctrine of the Reasonable Alternative*, 9 UTAH L. REV. 254 (1964).

UNSIGNED LEGAL ARTICLES

Comment, *Justice Douglas' Sanctuary: May Churches Be Excluded from Suburban Residential Areas?* 45 OHIO ST. L.J. 1018 (1984).

————, *Defining Religion: Of God, the Constitution, and the D.A.R.*, 32 U. CHI. L. REV. 533 (1965).

Note, *A Braunfeld v. Brown Test of Indirect Burdens on the Free Exercise of Religion*, 48 MINN. L. REV. 1166 (1964).

————, *Compulsory Flag Salutes and Religious Freedom*, 51 HARV. L. REV. 1418 (1938).

————, *Constitutional Law—Freedom of Religion—Exemption of Conscientious Objectors from Military Service*, 43 COLUM. L. REV. 112 (1943).

————, *Freedom of Expression in a Commercial Context*, 78 HARV. L. REV. 1191 (1965).

————, *Freedom of Religion—Regulation of Solicitation of Charitable Funds by Religious Organizations*, 15 FORDHAM L. REV. 113 (1946).

————, *Review of Ecclesiastical Decisions by Civil Courts*, 46 YALE L.J. 519 (1937).

————, *The Sacred and the Profane: A First Amendment Definition of Religion*, 61 TEX. L. REV. 139 (1982).

————, *Toward a Constitutional Definition of Religion*, 91 HARV. L. REV. 1056 (1978).

Symposium, *Policy-Making in a Democracy: The Role of the United States Supreme Court*, 6 J. PUB. L. 2 (1957).

————, *Statutory Construction*, 3 VAND. L. REV. 1 (1950).

————, *The Role of the Supreme Court in the American Constitutional System*, 33 NOTRE DAME LAW. 521 (1956).

INDEX

Abraham, Henry J., 62, 68, 102, 128, 137 (n.27), 150 (n.21), 152 (n.56), 160 (n.11), 162 (n.40)
Absolute language, 108–109, 112, 161 (n.15)
Accommodation, 30–31, 63, 121, 167 (n.73)
Actionable behavior. *See* Religious liberty, proselytizing
Activist libertarian, xv–xvi, 18–22, 27, 31–34, 38–41, 49, 63–71, 108–110, 112, 160 (n.7)
Administrative convenience, 70
Admission to the bar, 67, 86, 159 (n.1–2)
Adult/child distinction, 9–10, 141 (n.47, 52), 149 (n.7, 10), 151 (n.37)
Allport, Gordon W., 126
Alternative means. *See* Tests of freedom
Ali, Muhammad (Cassius Clay), 65
American Bar Association (ABA), 44, 152 (n.46)
American Civil Liberties Union (ACLU), 44, 152 (n.46)
Amish children, 49–50
Amish Mennonite Church. *See* Old Order Amish
Antihandbill ordinance, 24
Antisocial behavior, 1–16, 26
Arsenal of protective devices. *See* Tests of freedom
Article I, Section 8, Clause 4, 53; Clause 7, 5; Clauses 11,12,14, 55, 92
Article IV, Clause 3, xix, 55, 68, 71
Article 37, Declaration of Rights (MD), 71

Atheists/agnostics. *See* Nonbelievers
Auxilliary precautions, xvi

Bad tendency, 114
Balancing test. *See* Tests of freedom
Ballard family, 6–7, 140 (n.31, 33, 40)
Bear arms, 53–55
Belief. *See* Religious liberty
Belief/action distinction, 6, 12–15, 42, 72, 161 (n.15)
Bernard, Burton C., xxiii
Bill for Establishing Religious Freedom, *See* Virginia Statute of Religious Liberty
Bill of Rights, xvi, xix
Black, Hugo L., 23–26, 31, 44–46, 58, 63–68, 71, 94, 97, 144 (n.31, 37), 146 (n.66), 148 (n.84), 152 (n.46), 158 (n.51), 160 (n.4)
Blackman, Harry A., 77–80
Bodenheimer, Edgar, 109, 135, 138
Bona fide claim/believer, 61, 73–74, 97
Bradley, Joseph P., 4
Braden, George D., 111
Brandeis, Louis D., 54–55, 143 (n.14), 149 (n.8), 155 (n.9)
Breach of the peace, 19–22
Brennan, William J., 70–74, 77–80, 101, 153 (n.63), 159 (n.62), 162 (n.31), 163 (n.43), 166 (n.69–70)
Breyer, Stephen, 169 (n.89)
Burden of proof, 74, 116, 128, 141 (n.57), 163 (n.41–43), 165 (n.60), 166 (n.70), 168 (n.80), 177 (n.36), 178 (n.45, 50)
Burger, Warren E., 47–49, 64–66, 75, 93, 107, 142 (n.60), 165 (n.60)

205